Essays in Honor of Lois
Parkinson Zamora

Essays in Honor of Lois Parkinson Zamora

From the Americas to the World

Edited by
Monika Kaup and John Ochoa

LEXINGTON BOOKS
Lanham • Boulder • New York • London

'Often I Am Permitted To Return To A Meadow'' by Robert Duncan, from THE OPENING OF THE FIELD, copyright ©1960 by Robert Duncan. Reprinted by permission of New Directions Publishing Corp.

"Letter to León Felipe," "Near Cape Comorin," "Exclamation," "Distant neighbor," "The balcony," "Delhi," "Reading John Cage," "A tale of two gardens," "Blanco," and "The mausoleum of Humayan," by Octavio Paz, translated by Eliot Weinberger and Charles Tomlinson, respectively, from THE COLLECTED POEMS 1957-1987. Copyright ©1965 by Denise Levertov Goodman. Copyright © 1967 by Octavio Paz and Lysander Kemp. Copyright © 1968, 1981 by Octavio Paz and Charles Tomlinson. Copyright © 1970 by Octavio Paz and Paul Blackburn. Copyright © 1971 by New Directions Publishing Corp. Copyright © 1972, 1973, 1978, 1979, 1986 by Octavio Paz and Eliot Weinberger. Copyright © 1979 by Editorial Seix Barral S. A. Copyright © 1979, 1985, 1987, 1988 by Octavio Paz. Copyright © 1983, 1984, 1985, 1986, 1987, 1988, 1990 by Eliot Weinberger. Reprinted by permission of New Directions Publishing Corp.

Excerpts from IN LIGHT OF INDIA by Octavio Paz, translated from the Spanish by Eliot Weinberger. Copyright © 1995 by Octavio Paz. Copyright © 1995, Editorial Seix Barral, S.A.- Barcelona (Espana). English translation copyright © 1997 by Eliot Weinberger. Reprinted by permission of Houghton Mifflin Harcourt Publishing Company. All rights reserved.

Excerpts from THE MONKEY GRAMMARIAN by Octavio Paz. Used with permission of Arcade Publishing © 1990.

Published by Lexington Books
An imprint of The Rowman & Littlefield Publishing Group, Inc.
4501 Forbes Boulevard, Suite 200, Lanham, Maryland 20706
www.rowman.com

6 Tinworth Street, London SE11 5AL, United Kingdom

Copyright © 2021 The Rowman & Littlefield Publishing Group, Inc.

All rights reserved. No part of this book may be reproduced in any form or by any electronic or mechanical means, including information storage and retrieval systems, without written permission from the publisher, except by a reviewer who may quote passages in a review.

British Library Cataloguing in Publication Information Available

Library of Congress Cataloging-in-Publication Data

Names: Ochoa, John A. (John Andres), 1967- editor. | Kaup, Monika, editor. | Zamora, Lois Parkinson, honouree.
Title: Essays in honor of Lois Parkinson Zamora : from the Americas to the world / edited by John Ochoa and Monika Kaup.
Description: Lanham : Lexington Books, [2021] | Includes bibliographical references and index. | Summary: "Honoring the lifework of comparatist Lois Parkinson Zamora, this collection traces artistic pathways that connect Latin American culture to the Americas, and to the world beyond. Its essays range from canonical writers like Roberto Bolaño and Gabriel García Márquez to non-canonical forms such as contemporary developments of Mexican folk Baroque"—Provided by publisher.
Identifiers: LCCN 2021038093 (print) | LCCN 2021038094 (ebook) | ISBN 9781793636669 (cloth ; alk. paper) | ISBN 9781793636683 (paperback) | ISBN 9781793636676 (ebook)
Subjects: LCSH: Latin American literature—History and criticism. | Literature and transnationalism—Latin America. | LCGFT: Literary criticism. | Festschriften. | Essays.
Classification: LCC PN36.Z36 E87 2021 (print) | LCC PN36.Z36 (ebook) | DDC 809/.898—dc23
LC record available at https://lccn.loc.gov/2021038093
LC ebook record available at https://lccn.loc.gov/2021038094

For Lois Parkinson Zamora,
distinguished scholar, devoted teacher, caring mentor, and admired friend.

Contents

List of Figures ix

Introduction xi
Monika Kaup and John Ochoa

PART I: INTER-AMERICANISMS 1

1 A Hemispheric World of Differences: Literature of the Americas (1982–2020) 3
  Antonio Barrenechea

2 Mistranslation and Catastrophe 27
  Anna Brickhouse

3 Transamerican Friendships and American Utopias: José Carlos Mariátegui, Waldo Frank, and Victoria Ocampo 37
  Priscilla Archibald

4 Dark Meadows of Gnosis: Robert Duncan and José Lezama Lima's Inter-American Mythopoetics 57
  Christopher Winks

PART II: BAROQUES 73

5 La Santa Muerte: Necroaesthetics and the Folk Baroque 75
  Silvia Spitta

6 Carpentier's *Concierto barroco*: Transoceanic Picaresques and Revolution, or All that Glitters Is Not Gold 93
  John Ochoa

| 7 | "Breaking the Circle of Perfection": Baroque Form from Johannes Kepler to Isabelle Stengers
Monika Kaup | 109 |

PART III: LATIN AMERICA IN THE WORLD — 123

8	Magical Realism's Synecdoche *Stephen M. Hart*	125
9	Epistemology of the Ineffable: Octavio Paz and India *Wendy B. Faris*	143
10	Alchemist of the Tropics: Alexander von Humboldt and Gabriel García Márquez's *Cien años de soledad* *Ralph Bauer*	173

Afterword — 205
Djelal Kadir

Index — 209

About the Contributors — 225

List of Figures

Figure 5.1	Calaveras, Altar, Museo Dolores Olmedo, Mexico City, Mexico	76
Figure 5.2	Detail, Altar, Museo Dolores Olmedo, Mexico City, Mexico	77
Figure 5.3	Street Altar, Mexico City, Mexico	79
Figure 6.1	*Granma* landing in Oriente Province, December 2, 1956	99
Figure 6.2	Total Mexican Silver Production, 1559–1810	100
Figure 10.1	Francis Bacon, frontispiece, *Instauratio Magna* (1620)	187
Figure 10.2	Andrés García de Céspedes, Regimiento de navegación (Madrid, 1606)	188

Introduction
Monika Kaup and John Ochoa

Honoring the lifework of comparatist Lois Parkinson Zamora, this collection is organized around the basic premise of comparative studies—interconnectedness. First and foremost, it traces intimate links and interactions between cultural spheres conventionally marked as "Latin America" and "North America," testifying to the ongoing vitality of hemispheric studies, a discipline to whose revival and massive expansion since the 1990s Lois Zamora's work has been instrumental. One of the manifestations of the paradigm shift from self-contained nation-based to translocal and transnational approaches to literary studies, the fresh burst of hemispheric literary and cultural studies in the past three decades is ultimately linked to the study of literature in a globalizing age: the reconfiguration of comparative literature on a truly global scale, as world literature. It is at the juncture of these two critical landscapes that our collection is located.

In a statement equally applicable to hemispheric literary studies, David Damrosch notes that world literature does not afford a detached "view from nowhere," but always remains locally inflected. Literary works "continue to bear the marks of their national origin" even after they have entered into global circulation.[1] So do critical studies. Therefore, comparative literary studies at any scale must always declare their local inflection or point of access. In keeping with the focus of Lois Zamora's own work, this collection's primary point of entry to comparative and hemispheric literary study is Latin American literature. Our essays cover three major critical fields—comparative hemispheric American literature, magical realism, as well as the Baroque, New World Baroque, and Neobaroque—which have drawn upon, and been decisively shaped by, Latin American literature, culture, and art. That this is the case is in no small part due to Lois Zamora. Zamora's critical vision played a foundational role in the development of these three related fields. Her comparative work first stimulated the emergence of contemporary transamerican literary studies (in *Writing the Apocalypse: Historical Vision in Contemporary U.S. and Latin American Fiction* ([1989]), then it continued to advance the field through the following decades, in *The Usable Past: The Imagination of History in Recent Fiction of the Americas* (1997) and *The Americas, Otherwise* (2009; coedited with Silvia Spitta). Next in chronological order, the collection *Magical Realism: Theory, History Community* (1995; co-edited with Wendy Faris) was the first study to treat magical realism as a global phenomenon, illuminating the continuities between magical realism's Latin American roots and the international boom of the genre beginning in the 1980s. Finally, with *The Inordinate Eye: New World Baroque and Latin American Fiction* (2006) and in the collection *Baroque New Worlds: Representation, Transculturation, Counterconquest* (2010; co-edited with Monika Kaup), Zamora expanded a surge of new scholarship on the Baroque/New World Baroque/Neobaroque. *The Inordinate Eye* examines the transcultural dynamics by which the New World Baroque emerged by way of the rebellious consumption of the European Baroque, and it further demonstrates how twentieth-century Latin American literature's verbal artworks were informed by the cultural history and exuberant visual forms of the New World Baroque. Looking back from our perspective three decades after her first major publications, the impact of Lois Zamora's comparative work has been to illuminate, and to stimulate further exploration of, important artistic pathways that link Latin American culture and literature to the Americas and the world beyond. In particular, it does so by shedding light on two artistic forms, magical realism and the Baroque, which have been either generated (magical realism) or revolutionized (the Baroque) in Latin America, and through which Latin American literature and culture have achieved prominence on a global stage. Broadly inspired by Zamora's example, the essays that follow demonstrate this fact.

A transnational entity in itself, Latin America shares an important interface with North America, but it is also bound up in other transnational contexts that do not involve the United States and Canada. Our collection is organized to reflect this point. We begin with hemispheric perspectives in part I (Inter-Americanisms) and end with essays tracing global comparative trajectories in part III (Latin America in the World). The essays in part II (Baroques) occupy an intermediate position between these two poles. It is in this way that this volume aligns with the recent reconfiguration of world literature as a rubric intended to connect various regimes of comparative literary studies. Indeed, world literary studies also endeavors to bridge the division between newer postcolonial and traditional Western canons, a dichotomy that has never worked well for Latin America, whose cultures straddle Western and non-Western realms.

Along with our focus on close readings of representative works of literature and art comes a return to the genuinely dialogic spirit that marked the surge of inter-American literary studies circa 1990. The goal was to overcome the siloed nature of the study of literature and culture of the Americas, and to stimulate mutual engagements between "Americanists," focused on an "America" synonymous with the United States and generally oblivious of its namesake, the continent to which it belongs, and "Latin Americanists," hyperaware of the anglophone nation to the north but hesitant to engage intersections in light of the unequal balance of power between north and south.[2] This spirit was modeled by Lois Zamora's work. It is a testament to Zamora's genuinely dialogic vision that her principal three monographs were translated into Spanish: *Writing the Apocalypse* as *Narrar el apocalipsis: La visión histórica en la literature estadounidense y latinoamericana contemporánea* (1994); *The Usable Past* as *La construcción del pasado: La imaginación histórica en la literature americana reciente* (2000); *The Inordinate Eye* as *La mirada exuberante: Barroco novomundista y literature latinoamericana* (2011). (They continue to be in print and available, as we have had the pleasure to discover on periodic visits to Mexico City's bookstores over the past decade.)

The so-called transnational turn of American studies since the late 1990s has brought welcome fresh attention to hemispheric American studies in departments of English and American studies. But it has also raised concerns among scholars long active in the field as well as Latin Americanists and Comparatists. As Claudie Sadowski-Smith and Claire Fox, Sophia McClennen, and Ricardo Salvatore have remarked elsewhere, some recent hemispheric studies emerging from departments of English and American studies cite mostly U.S.-based or Americanist scholars, slighting Hispanist and Latin Americanist scholarship, especially if published in Spanish, Portuguese, and languages other than English. In the first essay in Part I ("Inter-Americanisms"), entitled "Hemispheric World of Differences: Literature of the Americas," Antonio Barrenechea addresses such concerns of what counts as hemispheric American studies, and how it should be put together. What is the right balance between parts and whole, the many linguistic, national, and ethnic traditions that make up the Americas, and the continental entity that these form together? In his reassessment of the field, Barrenechea traces the transformation of academic inter-Americanism from a "Literature of the Americas" wave of development founded within comparative literature (1982–2000) into a more U.S. critique-centered, and by extension more skeptical, Hemispheric Studies wave as defined by English and American studies (1998–present). He argues that the gradual subtraction of literatures and languages from the second incarnation is largely responsible for the less comparative aspect of today's hemispherism, the raison d'être of the first wave. What the field needs now, he contends, are new multidisciplinary studies that immerse themselves into the different languages and literatures outside as well as inside of the United States. While forwarding a critique of the existing field, Barrenechea offers a corrective through what he calls the *Summa Americana*, a variant of the encyclopedic novel that stages a hemispheric gathering of differences across cultures and epochs.

This volume gives equal attention to the work of scholars based in Spanish and English departments, seeking to rectify the reputation of "hemispheric studies" as a grander version of American studies. In exploring hemispheric American literary studies, this collection adopts a dual strategy, combining questions of theory and methodology with individual case studies and critical practice. Hemispheric studies is not new; its ongoing revival takes place against the foil of two centuries of hemispheric thinking. The inception of inter-Americanism is in the era of the struggle for independence in the late eighteenth and early nineteenth centuries. Subsequently, in the century of Manifest Destiny, the rhetoric of "fraternal republics in arms" against European colonialism was increasingly hollowed out by the reality of U.S. expansionism. Hemispheric thinking thus emerged under the cloud of America's rise as a neo-imperial power, a development denounced by José Martí in his landmark essay, "Our America" (1891). The subsequent founding of the Pan-American Union in 1889 took place in these historical conditions, and the PAU's institutional rhetoric of hemispheric dialogue and collaboration in the Pan-American era (1890–1940)[3] sat uncomfortably against the political reality of the U.S. neo-imperial status in the hemisphere.

Hemispheric literature—and, needless to say, world literature—does not constitute an essence or a unified whole. Rather, both are the sum of a transfinite plurality of contexts, networks, and potential access points to places elsewhere. To eschew the dynamics of othering that vitiates hemispheric studies (Latin America as the Other of the United States; the United States as the Other of Latin America) and to overcome "the North/South Divide," as has been suggested by Zamora and Spitta,[4] and to avoid projecting the outlook of our home cultures onto the wider world, it is best to conduct hemispheric studies as a polycentric endeavor, the collaborative effort of scholars from distinct disciplinary locations. This is the approach adopted here.

Polycentrism implies asymmetry. For this reason, this collection seeks to overcome the popular "two Americas" thesis in hemispheric studies—the reductively schematic dichotomy between an English-speaking America in the north and a Spanish-speaking America in the south, whose beginnings hark back to exiled Cuban writer José Martí's concept of a multiracial, Hispanophone, Catholic "Our America" that is in conflict with a racially segregated, Anglophone and Protestant North America—emphasizing considerable affinities instead. Christopher Winks's reading of poetry by Robert

Duncan and José Lezama Lima, for example, illuminates a shared mythopoetics of world-making in these two poets, American and Cuban, respectively. Here, myth is not the "obscurantist" antithesis of knowledge; it is a form of knowledge. Beginning with a discussion of Martin Heidegger's consideration, following Hölderlin, of the task of the poet in times of destitution, "Dark Meadows of Gnosis: Robert Duncan and José Lezama Lima's Inter-American Mythopoetics" proposes an inter-American repurposing of the German philosopher's insights through two poems. Written twelve years apart and in different languages and countries, Cuban poet José Lezama Lima's "Una oscura pradera me convida" (newly translated here) and American poet Robert Duncan's "Often I Am Permitted to Return to a Meadow" are both governed by the metaphor of the meadow. Both poems are closely analyzed, through a comparatist perspective, as moments of the authors' poetic epistemologies and pilgrimages, refracted through and illuminated by Heidegger's thoughts on poetic language and Spanish philosopher María Zambrano's meditations on clearings in the forest as instantiations of a Dantean "vita nova." In both poems, the meadow, Winks shows, figures as a liminal figure connecting death and eros/life, governing the process of transformation from one pole to the other that occurs in the act of poetic creation. As Winks concludes, "Lezama's pagan Catholicism and joyful knowledge and Duncan's syncretic myth-and-soul-making are both poetic systems of ingathering that not only seek out the traces of the fugitive gods but re-animate them in the realm of that language which, in Heideggerian terms, speaks."

Like Barrenechea, who recommends a "multidirectional" approach, Priscilla Archibald further helps model what she describes as an "alternative and distinctly polycentric pan-Americanism." In "Transamerican Friendships and American Utopias: José Carlos Mariátegui, Waldo Frank, and Victoria Ocampo," Archibald examines Anglo American novelist and cultural critic Waldo Frank's intervention in Latin America in the 1920s, 1930s, and 1940s, specifically his intellectual collaboration with Peruvian Marxist José Carlos Mariátegui, and with Argentine woman of letters, Victoria Ocampo. Just as the United States had established its dominance in the Western hemisphere and Latin America's peripheralization was being consolidated in new ways, Frank was welcomed into the Latin American intellectual community as "one of [their] own." Yet the ideological, political, and cultural projects of these three figures—all prominent public intellectuals—were extremely heterogeneous: Frank was a leftist intellectual who practiced an elite humanism and was never entirely comfortable with party politics; José Carlos Mariátegui, by contrast, was the founder of the Peruvian Socialist Party and developed a groundbreaking Indo-American socialism; Victoria Ocampo, finally, a member of Argentina's elite and one of its staunchest apologists, advocated an ostensibly apolitical cultural agenda.

Frank made a point of extending himself to the Latin American intelligentsia quite pointedly as a "friend." What, Archibald asks, made this unusual transamerican friendship possible, and what does it mean? She argues that the unlikely affiliation between a leftist, an unorthodox Marxist, and an elitist cosmopolitan highlights the disparate forces operating in the Americas in the first half of the twentieth century. Against the grain of the official pan-Americanism of the era, which reinforced the United States as center and singular political actor, the collaborations of Frank and Mariátegui and Frank and Ocampo demonstrate the pivotal role that polycentric transamerican collaboration played during the 1920s, 1930s, and 1940s, something that hindsight (and Western hegemony) frequently mask.

While this collection thus establishes hemispheric continuities, it does not picture the hemispheric as a transcendent ideal of hemispheric unity, perhaps reminiscent of the pan-Americanism of the Pan-American Union in the early twentieth century, promoted by Teddy Roosevelt to cement U.S. domination in the Americas. Instead, we simply intend the concept as an alternative perspective to the centering and self-contained paradigm of national literature—the de-centering optic of interconnectivity, contact, and comparison.

A note on the vexed problem of relations between the national/local and the transnational is warranted here. Rather than a rigid dichotomy, this collection views the shift from nation-based to hemispheric (and global literary) scales as a figure/ground shift from objects to relationships. In the nation-based paradigm, autonomous objects (identity-based collectives such as national, ethnic, or language groups) are primary and the relationships between them, secondary. Conversely, in the hemispheric or comparative world literary paradigms, interrelationships are primary and the objects they connect, secondary. Both views are equally valid and equally indispensable. At the same time, they are opposites, and they co-exist in each other's blind spots.

This in turn brings up a related predicament addressed in Antonio Barrenechea's essay: it has generally been accepted that the rubric of the nation is an invention. Nations are imagined communities. But so is the notion of the American hemisphere, as Edmundo O'Gorman insisted in his landmark thesis of the invention of America. As central organizing principles, neither "nation" nor "hemisphere"—nor, for that matter, "world"—can thus escape the hermeneutics of suspicion. Yet in the event, critical suspicion targeting such cultural constructs makes but a trivial point. As philosopher John Searle has shown, the world humans inhabit is a world of social constructs: its furniture, encompassing phenomena such as citizenship, government, marriage, human rights, private property, and so on, are entities that are fabricated rather than found. Yet their impact on our lives is no less objective than that of material objects like rocks. Inspired by theorists such as Searle and Bruno Latour, this collection espouses a new realist view: if something is culturally constructed, it does not follow that it is therefore unreal, as posited by both postmodern constructivism and reductive materialism. A contemporary philosophical movement and participant in the wider and much more heterogeneous so-called ontological turn, which is devoted to the recovery of the real after postmodernism, new realism searches for an escape from the impasse between universalized, radical constructivism, and reductive materialism plaguing the humanities and social sciences. While a deeper exposition is beyond our interests or scope, specific applications of new realism exist for the study of the Baroque, which are explored in Monika Kaup's essay, "'Breaking the Circle of Perfection': Baroque Form from Johannes Kepler to Isabelle Stengers." Ultimately, new realism's helpfulness is in establishing a new footing for—or in recomposing, in Bruno Latour's words—humanistic study in the twenty-first century. Instead of debunking social constructs, new realism seeks to establish the singular reality that obtains for humanistic objects of study. It offers alternatives by illuminating a process- and context-oriented, that is to say, a non-materialist notion of the real. The real is not identical with the material: not everything that exists is material. Social, cultural, and linguistic artifacts are both constructed and real. The difference is that such entities—in contrast to brute facts like earthquakes—are objective realities that are collectively instituted (Searle). Thus, for imagined communities such as nation, hemisphere, or world, the question is not whether they are real or constructed. The proper question is *where* they are real, and *how* they become real. Accordingly, guided by the new realist maxim that not everything that exists is material, this collection is thus less troubled by the dilemma of "invention." As shown in Barrenechea's essay, it is therefore also less preoccupied with the attitude of critical suspicion.

So, yes, America—the continent—is an invention. But it is nevertheless real. Like nations in the Americas, it is a construct, but one that foregrounds interconnections, contacts, and exchanges across national and cultural borders. Unthinkable without the inaugural inscription of a Eurocentric worldview, the Americas are nonetheless not frozen at their beginnings. Ongoing processes of translation, transculturation, recycling, and appropriation—the dynamics of travel and cultural contact—have resulted in the deformation and recreation of these cultural constructs. These essays in their own ways look at how "America" is a product of collective creativity always, but with an outside referent, as well as a part of an ongoing chain of signification. Incidentally, this is also a point made by O'Gorman. What O'Gorman's doctrine of the Invention of America pointed to was in fact a double-discourse: America was a mirror of the European imagination, but at the same time it was radically new, a New World whose actual setting was located by Columbus. America, in his view, was at once another step in a cumulative process of Western creation, and a swerve away from it. There is a subtle meaning to the word "invención," as the *Diccionario* of the Spanish Royal Academy tells us. "Invención" is also a rhetorical strategy whose function is to "encontrar las ideas y los argumentos necesarios para desarrollar un asunto" (find the ideas and necessary arguments to develop a matter).[5] It is *discovery*, in the legal or heuristic sense, meaning that it is not definitional, but rather part of a process. The running paradox is that America is an ongoing discovery.

Because translation is one of principal modes of the transnational circulation of texts, mistranslation is one of its chief pitfalls. Yet, rather than embarking on a critique of untranslatability or of the politics of translation, in "Mistranslation and Catastrophe," Anna Brickhouse explores its creative outcomes. Brickhouse discusses late Chilean writer Roberto Bolaño's 1996 novel *Estrella distante*, translated into English as *Distant Star*, which features an obscure epigraph by William Faulkner, translated into Spanish. Issues of translation arise: if world literature is generated, at least by some definitions, when works gain broader significance and reach through translation, then Bolaño's translation of Faulkner appears to operate in the reverse direction. Indeed, the epigraph turns out to come from an obscure early-career Faulkner work, a book of poetry from 1924 that Faulkner wrote before he started writing the novels and stories for which he became famous: *The Marble Faun*—a long pastoral poem by Faulkner that is simply not very compelling, spoken as it is by the titular faun himself, who meditates on art and beauty, lamenting his inanimate status: "What star is there that falls, with none to watch it?" Hence the title of the novel. As Faulkner asks of the falling star, Brickhouse suggests, we might ask here: Does the original poet's work exist if it is never recognized after its translation and citation?

Bolaño's *Distant Star* is concerned with poetic recognition, too, though in a far darker guise: it asks if his main character, the fascist and torturer Wieder can be tracked down across the transmission and translation of his many pseudonymous verses and aesthetic manifestoes. As Brickhouse elucidates, the novel pursues the problem of finding a criminal through his art while exploring the larger intertwining of aesthetics and politics in the midst of the Cold War Americas. Faulkner, in the 1950s, was himself a Cold War cultural ambassador, sent by the State Department to Brazil, Peru, and Venezuela, where he promoted pro-U.S. sentiments. He worked on projects to translate Latin American writers into English, but these efforts failed to yield much. *Distant Star*, set in the midst of the CIA-encouraged coup in Chile, and the aftermath of torture and disappearances, thus elaborates through its epigraph a miniature version of Faulkner's Ibero-American translation project in which, effectively, little to nothing gets transmitted. Bolaño died the year before the English translation of *Estrella distante* was published, but, Brickhouse speculates, perhaps he too would have seen some glimmer of meaning in the way the retranslation of his epigraph effects a kind of mistranslation:

an effacement of the original. It is in part from Bolaño's *Distant Star* that Brickhouse takes the working hypothesis of a current project, one indebted to Zamora's work: that the long history of the Americas may be read in part as a series of mistranslated catastrophes, as a history *of* the mistranslation of catastrophe.

As noted at the outset, this collection showcases the Baroque/New World Baroque/Neobaroque. As Lois Zamora establishes in *The Inordinate Eye*, the Baroque is a critical currency with deep roots in Latin American and Caribbean literary and art history and critical traditions: Latin America played a key role in the transformation of what was originally an European colonial form into something new—a transhistorical, transcultural, and interartistic expression that must be thought across the boundaries of period, nation, race, and discipline. These developments have tipped the scales of the Baroque's reputation from the retrograde to the innovative: from the vantage point of the twenty-first century, there can no longer be any doubt about the importance of the Baroque as a modern expression, and its ongoing vitality. No longer confined to its seventeenth-century European origins, the Baroque is now recognized as both polyglot and contemporary: it encompasses five centuries and multiple continents, nations, and artistic forms. This is the result of the Baroque's prolific offshoots and reincarnations: the New World Baroque that grew up in the Americas in the colonial period, and the Neobaroque, which denotes the multiple waves—modernist, postmodernist, postcolonial—of twentieth- and twenty-first-century revivals of the Baroque. Hence, the Baroque, Neobaroque, and New World Baroque today are posterchildren of an "antiproprietary" expression that belongs to not one, but many distinct ethnic and national groups at the same time.[6] The Baroque's contemporary status as a global expression is reflected in a notable shift in the critical orientation of Baroque studies conducted since the 1990s, a redirection to which Zamora's work has been central. Until the 1970s, Baroque studies was animated by questions adjudicating national and disciplinary boundaries such as: Was there a Baroque in England and in Northern Europe? How to handle differences between the Baroque and mannerism? Is there a baroque philosophy? In contrast, the new Baroque studies acknowledges the inevitability of thinking the Baroque across the divides of period, history, region, and discipline—in short, of viewing the Baroque as a transatlantic and transamerican expression and, therefore—considering additional Asian transculturated Baroques in Goa, Macao, and the Philippines—a global category. Despite the considerable fresh attention it has recently received, the Baroque/Neobaroque/New World Baroque still remains to make its mark on the burgeoning field of world literature (or planetary or global literary studies). By spotlighting the rich and varied landscape of the Baroque's transnational and transhistorical travels in the three essays of Part II ("Baroques"), our goal is to help rectify this situation.

In "La Santa Muerte: Necroaesthetics and the Folk Baroque," Silvia Spitta considers the expanding contemporary Mexican popular cult of La Santa Muerte. The essay reads the theatricalization of death in contemporary Mexican narcoculture as folk Baroque. Rivaling, even displacing, the traditional Mexican cult of la Virgen de Guadalupe among the poor in certain locations, La Santa Muerte emerged in the 1990s with the expansion of the drug cartels. Censored by the Catholic Church, it nonetheless thrives as a new protector figure of the Mexican underclasses that have been abandoned by the neoliberal state to drug-related violence. Spitta reports that altars for and rituals related to La Santa Muerte (la Huesuda, la Flaquita) abound in Mexico City's working-class neighborhoods, border cities, and the sites of infamous brutal serial murders of women (femicides) and cartel warfare. La Santa's followers "believe that she protects people against *violent death*" such as the "muerte artera," as seen in the theatricalized torture-assassinations of narcoviolence (such as *narcomensajes* displayed on the bodies of victims). Spitta argues that for better or worse, the cult of La Santa Muerte (along with narcocemeteries, narcosatanic cults, and so on) is a rearticulation of the Mesoamerican cult of death that survives in contemporary Mexico in popular Day of the Dead celebrations. As such, it is also an instance of the folk Baroque, an exuberant sensibility that permeates Mexican (and Latin American) popular and visual culture. As Spitta affirms, La Santa Muerte is both evidence and a sobering reminder of the darker aspect of the Baroque: the Baroque has always been "both an aesthetics of plenitude and exuberance and one of monstrosity and horror," a lineage that reaches back to baroque paintings of the decapitated head of St. John the Baptist. Spitta further suggests that the Mexican media's "sensationalist and grotesque fascination with death particularly that of the so-called *nota roja* or crime-beat press, has to be seen as part of the same underlying folk Baroque sensibility that exists alongside the Day of the Dead altars and Trees of Life." Spitta concludes by speculating whether the narcotheatrics of death, a relapse into savagery of which La Santa Muerte is an epiphenomenon, may also be an expression of an age-old phenomenon present across cultures and epochs, stretching back to primitive head-hunting.

In "Carpentier's *Concierto barroco*: Transoceanic Picaresques and Revolution, or All that Glitters Is Not Gold," John Ochoa reframes Alejo Carpentier's novel, *Concierto barroco* (1974) by exploring intersections between the Neobaroque and the picaresque. Running through the heart of the Baroque-Neobaroque continuum, Ochoa observes, is a geographic axis: Europe, Cuba, Mexico, and its reverse, Mexico, Cuba, Europe. Numerous historical and literary journeys go back and forth along this route. A postcolonial revision of the twinned themes of travel, discovery, and conquest, Carpentier's short novel reverses the direction of European colonization. It draws on the eighteenth-century version of the picaresque mode to tell the tale of a rich *Indiano* who goes to Europe to experience the pomp and wealth of the continent. By inviting the picaresque into the Baroque, which is traditionally associated with abject penury, Ochoa observes, Carpentier turns the picaresque on its head. Ochoa suggests that he does so with subversive intent: *Concierto barroco* gets to the heart of a sobering reality of the Neobaroque: a lot of its opulence and rich ornamentation is skin deep (to paraphrase Severo Sarduy), it is all gold-leaf, illusion of weightiness and representation and little substance. This complicated dynamic, according to Ochoa, extends to the political/revolutionary value of both the historical Baroque and the Neobaroque: the first was associated with the Counter-Reformation, which relied on wealth from the mines of the American mainland to carry out its depleting struggle. The Neobaroque, on the other hand, is associated with the Cuban Revolution (which also unfolded along this axis, launched from Mexico and featuring picaresque adventurers). What, Ochoa asks, follows from Carpentier's exposure of the Baroque's unstable "blend of lack and opulence" for the debate about the Baroque's politics? In the end, he concludes, the novel sidesteps a serious answer to this question. Instead, it opts for an evasive baroque response: the "actual worth of what travels ... is immaterial, because the real value is the effect, the poetic illusion itself: false gilt."

In "Breaking the Circle of Perfection": Baroque Form from Johannes Kepler to Isabelle Stengers," Monika Kaup foregrounds considerations of form. How to make sense of the problem of disorder and irregularity at the heart of debates on the Baroque? Kaup makes the case that the vexed debate over baroque form can usefully be reframed through a new realist approach. The essay begins by recalling familiar parallels between the rise of baroque art and modern science in the seventeenth century: echoes of the cosmology of Johannes Kepler, for example, are found in the geometry of ellipses organizing baroque architecture and visual art. Baroque visual and verbal arts are a response to the shattering of the Ptolemaic universe, putting in its place the de-centered modern universe stretching out to infinity. Kaup's essay examines correspondences between baroque form and so-called systems thinking, the alternative science of self-organizing systems that emerged in the twentieth century. Systems thinking is one major tributary of new realism, which adopts a contextual concept of the real. New realism is new because it shifts the focus from seeing pieces to describing relationships and organized patterns of meaning. According to Kaup, there are compelling parallels between the history of systems thinking and the so-called baroque-neobaroque *retombée,* a term Severo Sarduy coins to picture interdisciplinary correspondences between art and science in the seventeenth-century Baroque and the twenty-first-century Neobaroque.

These analogies can be gleaned from philosopher of science Isabelle Stengers's essay "Breaking the Circle of Sufficient Reason," which discusses the work of chemist Ilya Prigogine, one of the co-founders of complexity theory. Stengers compares the new science of self-organization to Kepler's cosmology, contending that "Prigogine is a descendant of Kepler, who dared to break the perfection of the circle." Complexity theory describes self-organization in complex systems at critical points of instability, creating order out of disorder. The higher-order system possesses emergent properties, properties that arise at higher levels of complexity but that are absent in any of the lower-level parts. Emergence thus produces irreducible wholes that are more than the sum of its parts. These processes of emergence and self-organization, Kaup proposes, had earlier been identified by Heinrich Wölfflin as one of the characteristic features of baroque compositions (Wölfflin's category of unity vs. multiplicity): in the Gesamtkunstwerk, for example, the baroque effect stems from the Gestalt of an organized pattern. Hence, Kaup contends, Wölfflin was a systems theorist. From the seventeenth to the twentieth centuries, the Baroque has been modeling a new kind of disorderly order as an alternative to ancient ideal of timeless perfection that was eventually overthrown by contemporary science. In so doing, and unnoticed by most observers, the Baroque thus pioneered a new definition of the real that only gained wide recognition in the twentieth century: a context-based notion of the real that prioritizes relationships, interdependency, and organized processes and patterns over elemental parts and isolated objects.

This brings us to our third and final section ("Latin America in the World"), which looks beyond the Americas to explore continuities between Latin America and the world. First comes Stephen Hart's essay on what is easily the best-known Latin American contribution to world literature: magical realism. The "literary language of the emergent postcolonial world" (Homi Bhabha),[7] magical realism was born in Latin America (even if its conception may have happened in Paris between the wars, where its early Latin American proponents—Carpentier, Miguel Angel Asturias, and Arturo Uslar Pietri—met and came into contact with surrealism).[8] Risen to the status of a global genre in the 1980s, magical realism is special for being born in the Global South. What, Hart asks, made it possible for the genre to be detached from its cultural origins and appropriated by writers from India, Africa, China, as well as Europe? In "Magical Realism's Synecdoche," Hart re-evaluates magical realism, starting with the ingredients as they came together in Gabriel García Márquez's pathbreaking novel *One Hundred Years of Solitude* (1967), and concluding with a brief discussion of the magical realist formula as it has been exported to the rest of the world in the fifty years or so since that event. Hart analyzes its five significant literary techniques or "essences"—that is (i) old wives' tales, (ii) popular Catholicism, (iii) phenomenological morphing after Kafka, (iv) irony, and (v) the political allegorization of the divide between the West and the non-West. Once these were gathered together, he contends, they produced the new style of magical realism that would make García Márquez perhaps the most famous Latin American writer in the world. Hart focuses, in particular, on the fifth "essence," which, he suggests, was the quintessence of magical realism exported to the rest of the world.

Next, Wendy Faris's "Epistemology of the Ineffable: Octavio Paz and India," turns to another Latin American Nobel laureate, Mexican modernist poet, and critic Octavio Paz. Faris examines Octavio Paz's encounter with India in his 1995 essay *Vislumbres de la India* (*In Light of India*), poems written during his appointment as ambassador to India (1962–1968) and published in *Ladera este*, *Hacia el comienzo* and *Blanco*, as well as his 1974 narrative *El mono gramático* (*The Monkey Grammarian*). She argues that these works reveal what we might call an epistemology of the ineffable, in which Paz employs a strategy of the glance to discern and register delicate moments of Indian sensibility. Paz's art of the glance (*vislumbre*) is a double mode; we perceive, but just barely; we only glimpse. Adopting an often visionary mode, Faris contends, Paz relies on intuitive knowledge gleaned from visual glimpses and fleeting moments of perception rather than on rational knowledge obtained by methodically gathered information, a way of knowing India that is oblique rather than direct. Beside *In Light of India*'s cultural explorations, its translations of Indian epigrams provide examples of such oblique glances—and a metapoetical image of that sensibility: "Beauty is not / in what words say / but in what, without saying, they say." Similarly, Paz often abandons a logically structured account in favor of listing glimpses of miscellaneous sights: "waves of heat," "torrents of cars," "the apparition of a girl like a half-opened flower," and so on. What's more, within Paz's *vislumbres*, we catch glimpses of an implicit sense of the sacred, allied to an aspect of Indian sensibility close to his own: the combination of the sensual, sometimes embodied in the erotic, and the spiritual. Finally, the strategy of *vislumbres*, or incomplete glimpses, inasmuch as they acknowledge incomplete knowability of another culture, reveals Paz as a sensitive cultural comparatist.

Our final essay is Ralph Bauer's "Alchemist of the Tropics: Alexander von Humboldt and Gabriel García Márquez's *Cien Años de soledad*." Also centering on Gabriel García Márquez's iconic novel, Bauer explores its engagement with the European archive. Specifically, he examines its intertextual dialogue with the travel writings about South America written by the nineteenth-century Prussian polymath Alexander von Humboldt through the enigmatic character of Melchíades the alchemist in *Cien años de soledad*. A major subject of the novel's meta-historical critique, Humboldt's travel writings about the American tropics are an important source of inspiration not only for the novel's central motif of Latin America's "solitude" but also for several of its ancillary themes, such as the tropical entanglement of nature and culture in Macondo as well as its historical amnesia. Moreover, Bauer argues that a re-reading of Humboldt as a Melchíaden "alchemist of the tropics" has a bearing not only on the criticism of García Márquez's novel but also on the recent critical debate about the role that Humboldt's legacy played in the history of neocolonialism in Latin America. Specifically, García Márquez's meta-fictional engagement with Humboldt through the character of Melchíades the alchemist forces us to see the significance of Humboldt's nineteenth-century writings in the context of the longue durée of a European discourse of discovery that reaches back to the sixteenth century—and even beyond to the late Middle Ages, when alchemy first entered the Latin West through transmission from the Arabic. By his association with the character of Melchíades, Humboldt is placed in a long line of European conquerors, travelers, and natural philosophers who participated in the ideological project that the Mexican philosopher of history Edmundo O'Gorman once called "the history of the idea that America was discovered" by Europeans.

The final word in this volume belongs to Djelal Kadir, a foundational figure, alongside Lois Parkinson Zamora, of comparative hemispheric American studies and fellow aficionado of organizing these in the form of "multicentered, multivocal" dialogues. Beginning with a reflection on the impossibility of afterwords ("except as more words they come after"), Kadir invites us into a personal dialogue with Lois Parkinson Zamora, reviewing four decades of shared and companionable academic pathways. Amplifying the chorus of voices gathered here, Kadir's Afterword brings the purpose of this volume into focus: We dedicate this collection of essays to Lois Parkinson Zamora in profound admiration. Her contributions to the study of the New World Baroque and her deep love of Mexico have resulted in a transcendental sea change in Hemispheric American studies.

NOTES

1. Damrosch, 283.
2. On this goal, see, for example Pérez Firmat, "Introduction," in *Do the Americas Have a Common Literature?*, 2. Zamora was a contributor to this landmark collection of essays.
3. See Fox, 3.
4. Zamora and Spitta, "Introduction," 192.

5. *Diccionario de la real academia española*, s.v. "invención; ttps://dle.rae.es/invenci%C3%B3n
6. We borrow this concept from Posnock, 144.
7. Bhabha, 7.
8. See Siskind, 65.

WORKS CITED

Bhabha, Homi. "Introduction: Narrating the Nation." In *Nation and Narration*, edited by Homi Bhabha, 1–7. London: Routledge, 1990.

Damrosch, David. *What is World Literature?* Princeton: Princeton University Press, 2003.

Fox, Claire. *Making Art Panamerican: Cultural Policy and the Cold War.* Minneapolis, MN: University of Minnesota Press, 2013.

Hanke, Lewis, ed. *Do the Americas Have a Common History? A Critique of the Bolton Theory.* New York: Knopf, 1964.

Latour, Bruno. "An Attempt at a 'Compositionist Manifesto.'" *New Literary History* 41, no. 3 (2010): 471–90.

———. *Reassembling the Social: An Introduction to Actor-Network Theory.* Oxford: Oxford University Press, 2005.

Martí, José. "Our America." In *The America of José Martí*, edited and translated by Juan de Onís, 138–51. New York: Farrar, Straus & Giroux, 1968.

McClennen, Sophia. "Inter-American Studies or Imperial American Studies?" *Comparative American Studies* 3, no. 4 (2005): 393–413.

O'Gorman, Edmundo. *The Invention of America: An Inquiry into the Historical Nature of the New World and the Meaning of Its History.* 1958. Bloomington, IN: Indiana University Press, 1961.

Pérez Firmat, Gustavo. "Introduction: Cheek to Cheek." In *Do the Americas Have a Common Literature?*, edited by Gustavo Pérez Firmat, 1–5. Durham, NC: Duke University Press, 1990.

Posnock, Ross. "Planetary Circles: Philip Roth, Emerson, Kundera." In *Shades of the Planet: American Literature as World Literature*, edited by Wai Chee Dimock and Lawrence Buell, 141–67. Princeton: Princeton University Press, 2007.

Sadowski-Smith, Claudia and Claire F. Fox. "Theorizing the Hemisphere: Inter-Americas Work at the Intersection of American, Canadian, and Latin American Studies." *Comparative American Studies* 2, no. 1 (2004): 5–38.

Salvatore, Ricardo D. "On Knowledge Asymmetries and Cognitive Maps: Reconsidering Hemispheric American Studies." *MLN* 130, no. 2 (2015): 362–89.

Searle, John. *Making the Social World: The Structure of Human Civilization.* Oxford: Oxford University Press, 2010.

Siskind, Mariano. *Cosmopolitan Desires: Global Modernity and World Literature in Latin America.* Evanston, IL: Northwestern University Press, 2014.

Zamora, Lois Parkinson and Monika Kaup, eds. *Baroque New Worlds: Representation, Transculturation, Counterconquest*. Durham, NC: Duke University Press, 2010.

Zamora, Lois Parkinson and Silvia Spitta, eds. *The Americas, Otherwise*. Spec. Issue, *Comparative Literature* 61, no. 3 (2009) 189–365.

———, "Introduction." In Zamora and Spitta, *The Americas, Otherwise*. 189–208.

Zamora, Lois Parkinson and Wendy Faris, eds. *Magical Realism: Theory, History, Community*. Durham, NC: Duke University Press, 1995.

Zamora, Lois Parkinson. *The Inordinate Eye: New World Baroque and Latin American Fiction*. Chicago: University of Chicago Press, 2006. Translated by Aura Levy as *La mirada exuberante: Barroco novomundista y literatura latinoamericana*. Madrid: Editorial Vervuert, 2011.

———. *The Usable Past: The Imagination of History in Recent Fiction of the Americas*. Cambridge: Cambridge University Press, 1997. Translated by Maria Podetti as *La construcción del pasado: La imaginación historica en la literatura americana reciente*. Mexico City: Fondo de Cultura Económica, 2004.

———. *Writing the Apocalypse: Historical Vision in Contemporary U.S. and Latin American Fiction*. Cambridge: Cambridge University Press, 1993. Translated by María Antonia Neira Bigorra as *Narrar el apocalipsis: La visión histórica en la literatura estadounidense y latinoamericana contemporánea*. Mexico City: Fondo de Cultura Económica, 1994.

Part I

INTER-AMERICANISMS

Chapter 1

A Hemispheric World of Differences
Literature of the Americas (1982–2020)
Antonio Barrenechea

Whether understood as a globalist expansion of American Studies, or as a branch of Comparative Literature, what scholars today call "Hemispheric Studies" has its conceptual roots in a presidential address to the American Historical Association (AHA) from 1932. In Toronto on December 28 of that year, Herbert E. Bolton, a historian from UC Berkeley, delivered "The Epic of Greater America." In an effort to inspire the AHA membership to consider "America" in its entirety, Bolton supplanted the typical yearly address with one outlining "the larger aspects of Western Hemisphere history."[1] Bolton's speech reflected the type of diplomatic optimism that would lead President Franklin D. Roosevelt to declare a U.S. "Good Neighbor" policy three months later. Yet, according to the U.S. historian, "a broader treatment of American history, to supplement the purely nationalistic presentation" was necessary not only to foster goodwill between neighbors, but "from the standpoint of correct historiography."[2] For Bolton, whose research had taken him to colonial archives in Latin America, forging this perspective meant rejecting all vestiges of the "Black Legend." This fixation on Spanish cruelty and Catholic mania began as sixteenth-century Anglo-Dutch propaganda, and skewed hemispheric timelines.

Bolton renounced Anglocentrism, and its distortion of Hispanic contributions to U.S. development. Starting in the 1920s, he gained esteem as the founder of Spanish borderlands history.[3] Yet, his greater ambition was a historiography that not only engaged Florida, California, and other national domains shaped by the Iberian presence, but that made Spanish America into a hemispheric bedrock. In his work, Puritan New England receded before the spread of European civilization from indigenous kingdoms in Mexico and South America, and across multiple and multidirectional frontiers. What became known as the "Bolton thesis" (a hemispheric analogue to Jackson

Turner's "frontier thesis" of U.S. formation) told a longer and more tangled tale than acknowledged by Anglo-Protestant historians at the time.[4] The scale of Greater America—with Spain, Portugal, France, and Britain as key players—led Bolton to promote a new paradigm for the study of the Western Hemisphere. "The Epic of Greater America" ends with a carpe diem:

> Who has written the history of the introduction of European plants and animals into the Western Hemisphere as a whole, or the spread of cattle and horse raising from Patagonia to Labrador? Who has written on a Western Hemisphere scale the history of shipbuilding and commerce, mining, Christian missions, Indian policies, slavery and emancipation, constitutional development, arbitration, the effects of the Indian on European culture, the rise of the common man, art, architecture, literature, or science? Who has tried to state the significance of the frontier in terms of the Americas?[5]

A progenitor of Hemispheric American Studies, Bolton sketches a multidisciplinary field to encompass branches of learning in the sciences and the humanities. The scope of America is New World-wide, both in geography and sweeping subject matter. As the historian makes clear by lacing his pointed inquiries with tantalizing litanies (inclusive of "literature"), the academy had drawn only parts of a bigger picture. Bolton, who would go on to direct over 100 Ph.D. dissertations and create an inter-American concentration at Berkeley, invites specialists of all stripes to render moot his rhetorical questions by enlisting to complete a hemispheric project.[6]

Since Bolton outlines a polycentric approach, it follows that scholars heeding his call would need to study units of analysis, big and small. Besides acquiring expertise in a particular subject ("art . . . architecture," etc.), they would have to work dialectically by zooming into and out of single strands of development. For scholars of literature, this might take the collective form of general training in world letters while specializing in genres, periods, and movements that took root in the Americas before and after European arrival. A basic prerequisite might be reading literature in the primary languages of the Western Hemisphere. It would also mean engaging scholarship on national or regional literatures within local (i.e., non-explicitly "hemispheric") contexts. Multidisciplinary work would be a requirement for accessing "Greater America," the point being to connect several parts learned from the ground up for a better grasp of the whole.

Despite its heavy demands upon scholars, a Boltonian approach is compelling today because it offers a way of studying literature of the Americas up close, rather than as part of a distant ideological critique that stands in for the difficult (but potentially more rewarding) task of multilingual literary analysis. The Bolton thesis embraces a humanistic philosophy about what we can learn about our hemispheric neighbors. Although emerging out of the pan-Americanist ethos of the 1930s (and marked by a Eurocentric bias), "The Epic of Greater America" provides a model adaptable to our time and place. Earl E. Fitz, who created the first U.S.-based "Inter-American Literature" curriculum while teaching at Penn State University, credits Bolton with establishing "a conceptual basis for inter-American commentary and analysis."[7] More recently, Ralph Bauer, a scholar of colonial American literatures, describes Bolton as "the founding father of comparative hemispheric scholarship in the U.S."[8] Still, Bolton's amplitude is missing from most twenty-first-century scholarship, which proves less "inter-American" and "comparative" than one might think.[9] Moreover, the hemisphere has gone missing not through some unintended oversight, but—as I shall argue—due to an entrenched mode of suspicion. The latter privileges auto-critiques of academia, and its U.S. imperial handmaiden, at the expense of literary insight. Today, a meta-discursive theorizing of hemispheric avenues and, most of all, *impasses* tends to substitute for a more direct (and essentially disorienting) engagement with languages, literatures, and authors whose perspectives come from outside the United States. Considering the South American and Hispanophone roots of "Literature of the Americas" as planted by the Peruvian intellectual Luis Alberto Sánchez starting in the 1940s, this trend is troubling, and amnesiac.

In the spirit of the present volume celebrating the lifetime achievement of Lois Zamora, this essay proceeds by revisiting her first book, *Writing the Apocalypse: Historical Vision in Contemporary U.S. and Latin American Fiction* (1989). Here, and in the studies Zamora influenced, we find conceptual unity with Sánchez's groundbreaking *Nueva historia de la literatura americana* (1944), which culminates in his four-volume *Historia comparada de las literaturas americanas* (1973–1976), the most ambitious literary history of the Americas in the scholarly record. This would be a less fashionable basis for Literature of the Americas as grounded in Latin American and Comparative Literature.[10] In connection with *Writing the Apocalypse*, I explore literature-centered directions for Hemispheric Studies through what I call a *summa Americana*, that is, an encyclopedic novel that assumes a Boltonian grand scale with an aim to recuperate, and reinvent, New World histories. My principal aim is to consider how a reengagement with fiction attuned to an American *longue durée* (and not to an a priori ontology of "America" as geographical fixture) can effect a meaningful dialogue with those neglected and/or colonized neighbors who remain silent in Hemispheric Studies scholarship. Instead of drawing disciplinary lines or forwarding yet another pro-forma critique of the walls we build as hemisphericists, I contend that literature still holds the best promise for bridging cultural divides.

ONE HEMISPHERE, MANY NATIONS: LITERATURE OF THE AMERICAS (1982–2000)

As an academic discipline, "Literature of the Americas" has been challenging the traditional study of American Literature for decades. Definitions remain fluid, however, and separate terms now describe a number of academic approaches. Some of these—including "Inter-American Studies" and "Hemispheric Studies"—are (by definition) less committed to the particularities of language and literature, and adopt instead a cultural "studies" macro-approach attuned to politics and ideology. Closer to the origins is "inter-American," which suggests a meeting of international participants on both sides of a punctuation dash. "Hemispheric," on the other hand, opens up a grammatically modified path for a new American Studies based on U.S. "hemispheric" relations with neighboring Spanish America, Brazil, Canada, and the Caribbean.

Before it had a name, "Literature of the Americas" began as the study of the Western Hemisphere, that is, the literary output of the nations comprising "the Americas." One finds the origins in lengthy, untranslated, and out-of-print volumes penned by postwar intellectuals from around the world. Foremost among these is Luis Alberto Sánchez (the unacknowledged founder of "Literature of the Americas"). A leftist APRA dissident, Sánchez began writing encyclopedic histories of Literature of the Americas while exiled in Chile during the 1930s. Following suit is the Lusophone scholar Joaquim de Montezuma de Carvalho, whose *Panorama das literaturas das Américas* (4 volumes, 1958–1965) is a nation-by-nation, multiauthored history written in Spanish, English, French, and Portuguese.[11] The project emerged as Erich Auerbach and other scholars planted the modern roots of Comparative Literature in the United States. Despite U.S. Cold War geopolitics, the global orientation produced a lettered sphere beyond any one nation.[12]

A quarter century later, the title of Gustavo Pérez Firmat's critical anthology *Do the Americas Have a Common Literature?* (1990) summons the ghost of Bolton.[13] In its preface, the Cuban-born poet and editor argues that "the lack of dialogue between 'Americanists' and 'Latin Americanists,'" had made it so that "inter-American literary studies is something of a terra incognita."[14] Less than a year earlier, Zamora had published *Writing the Apocalypse*. A book with multidisciplinary ambitions, it battled the skepticism of scholars who resisted redrawing academic boundaries. Inquiring into fictions in the United States and Latin America, Zamora undertook side-by-side readings of major novels from cultures seen as radically different (if not downright opposite). Her analysis disrupted established lines of training and assigned university turf. Pérez Firmat's pronouncement notwithstanding, *Writing the Apocalypse*, emerged as inter-Americanism took shape within Comparative

Literature. This newly minted "Literature of the Americas" was the first collective response to Bolton's call for hemispheric scholarship beyond Sánchez, Carvalho, Canadian-born George W. Umphrey, and a handful of other iconoclasts.[15] The field entered the U.S. academic mainstream with the tenth congress of the International Comparative Literature Association (ICLA), hosted by New York University in August 1982.

There are at least four reasons why the ICLA conference, which featured a major unit on "Inter-American Literary Relations," is significant for the discipline during the first wave. First, it regarded American Literature as the fiction and non-fiction of the Western Hemisphere (i.e., the United States, Spanish America, Brazil, and Anglo-French Canada). The emerging discipline's primary object of study was a multinational and multilingual canon of *literature*. Second, papers were in multiple languages (English, Spanish, and French), the work of scholars hailing from universities across North and South America. Third, critiques of methodology (the largest contribution of Hemispheric Studies since 2000) did not substitute for the close reading of literature of the Americas. As cataloged in volume three of the conference proceedings (published in 1985), juxtapositions were integral. These ranged from: (1) place and selfhood ("The Metropolis and the Nation in American Literatures" / "Regional and National Identity in American Literatures"); (2) aesthetics and traditions ("Crosscurrents in the Development of Narrative Form in American Literatures" / "Literary Movements in American Literatures"); (3) genres ("Crosscurrents in the Development of Poetry in American Literatures" / "The Fantastic in American Literatures"); (4) North-South artistic flows ("Toward a History of Cultural Relations" / "Canadian and Latin American Literatures and their Interdependence"); and (5) intellectual history ("Crosscurrents in the Development of Comparative Literature in Latin America" / "History of Genre Criticism in American Literatures"). Four, the conference featured the contributions of several young scholars who would go on to write influential studies of the Americas (among them, Zamora, Fitz, Wendy Faris, Jorge Schwartz, Cynthia Steele, A. Owen Aldridge, Mary Louise Pratt, and Elizabeth Lowe). The collected papers in the conference volume document this early work's care for traditions placed in two and three way dialogues. The dialogues themselves took the form of literary analysis marking continuities and differences.

Furthermore, a keynote address by the Mexican novelist Carlos Fuentes confirmed the centrality of Latin America to the topic of "Inter-American Literary Relations." At the time, Comparative Literature saw its principal concern as European national literatures (with French, German, and English forming a holy trinity of tongues). The ICLA conference signaled a shift wherein Comparative Literature's attention to languages and literatures would refocus upon the Americas. Since its emergence in the nineteenth century, Comparative Literature had not really dialogued with Latin America (Spanish and Portuguese), and even less so with Francophone literatures outside of France. Recalling the event in a personal email, Fitz writes: "Everyone seemed fired up and inspired by the idea of freeing our dear old discipline of Comparative Literature from its old, but truly venerable, European moorings and (without forgetting those) creating something new, exciting, and comparative in all the best ways. There was a palpable sense of excitement, of getting into something really new and really comparative, in meaningful and productive ways. And that it (the inter-American project) could be done and done well."[16] As Fitz suggests in this recollection, the critique of Comparative Literature was constructive. The inter-Americanists at NYU performed a balancing act. They rejected Eurocentrism, but held on to the discipline's raison d'être: an international multilingualism for crossing literary terrains.

This model of American Literature as Comparative Literature informed books that preceded *Writing the Apocalypse*. Published in 1982 and 1986, respectively, were A. Owen Aldridge's *Early American Literature: A Comparatist Approach* (the first monograph of its kind) and Bell Gale Chevigny and Gari Laguardia's *Reinventing the Americas: Comparative Studies of Literature of the United States and Spanish America* (the first such edited collection). Another popular pursuit was the two and three-author study, such as José Ballón's *Autonomía cultural americana: Emerson y Martí* (1986) and Vera M. Kutzinski's *Against the American Grain: Myth and History in the William Carlos Williams, Jay Wright, and Nicolás Guillén* (1987). This trailblazing scholarship continued with Zamora, who brought together a range of authors for the first time: Gabriel García Márquez, Thomas Pynchon, Julio Cortázar, John Barth, Walker Percy, and Carlos Fuentes. *Writing the Apocalypse* served two purposes. It contributed to our understanding of apocalyptic themes and techniques in specific fictions; it also helped to define Literature of the Americas as a coherent field. Zamora introduced now-common themes in Hemispheric Studies, including Latin America-U.S. South literary relations (with Faulkner as master precursor), and caution over participating in U.S. academic imperialism. The book's chapters resonate with one another in pairs. Throughout, Zamora remains attuned to "the similarities and differences which become apparent when novels from different national and linguistic contexts are juxtaposed, opposed, superimposed."[17] As important to the comparative design is her immersive approach to individual texts within single chapters. She engages hemispheric voices in specific domains before relating them to each other. Most of all, for Zamora, U.S. relations and double-dealings are not required for Hispanic literatures to matter.

Still, Zamora is mindful of uneven U.S.-Latin American power dynamics, noting the "understandable (and necessary) skepticism about the plausibility of a hemispheric American comparative context."[18] This type of warning is rife in Hemispheric Studies today. The difference here is that *Writing the Apocalypse* is a testament to what committed scholars *can* accomplish when they study the literature of the Americas. Zamora proceeds with magnanimity, and with faith in the humanities as an agent of change. She challenges the naysayers: "To recognize *only* the differences between the United States and Latin America (admittedly great), *only* the abuses of the political past and present (also enormous), is to deter or defer comparative literary study and resign ourselves to further mutual misunderstanding."[19] As Zamora works to define an inter-American foundation for the imagination of history, literature matters. The apocalyptic authors here "are aware of humanity's propensity for communal self-destruction, and they are aware of the effects of crisis, for both good and evil, on the individual."[20] Yet, their feats of imagination reveal "the conviction that literature may yet influence that outcome."[21]

Thirty years after its appearance, *Writing the Apocalypse* strikes the reader with its sustained attention to literature. Zamora does not rummage through an undifferentiated deluge of culture, ripe for pre-scripted ideological repurposing. Rather, she approaches literature with a receptiveness to whatever emerges from the reading experience. One finds a profound allegiance to the world of letters, and a stance of humility before complex narrative worlds. As Zamora attests throughout the book, literature has a capacity for insight, contestation, and transhistorical impact. Her dialogue with some of the best and brightest from the Americas (via their greatest artistic contributions) makes her book into a hemispheric gathering of texts and voices.[22] At a time when such comparative projects might be considered beyond the scope of "Americanist" publishing lists, including those claiming a specialization in "New World," "Americas," and "Hemispheric" *Studies* (not literature), the ethos of close reading in *Writing the Apocalypse* dates the book to a more optimistic moment in academia. Several books followed suit, including Fitz's *Rediscovering the New World: Inter-American Literature in a Comparative Context* (1991), José David Saldívar's *The Dialectics of Our America: Genealogy, Cultural Critique, and Literary History* (1991), and Zamora's own *The Usable Past: The Imagination of History in Recent Fiction of the Americas* (1997). I date the closing of this phase of hemispheric study to books influenced by Zamora's modernist historical bent, as well as Saldívar's attention to race. Among these are Doris Sommer's *Proceed with Caution, When Engaged by Minority Writing in the Americas* (1999), Deborah Cohn's *History and Memory in the Two Souths: Recent Southern and Spanish American Fiction* (1999), George Handley's *Postslavery Literature in the Americas: Family Portraits in Black and White* (2000), and Santiago Juan-Navarro's *Archival Reflections: Postmodern Fiction of the Americas (Self-Reflexivity, Historical Revisionism, Utopia)* (2000). While providing a fitting end to an era keen on gathering outside voices, the international gains were already yielding to the scope and influence of English and American Studies departments. As it turned out, Americanists were undertaking a politically based "hemispheric turn" of their own. Declared unbound by comparatists in 1982, America was about to go national again.

ONE NATION, UNDER SUSPICION: HEMISPHERIC STUDIES (1998–2020)

The Oxford Online Dictionary defines a *professor* as "a person who affirms a faith in or allegiance to something."[23] As professors of literature know, that "something"—much as the liberal arts curriculum to whose mission it was once central—has been steadily losing ground in the neoliberal university. Reasons for the turn away from literature are varied, and no less politically contentious. Within language and literature departments, we might attribute at least some of them to poststructuralist modes of engagement that emerged in the 1980s and 1990s as theory (stemming from Comparative Literature's search for connections across traditions) and critiques of the Western canon overlapped into a neo-Marxian form of Cultural Studies. As contingencies of value eclipsed any remnant of "literariness," a New Historicist materialism set upon the task of mining cultural artifacts (literary or otherwise) with the express purpose of exposing the operations of power they concealed. American Literature professors turned to reading texts in two basic ways: (1) as enabling U.S. hegemony (and usually privileged within an arbitrarily assembled canon) and (2) as resisting this same oppression, especially in works by ethnic, border, and marginalized authors who needed championing. Despite appeals for an open canonicity, these non-mainstream and counter-hegemonic writings soon made up an alternative U.S. multiculturalist canon, which suited Americanist scholars newly attuned to post-colonialist critiques of culture. What this orientation lacked, however, was an awareness of how—in the interest of achieving social and political justice—Americanists were inevitably imposing their will upon literary texts. The strategy of criticizing U.S. imperialism by equating literature with ideology became a hallmark of the "New Americanists," whose strong influence begins with Amy Kaplan and Donald E. Pease's collection *Cultures of United States Imperialism* (1993), a volume privileging race, gender, and resistance as inscribed in cultural productions.

Over the last twenty-five years, the approach the volume helped to establish has become de rigueur within departments of English and American Studies. One unintended consequence of its attendant anxieties, however, has been its contribution to the unseating of literature from the throne of the humanities. As literary craft and cultivation became synonymous with a politically inscribed rhetoric of exclusion, context (rather than the text) became most important. Literary works were now historical documents by another name. On the one hand, this cultural materialism dislodged nationalistic and patriarchal assumptions responsible for placing European and Euro-American literature into incomparable universal categories. On the other, the new critiques possessed an unexamined certainty that, beyond the textual surfaces, there lay hidden the truth of the work as an instrument of power. As if offering an apologia for centuries-old traditions that had praised literature as a humanistic enterprise, scholars looked newly askance at the imagination of authors, and at the uniqueness of literary creation. Yet, the development of this more "serious" sociological approach, unwittingly placed texts into an ideological box. The call of professorial duty was now getting beyond the aesthetic effects of the literature professed. Criticism became the negative—and more responsible—task of anti-imperial "demystification." In *Touching Feeling: Affect, Pedagogy, Performativity* (2003), Eve Sedgwick aptly describes academic epistemologies after New Historicism as ones in which "the methodological centrality of suspicion to current critical practice has involved a concomitant privileging of the concept of paranoia."[24] By comparison with this preemptive and distrustful approach (which I believe currently bolsters the university's fatal auto-skepticism regarding the intrinsic value of the liberal arts), "anything *but* a paranoid critical stance has come to seem naïve, pious, or complaisant."[25]

More recently, Rita Felski has denounced this mindset for lacking the moral capacity to study literature in proper depth. In her own work, Felski borrows Paul Ricoeur's definition of "the hermeneutics of suspicion" to characterize the symptomatic reading strategies offered by Marx, Freud, and Nietzsche. She argues that, despite revolutionary intentions, the practice of reading against the grain conceals the critic's own biases. It does so, in part, by foreclosing a full range of textual associations for the sake of reproducing a privileged mode of critique that is central to its legitimacy. This stands in as a seal of professionalization in language and literature departments today. Following Sedgwick, we might say that the hermeneutics of suspicion results in a kneejerk complacency that prefers critical tautology to literary novelty. The main problem with this critique is that it does not approach polysemous worlds anew each time it encounters (and reencounters) literature. Instead, it finds comfort—and academic authority—in a fundamentalist skepticism. As vigilance becomes an academic mantra, deep insight means never falling for the machinations of art. Where literature is a ruse, only suspicion remains.

Contrary to poststructuralist critiques of value, in *Uses of Literature* (2008), Felski claims that "evaluation is not optional: we are condemned to choose, required to rank, endlessly engaged in practices of selecting, sorting, distinguishing, privileging, whether in academia or in everyday life. We need only look at the texts we elect to interpret, the works we include in our syllabi, or the theories we deign to approve, ignore, or condemn."[26] This questioning of critical norms forms part of a turn-of-the-century movement set upon recovering the aesthetic, as well as the role of affect mostly absent from literary studies.[27] Felski's call for reassessing what were once counterintuitive reading practices follows upon the French philosopher Bruno Latour, who tackles the unintended consequences of relativist epistemologies in "Why Has Critique Run Out of Steam? From Matters of Fact to Matters of Concern," a 2004 article published in *Critical Inquiry*. More specifically, Derek Attridge's 2004 book *The Singularity of Literature* provides a view of the literary text as allergic to critical dogma. Literature, in this vein, functions not as a collection of passive objects to demystify with predetermined aims. Rather, texts are irreducible artifacts that change with each reader's encounter. Treating each act of reading as a novel experience, Attridge embraces "an openness that allows for a range of possible outcomes."[28] Such a restorative approach to texts—and (in Attridge's case) to a string of responses constituting literary originality and qualitative differences—has opened up an avenue for exploring literature's power to impact the reader across time and place. For Felski, these include visceral aspects of the reading experience (shock, enchantment, disgust, etc.). Far from espousing a traditionalism (or being unaware of contingencies of value), the work of these scholars is essential because it reminds us that all literary texts resist our efforts to make them mean something. This is not tantamount to a reactionary "naïve reading" to oppose a "suspicious reading," or one that seeks to resurrect an *explication de texte* where literature eclipses readers. Texts are unique. They possess an unruly vitality worth engaging not from some safe critical distance and with the aim of coercing a single confession. Rather, texts command attention to linguistic expression, strangeness, and nuance gleaned through close-readings that measure the effects of language on the page. Human products, texts are literal embodiments of difference. A responsible reading of literature requires a willingness to meet otherness head on, registering its effects both on the brain and on the body. It is in this configuration—where literature remains an active disciplinary object—that I would like to consider how immersing oneself in encyclopedic novels—some of which Zamora dialogues with in *Writing the Apocalypse*—might strengthen the "Inter-" prefix in "Inter-American" Studies. For that to happen, hemisphericists would need to overcome "the aversion to surprise" that Sedgwick considers a cornerstone of paranoid reading.[29] On some level, this work requires rethinking the political basis (and biases) of literary studies after New Historicism. Does my questioning of the ensconced skepticism of the field not risk weakening the anti-imperialism that motivates much of U.S.-based Hemispheric Studies today?

In a 2004 special issue of *Comparative American Studies*, Claudia Sadowski-Smith and Claire F. Fox make the case that "inter-Americas scholars need to establish closer contact with one another across disciplinary, regional, and national borders and to urge the reconfiguration of existing interdisciplinary fields in the United States and elsewhere."[30] Sadly, the international amplitude and cooperation that these inter-Americanists prescribe are sorely missing from Hemispheric Studies today. It would seem that institutional, organizational, and linguistic asymmetries have continued to pose insurmountable challenges for scholars working in separate parts of the Americas, and within separate gathering and publishing venues. I believe that we would go a long way toward repairing the divide by taking a second look at earlier incarnations of hemispherism, whose core aim was to speak across nations by treating both "Literature" and "Americas" as plural disciplinary objects. Any revisiting of Zamora's generation also calls for a sobering clarification of what remains a missing page in intellectual history, and reveals aspects of an uneven development. Indeed, a U.S. historian called for the discipline in 1932, and literary comparatists answered the call collectively half a century later. It is also true that, in keeping with changing tides, the hermeneutics of suspicion is responsible for turning "Literature of the Americas" into something more U.S-centric: "Hemispheric Studies." Its imagined orphanhood clears a pathway for promoting future interests, untethered to a collective disciplinary history.

I do not conclude that Hemispheric Studies is invalid, but only that we are currently in need of an immersive and international literary supplement to the perspectives of English and American Studies.[31] The unfolding of the Americas discipline since 2000 has addressed one part of a whole. It is something akin to the Spanish borderlands history that Bolton founded before establishing a hemispheric field inclusive of smaller disciplines (but here the development has occurred in reverse: from Greater America to U.S.-America). Without this essential inclusion, one of the most regrettable aspects of Hemispheric Studies comes into view and exacerbates the cross-cultural divide: "hemispheric," like the U.S. appropriation of the signifier "America," is U.S. privilege by another name. In 2000s scholarship, it denotes mostly U.S. hemispheric *relations*, *migrations*, or *imaginaries* (with a one-sided emphasis on nearby Mexico and the Caribbean). Whereas Literature of the Americas used disciplinary critique as a mental catapult beyond any one nation, Hemispheric Studies privileges self-reflexivity to challenge the single most powerful nation's deleterious impact on the Western Hemisphere. Since only the presence of the United States guarantees a designation of "hemispheric" in this work, Pérez Firmat's "terra incognita" is a prophecy thirty years in the making. The admonishment now describes, accurately, the non-U.S. literatures that Americanists have grown too skeptical to read in their "hemispheric" work. A navel-gazing approach trumps the hemisphere as object, something comparatist Djelal Kadir calls out in the most brilliant dissection of New and Post National American Studies on record. While Kadir (19) does not blame suspicion directly, he decries U.S. academic solipsism as "a more capacious nationalism that reinscribes a nationalist project."

The national fixture remains in place in Janice Radway's presidential address to the American Studies Association (ASA), which inaugurated the U.S.-based "hemispheric turn" in 1998. The conference took place in Seattle and operated under the title "American Studies and the Question of Empire: Histories, Cultures and Practices." This effort culminated in the flag-bearing anthology *Hemispheric American Studies* (2008), "a sort of handbook (or guidebook) to a burgeoning field," as editors Caroline F. Levander and Robert S. Levine claim.[32] Sophia McClennen has offered an assessment of Radway's address and traced its implications for Hemispheric Studies. She denounces the ASA speech as forwarding lines of thinking that "represent themselves as post-national, but which ultimately have no cultural referents beyond the borders of the United States, and consequently are not post-national in any meaningful way."[33] As indicated by the title of the ASA conference, "Empire" (not hemispheric traditions) and "Cultures" (not literatures) attests to the influence of *Cultures of United States Imperialism*. Radway's speech is a reference point for influential books whose capacious titles claim to take American Studies global, among them *Hemispheric American Studies* and Wai Chee Dimock and Lawrence Buell's *Shades of the Planet: American Literature as World Literature* (2007). Neither book immerses itself in non-U.S. American literatures or critical traditions.[34] The shift from location to method in the titles of the two flagship hemispheric anthologies, from 1990 and 2008, respectively, is significant. The first announces a multidirectional quest within a grounded civilization (*Do the "Americas" Have a Common Literature?*), while the second asserts a new and improved *"Hemispheric" American Studies* that refashions itself to float over and through the Americas.[35] The latter has become such a preferred term in 2020 that "Hemispheric Studies" suffices; no hemispheric alternates exist for the invisible yet omnipresent (U.S.) "American."[36]

Furthermore, given the 2000s decline of Literature of the Americas, scholars might be surprised to learn that *The Cambridge History of the American Novel*, a 1272-page volume from 2011, includes entries that would seem to expand its titular "American" designation via fiction. "The Hemispheric Novel in the Post-Revolutionary Era" by Gretchen Murphy and "Hemispheric American Novels" by Rodrigo Lazo (chapters 33 and 65, respectively), prove that there is still interest in literature, at least as it pertains to U.S. relations with the Western Hemisphere. Not surprisingly, both essays pause to reflect on the parameters of the "hemispheric" subject matter under question. While defending *Hemispheric American Studies*, Lazo argues for delimiting the Americas field "toward a hemispheric approach rather than a presumptuous designation of a new field that would include all novels published in the Americas."[37] I would like to interrogate, for a moment, this strategic and most-sensible narrowing, and explain what it signals to me about the critical aptitude of Hemispheric Studies. Echoing Levander and Levine's misapplication of the term "bourgeoning" to describe what began in Comparative Literature in 1982, here Lazo applies "new" for an impossible discipline, any "presumptuous" move to create one perhaps concealing an imperialistic hubris. He does not recognize continuity with earlier incarnations of the field because his concern is for the "how" rather than the "what." The latter, as he suggests, would comprise semi-planetary differences within a vast literary archive. Indeed, a tall order for any single scholar who does not embrace collaboration in the—admittedly—impractical ways that Sadowski-Smith and Fox do. Not by coincidence, this narrowing also makes "Hemispheric American Novels" more relevant for the U.S. target audience of the Cambridge volume. After all, *The Cambridge History of the American Novel* does not include articles on, say, the *novela de la tierra* or the *roman du terroir*, two telluric "American" genres from Latin America and French Canada, respectively. Consistent with the New Americanist mission, Lazo's definition of the hemispheric field "focuses on how the conception of an inter-American space is intertwined with the great violence that has been carried out in the name of colonial or imperialist triumph and economic success."[38] This delimiting finds coherence in an axis of power that makes the Americas manageable for Americanists with political commitments. What I object to here is only the elimination of a fuller span in favor of one overriding thrust for "Hemispheric American Novels." This remains the case despite Lazo's timely critique of nationalism as expressed in, for instance, U.S. immigration policy, no doubt a key pressure point of inter-American affairs today.

Americanist claims to originality neglect Luis Alberto Sánchez; they also elide the first wave of "Literature of the Americas" that followed the Peruvian's original achievements without acknowledging him. The conceptual origins of Hemispheric Studies, however, lie in a different neglected and out-of-print source: Stanley T. Williams's *The Spanish Background of American Literature* (2 volumes, 1955). Williams—a renowned Melville scholar and an early founder of American Studies while at Yale University—inquired into Hispanic contexts and sources for nineteenth-century U.S. letters. In his Cold War-era treatise, he provided a Hispanist alternative to F.O. Matthiessen's more expressly nationalistic *American Renaissance: Art and Expression in the Age of Emerson and Whitman* (1941). By contrast, Williams's offbeat emphasis on the contributions of Hispanic peoples to the cultural development of the United States challenged stereotypical views of Spain and its colonies. At the same time, his efforts steered Literature of the Americas toward one national literature looking in on itself. Instead of an archive of texts in many languages and representing several traditions (and inside which the value of the Hispanic world is plain to see), Literature of the Americas would give a "hemispheric" spin to American Studies. *The Spanish Background of American Literature* is a landmark whose importance has not carried over, despite the 1990s "hemispheric turn." It is Hemispheric Studies avant la lettre.

In keeping with the emphasis on approach over member nations, English over Babel, Hemispheric Studies developed quite differently from Literature of the Americas. One wonders if Lazo's "Hemispheric American Novels" can set in motion the forms of international dialogue espoused by Sadowski-Smith and Fox. By contrast, what would it mean for Hemispheric Studies to engage the Quiché-Maya *Popol Vuh*, the Inca *Ollantay*, or any other early/pre-Columbian indigenous texts from outside the current borders of the United States? What about Spanish American epics, such as *La Araucana* (1569–1589) by Alonso de Ercilla or *Martín Fierro* (1872–1879) by José Hernández, two cornerstones of Chilean and Argentine national identities, respectively? Should it be a concern of Hemispheric Studies that the existentialist novels of Clarice Lispector are milestones of Brazilian literary history?[39] How can we understand historical, cultural, and linguistic divisions in Canada if Margaret Atwood and Hubert Aquin are not on required reading lists?[40] What about Spanish American post-Boom authors indebted to the non-manifestly "hemispheric" fictions of Jorge Luis Borges? Indeed, the answers to these questions will differ depending on interests, background, and professional training. I would argue—impractically—against any limitations to intellectual discovery gained from approaching "The Americas" (in the parlance of Zamora and Silvia Spitta) "Otherwise."[41] Without advancing a Eurocentric ontology of America as critiqued by Mexican philosopher Edmundo O'Gorman, I embrace here—as did Sánchez and other Literature of the Americas scholars—an America that is geographically "correct." Based in the Bolton thesis, this approach is open to scholarship along a multidirectional spectrum. It observes a literary historical timeline based upon patterns of indigeneity, contact, conquest, colonization, slavery, miscegenation, independence, nations, migration, and globalization. In what follows, I offer an alternate version of "Hemispheric American Novels" that is a point of entry to those professing literature on this maximal scale.

SUMMA AMERICANA: FROM TERRA INCOGNITA TO TERRA NOSTRA

In *Writing the Apocalypse*, Zamora engages novels of the "encyclopedic" genre, among them García Márquez's *Cien años de soledad* (1967), Thomas

Pynchon's *Gravity's Rainbow* (1973), and Fuentes's *Terra nostra* (1975). In "Encyclopedic Narrative: From Dante to Pynchon" (1976), Edward Mendelson argues that literary compendia incorporate extended references to politics, science, technology, language, history, and art (as well as tropes of monstrosity and gigantism that reflect on the form itself). Mendelson singles out Melville, Dante, Rabelais, Cervantes, and other luminaries, for an encyclopedic author is one who attends to the whole social and linguistic range of his nation, who makes use of all the literary styles and conventions known to his countrymen, whose dialect often becomes established as the national language, who takes his place as national poet or national classic, and who becomes the focus of a large and persistent exegetic and textual industry comparable to the industry founded upon the Bible.[42]

Reflecting on *Terra nostra*, most would agree that Fuentes's magnum opus incorporates a linguistic world from the sixteenth century to the present, creating a Hispanic bible. This encyclopedic novel has gained the critical public afterlife Mendelson describes. Fuentes has become a key national author, although this is largely based upon the reputation of *La muerte de Artemio Cruz* (1962), his more accessible and personal novel about the failures of the Mexican Revolution. Indeed, in *Terra nostra*, Fuentes expands Mendelson's criteria beyond national self-sufficiency, and in keeping with the international identity of one of the most cosmopolitan of Latin American writers. *Terra nostra* is not so much the encyclopedic novel of Mexico, but a New World cathedral built from dazzling Hispanic literatures. I call it a *summa Americana*.[43]

Of course, not all encyclopedic literatures—even those from the Americas—fit into this category. In keeping with Boltonian sightlines, the *summa Americana* uses historical fiction to revive the hemispheric legacies of Greater America. Publishing lists attest that big novels have been popular in the United States over the past decade.[44] Yet, Hispanic authors have been producing the *summa Americana* since the 1960s. During the "Boom," national fictions gave way to an international scene of writing and politics among authors of what Emir Rodríguez Monegal called the "novela total." This "total novel" has more than a passing relationship to the scholarly "panorama" that Sánchez and likeminded scholars held up as a model of erudition. In line with the first New World chroniclers, intellectual breadth gives these academics, and the "novela total" itself, its encyclopedic basis. More recently, as an updating of Bolton's blindness to Black history in "The Epic of Greater America," I would include Manuel Zapata Olivella's Colombian masterwork *Changó, el gran putas* (1984), which places the African diaspora on a hemispheric post-Columbian scale. These and other Latin American texts fit this definition of a *summa Americana* better than most maximalist fictions by Pynchon, David Foster Wallace, Don DeLillo, and other Anglo-American authors. Leslie Marmon Silko's *Almanac of the Dead* is an exception, as it envisions American Indian history along a hemispheric plane of Maya- and Aztlán-based prophecy: "The Americas were full of furious, bitter spirits; five hundred years of slaughter had left the continents swarming with millions of spirits that never rested and would never stop until justice had been done."[45] I would also include Jacques Poulin's *Volkswagen Blues* (1984). Despite its shorter length, it mixes timelines and envisions the colonial theme of the fur trading *voyageur* beyond Canada. It imagines border-crossing as continuous with the travel of U.S. pioneers and Quebecois global citizens in search of a contemporary El Dorado, a South American legend that is among the earliest versions of "le Grande Rêve de l'Amérique."[46]

It is not by coincidence that I privilege Latin America in my definition of "Hemispheric American Novels." The region is a bedrock of "America," and is hardly the default Anglophone nation hosting millions of Hispanic immigrants. It is part of the Western Hemisphere, which has been speaking Spanish since before the sixteenth century. As Bolton and subsequent historians attest, Spain offered one example of imperialism and slavery for Britain and other rivals long before the establishment of the United States. Moreover, Spaniards living alongside indigenous populations destroyed and/or absorbed these communities. This history carries vast implications for the core identities of millions of people living far south of current U.S. borders. Professors of Latin American literature recognize that a history-based New World identity remains a pivotal theme in the region. In sum, the Hispanic story of America is irreducible to one of immigration into the United States by another "minority" group striving to attain Anglo-American citizenship. With *summa Americana* in hand—and with an equal helping of boldness, apprehension, curiosity, and openness to literature—the reader gradually approaches a hemispheric world of differences.

Most of all in Latin America, a hemispheric archive of documents is central to the origins and significance of the *summa Americana* as a New World variant of the encyclopedic genre. *Terra nostra* gathers sources comprising what Roberto González Echevarría calls the "Archive." These colonial writings start with Christopher Columbus and form "a repository for the legal documents wherein the origins of Latin American history are contained, as well as a specifically Hispanic institution created at the same time as the New World was being settled."[47] Hispanic civilizations have incorporated them into a complex historical reality of baroque accommodation and cultural *mestizaje*. *Terra nostra* imagines Europe meeting America as the *quarta orbis pars* to shatter the Catholic trinity. Fuentes's *summa Americana* transforms gradually into an archive of wisdom, myths, facts, and figures about New World identity (thus countering the other giant in the novel—El Escorial palace). *Volkswagen Blues* creates a scrapbook of a transamerican journey that the reader uses to retrace the steps of the Quebecois protagonists. *Almanac of the Dead* forges strong ties to the Mesoamerican codices, and seeks to materialize in the reader's hands to issue a prognostication. These hemispheric megafictions are monuments that attest to the endurance of literature. The *summa Americana* makes us think across hemispheric borders because it activates the Archive in its DNA. It also asks us to rethink the Archive in line with Fuentes's literary reinvention. Through "la suprema unión de la fábula y la realidad," the reader discovers a Greater American *Terra nostra* (literally "our land" in Latin).[48] The novel offers an invitation (and no less a challenge) to rediscovery through an encyclopedic program of lifetime reading, education, and engagement. To read the *summa Americana* well is to surpass academic limitations that privilege specializations in practice. Patience is more than the proverbial virtue here, for one does not dabble in the *summa Americana*. We must plunge and be happy to sink.

Moreover, the *summa Americana* undertakes a self-conscious expansion through words, and often in ways that cue readers to experience the text beyond the markings on a page. As if growing bigger to merge form and content, size matters here. Encyclopedic novels are at once literature and large artifacts (normally above 500 pages); as conceived through fictional conceits, their word-sculpted bodies are not reducible to transferable type on a digital tablet or screen. Their authors create tangible objects with a maximum gravity that turns them into one-of-a-kind book structures. We enter long-term relationship with them, and experience the weight of their ponderous knowledge. Their maximal scale results from words turning into matter, as authors from the Americas make words matter for their readers. By aligning the art of the novel with three-dimensional world building, they confront us with the power of artistic revelation. The *summa Americana* compels us to jump into the deep end of languages and to dialogue with New World cultures across space and time. Their towering intellect, erudition, and word counts overwhelm. These prodigious books seem to know more as fiction than we do as critical readers. Yet, we may find comfort in the fact that—through a single one of these encyclopedic books—we hold the knowledge of America in our hands, so long as we engage in the additional reading necessary to exist in their hemispheric webs. Only this devotion to literature can turn Pérez Firmat's terra incognita, which haunts Hemispheric Studies today, into a hard-earned *terra nostra*. Elsewhere, Fuentes writes: "The contemporary novelist uses fiction as an arena where not only characters meet, but also languages, codes of behavior, distant historical eras, and multiple genres, breaking down artificial barriers and constantly enlarging the territory of the human presence in history."[49] In the end, it is one thing to talk about the hemisphere, and quite another to inhabit this cultural complex. Is this not the task of the hemispheric American scholar?

No amount of suspicion can substitute for reading. This essay advocates for a renewed commitment to making Hemispheric Studies more international on the one hand, and literature-based on the other. True inclusivity allows nations to retain their literary sovereignty rather than always placing them in self-interested interactions, no matter how liberal-minded or nominally cosmopolitan. The aim is to recover the hemisphere, a multiperspectival entity that has spoken Romance languages for centuries, and not always with the United States in mind. Reading the *summa Americana*, one finds its textual nutrients everywhere, for the Archive is contained within it. Using a capacious vision to match its formal gigantism, the *summa Americana* demands a commitment to literature in the interest of a hemispheric gathering. It values inter-American dialogue and process rather than prescription and critical dogma. I believe that such immersion, and the reading facilitated by its total (but not totalizing) vision, would bring scholars to a fuller understanding of the Americas. Instead of remarking on impossible amplitudes yet again, we may find that the encyclopedic novel—the *summa Americana* in particular—provides a pathway to the hemisphere as charted by Zamora and kindred scholars of American difference.[50] In the 2020s, a resurgent U.S. nationalism has reduced Latin America to a caricature. I can think of nothing more vital to the future of the discipline than its hemispheric voices, past and present.

NOTES

1. Bolton, "The Epic," 448.
2. Ibid.
3. Hurtado provides a recent assessment of Bolton as a historian of the borderlands.
4. "The Epic of Greater America" was a response to James Truslow Adams's *The Epic of America* (1931), which recounted a U.S. national story. In 1937, a Spanish translation of the address appeared in Mexico as *La epopeya de la máxima América*. On the Bolton thesis, see Hanke.
5. Bolton, "The Epic," 474.
6. For a discussion of Bolton's teaching at Berkeley, see Truett, 223–30.
7. Fitz, "The Theory," 154.
8. Bauer, "Early American," 256.
9. A major exception is Early American Literature, where the scholarship of Bauer, Anna Brickhouse, and others advances a Boltonian reconfiguration of American Puritan origins.
10. Sánchez is one of the foremost Peruvian intellectuals of the twentieth century. He began authoring literary histories of the Americas after a 1930 military coup led

to his exile. Estuardo Núñez, Sánchez's student, was the first scholar to call for a marriage of Latin American and Comparative Literature. The two became colleagues at the Universidad de San Marcos in Lima.

11. Literary historians used the "panorama" to synthesize one national output (e.g., Sánchez's *Panorama de la literatura del Perú*, 1974), or to provide a general survey (e.g., Sánchez's *Panorama de la literatura actual*, 1934). The Washington DC-based *Panorama: Revista interamericana de cultura* also influenced Carvalho's hemispheric "panorama." Housed in the Department of Cultural Affairs of the Pan American Union from 1952 to 1955, the journal used a member-nations platform in the same four languages. *Panorama das literaturas das Américas* includes an "aprecentação" by the secretary general of the Organization of American States.

12. For a history of Literature of the Americas as a discipline, see Barrenechea, "Literature."

13. In the preface to the volume, Pérez Firmat acknowledges the title's relation to Lewis Hanke's anthology *Do the Americas Have a Common History?: A Critique of the Bolton Thesis* (1964).

14. Pérez Firmat, *Do the Americas*, 2.

15. Umphrey's thirteen-page essay, "Spanish American Literature Compared with That of the United States" (1943), is the first study of literature of the Americas in English.

16. Email to author, September 2, 2015.

17. Zamora, *Writing the Apocalypse*, 6.

18. Ibid, 21.

19. Ibid, 21–2, author's italics.

20. Ibid, 192.

21. Ibid.

22. *Writing the Apocalypse* appeared in Spanish translation in 1995 as *Narrar el apocalipsis: La visión histórica en la literatura estadunidense y latinoamericana contemporánea*.

23. "Professor." Oxford Dictionaries, accessed December 24, 2020, http://www.oxforddictionaries.com/us/definition/american_english/professor.

24. Sedgwick, *Touching Feeling*, 125.

25. Ibid, 126.

26. Felski, *Uses of Literature*, 20.

27. Cynics might see this shift as a post-9/11 return to illusory foundations, rather than a recuperation of sensorial experience that makes literature meaningful for readers in the first place. For a summation of affect theory in relation to aesthetics, see Gregg and Seigworth.

28. Attridge, *The Singularity*, 8.

29. Sedgwick, 130.

30. Sadowski-Smith and Fox, "Theorizing the Hemisphere," 22.

31. A book that manages to combine aspects of both waves is Kirsten Silva Gruesz's *Ambassadors of Culture: The Transamerican Origins of Latino Writing*

(2002). See also Anna Brickhouse's *Transamerican Literary Relations and the Nineteenth-Century Public Sphere* (2004).

32. Levander and Levine, *Hemispheric*, 3.
33. McClennen, "Inter-American Studies," 402.
34. This trend continues in *American World Literature: An Introduction* (2019). Here, however, Paul Giles (1–29) provides an excellent summation of intellectual history and terminology.
35. Pérez Firmat's volume began as a lecture funded by the Latin American and Caribbean Center at Florida International University in December 1987. Levander and Levine's anthology stems from a 2006 special issue of *American Literary History* on "Hemispheric American Literary History" (co-edited by Levander and Levine). This expanded into the 2007 NEH seminar at Columbia University, "Toward a Hemispheric American Literature," co-directed by Rachel Adams and Caroline F. Levander. The book version finally changed "Literature" into "Studies."
36. For example, Global South Studies marks the Southern Hemisphere as the Third World.
37. Lazo, "Hemispheric," 1086.
38. Ibid.
39. Throughout his career, Fitz has mounted a defense of Brazil within an inter-American literary project. Hemispheric accounts, however, mostly neglect it. For a recent exception, see Tosta.
40. As with Brazil, U.S.-Latin America-based comparatists mostly elide Canadian literature. For the most notable exception, see the scholarship of Patrick Imbert (for example, *Comparing*).
41. See the special issue "The Americas, Otherwise" in *Comparative Literature* 61, no. 3 (2009). The most active comparative studies platforms for inter-Americanists since 2000 are: the International American Studies Association (IASA) (est. 2000), *Comparative American Studies: An International Journal* (est. 2003), and the International Association of Inter-American Studies (IAS/EAS) (est. 2009). The IASA and IAS/EAS keep flagship journals. These are, respectively, *Review of International American Studies* (RIAS): https://iasaweb.org/rias-journal/ and *Forum for Inter-American Research* (FIAR): http://interamerica.de/.
42. Mendelson, "Encyclopedic Narrative," 1268.
43. For a discussion of encyclopedic novels of the Americas, see Barrenechea, *America Unbound*.
44. See the recent focus on "Big Novels" in *American Book Review* 37, no. 2 (2016).
45. Silko, *Almanac of the Dead*, 424.
46. Poulin, *Volkswagen Blues*, 109.
47. González Echevarría, *Myth and Archive*, 29.
48. Fuentes, *Terra nostra*, 466.
49. Fuentes, "Latin America," 5.
50. For a discussion of two recent comparative studies of the Americas, see Barrenechea (Review). Whether this signals a revived literary internationalism in the field remains uncertain.

WORKS CITED

Adams, James Truslow. *The Epic of America*. Boston: Little, Brown, and Company, 1931.

Aldridge, Alfred Owen. *Early American Literature: A Comparatist Approach*. Princeton: Princeton University Press, 1982.

Attridge, Derek. *The Singularity of Literature*. London: Routledge, 2004.

Ballón, José C. *Autonomía cultural americana: Emerson y Martí*. Madrid: Pliegos, 1986.

Barrenechea, Antonio. *America Unbound: Encyclopedic Literature and Hemispheric Studies*. Albuquerque: New Mexico University Press, 2016.

———. "Literature of the Americas." In *Encyclopedia of Contemporary American Fiction, 1980–2020*, edited by Leslie Larkin, Stephen Burn, and Patrick O'Donnell. London and New York: Wiley-Blackwell, 2021 (forthcoming).

———. Review of *Whiteness on the Border: Mapping the U.S. Racial Imagination in Brown and White*, by Lee Bebout (New York University Press, 2016); *The Poetry of the Americas: From Good Neighbors to Countercultures*, by Harris Feinsod (Oxford University Press, 2017); and *Anxieties of Experience: The Literatures of the Americas from Whitman to Bolaño*, by Jeffrey Lawrence (Oxford University Press, 2018). *American Literature* 92.1. (2020): 169–71.

Bauer, Ralph. "Early American Literature and American Literary History at the 'Hemispheric Turn'." *Early American Literature* 45, no. 2 (Summer 2010): 250–65.

Bolton, Herbert Eugene. "The Epic of Greater America." *The American Historical Review* 38, no. 3 (April 1933): 448–74.

———. *La epopeya de la máxima América*. Translated by Carmen Alessio Robles. México: Instituto panamericano de geografía e historia, 1937.

Brickhouse, Anna. *Transamerican Literary Relations and the Nineteenth-Century Public Sphere*. Cambridge: Cambridge University Press, 2004.

Burns, Daniel, ed. "Big Novels." Special Issue, *American Book Review* 37, no. 2. (January/February 2016).

Carvalho, Joaquim de Montezuma de, ed. *Panorama das literaturas das Américas*. 4 vols. Nova Lisboa, Angola: Município de Nova Lisboa, 1958–1965.

Chevigny, Bell Gale and Gari Laguardia, eds. *Reinventing the Americas: Comparative Studies of Literature of the United States and Spanish America*. Cambridge: Cambridge University Press, 1986.

Cohn, Deborah. *History and Memory in the Two Souths: Recent Southern and Spanish American Fiction*. Nashville: Vanderbilt University Press, 1999.

Dimock, Wai Chee and Lawrence Buell, eds. *Shades of the Planet: American Literature as World Literature*. Princeton: Princeton University Press, 2007.

Felski, Rita. *Uses of Literature*. Malden, MA and Oxford: Blackwell, 2008.

Fitz, Earl E. *Rediscovering the New World: Inter-American Literature in a Comparative Context*. Iowa City: University of Iowa Press, 1991.

———. "The Theory and Practice of Inter-American Literature: An Historical Overview." In *Beyond the Ideal: Pan-Americanism in Inter-American Affairs*, edited by David Sheinin, 153–65. Westport, CT: Greenwood, 2000.

Fuentes, Carlos. "Latin America and the Universality of the Novel." In *The Novel in the Americas*, edited by Raymond L. Williams, 1–12. Boulder: University of Colorado Press, 1992.

———. *Terra nostra*. México: Joaquín Mortiz, 1975.

Giles, Paul. *American World Literature: An Introduction*. Hoboken, NJ: Wiley, 2019.

González Echevarría, Roberto. *Myth and Archive: A Theory of Latin American Narrative*. Durham: Duke University Press, 1998.

Gregg, Melissa and Gregory J. Seigworth, eds. *The Affect Theory Reader*. Durham: Duke University Press, 2010.

Gruesz, Kirsten Silva. *Ambassadors of Culture: The Transamerican Origins of Latino Writing*. Princeton: Princeton University Press, 2001.

Handley, George. *Postslavery Literature in the Americas: Family Portraits in Black and White*. Charlottesville: University of Virginia Press, 2000.

Hanke, Lewis, ed. *Do the Americas Have a Common History?: A Critique of the Bolton Theory*. New York: Knopf, 1964.

Hurtado, Albert L. *Herbert Eugene Bolton: Historian of the American Borderlands*. Berkeley: University of California Press, 2012.

Imbert, Patrick. *Comparing Canada and the Americas*. New York: Peter Lang, 2019.

Juan-Navarro, Santiago. *Archival Reflections: Postmodern Fiction of the Americas (Self-Reflexivity, Historical Revisionism, Utopia)*. Lewisburg, PA: Bucknell University Press, 2000.

Kadir, Djelal. "Introduction: America and Its Studies." *PMLA* 118, no. 1 (January 2003): 9–24.

Kaplan, Amy and Donald E. Pease, eds. *Cultures of United States Imperialism*. Durham: Duke University Press, 1993.

Kutzinski, Vera M. *Against the American Grain: Myth and History in William Carlos Williams, Jay Wright, and Nicolás Guillén*. Baltimore: Johns Hopkins University Press, 1987.

Latour, Bruno. "Why Has Critique Run Out of Steam? From Matters of Fact to Matters of Concern." *Critical Inquiry* 30, no. 2 (Winter 2004): 225–48.

Lazo, Rodrigo J. "Hemispheric American Novels." In *The Cambridge History of the American Novel*, edited by Leonard Cassuto, Clare Virginia Eby, and Benjamin Reiss, 1084–95. Cambridge: Cambridge University Press, 2011.

Levander, Caroline F. and Robert S. Levine, eds. *Hemispheric American Studies*. New Brunswick: Rutgers University Press, 2008.

———, eds. "Hemispheric American Literary History." Special Issue, *American Literary History* 18.3 (2006) 1–17.

Matthiessen, F.O. *American Renaissance: Art and Expression in the Age of Emerson and Whitman*. New York: Oxford University Press, 1941.

McClennen. Sophia. "Inter-American Studies or Imperial American Studies? *Comparative American Studies: An International Journal* 3, no. 4 (2005): 393–413.

Mendelson, Edward. "Encyclopedic Narrative: From Dante to Pynchon." *MLN* 91 (1976): 1267–75.
Murphy, Gretchen. "The Hemispheric Novel in the Post-Revolutionary Era." In *The Cambridge History of the American Novel*, edited by Leonard Cassuto, Clare Virginia Eby, and Benjamin Reiss, 553–70. Cambridge: Cambridge University Press, 2011.
O'Gorman, Edmundo. *The Invention of America: An Inquiry into the Historical Nature of the* New World and the Meaning of Its History. Bloomington: Indiana University Press, 1961.
Pérez Firmat, Gustavo, ed. *Do the Americas Have a Common Literature?* Durham: Duke University Press, 1990.
Poulin, Jacques. *Volkswagen Blues*. Montréal: Leméac, 1988.
Radway, Janice A. "What's in a Name?: Presidential Address to the American Studies Association, 20 November 1998." *American Quarterly* 51, no. 1 (March 1999): 1–32.
Rodríguez Monegal, Emir. *El boom de la novela latinoamericana*. Caracas: Tiempo Nuevo, 1972.
Sadowski-Smith, Claudia and Claire F. Fox. "Theorizing the Hemisphere: Inter-Americas Work at the Intersection of American, Canadian, and Latin American Studies." *Comparative American Studies: An International Journal* 2, no. 1 (2004): 5–38.
Saldívar, José David. *The Dialectics of Our America: Genealogy, Cultural Critique, and Literary History*. Durham: Duke University Press, 1991.
Sánchez, Luis Alberto. *Historia comparada de las literaturas americanas*. 4 vols. Buenos Aires: Losada, 1973–1976.
———. *Nueva historia de la literatura americana*. Buenos Aires: Americalee, 1944.
Sedgwick, Eve. *Touching Feeling: Affect, Pedagogy, Performativity*. Durham: Duke University Press, 2003.
Silko, Leslie Marmon. *Almanac of the Dead*. New York: Simon & Schuster, 1991.
Sommer, Doris. *Proceed with Caution, When Engaged by Minority Writing in the Americas*. Cambridge University Press, 1999.
Tosta, Luciano. *Confluence Narratives: Ethnicity, History, and Nation Making in the Americas*. Lewisburg: Bucknell University Press, 2016.
Truett, Samuel. "Epics of Greater America: Herbert Eugene Bolton's Quest for a Transnational American History." In *Interpreting Spanish Colonialism: Empires, Nations, and Legends*, edited by Christopher Schmidt-Nowara and John Nieto Phillips, 213–47. Albuquerque: University of New Mexico Press, 2005.
Umphrey, George W. "Spanish American Literature Compared with That of the United States." *Hispania* 26, no. 1 (February 1943): 21–34.
Valdés, Mario J., ed. *Proceedings of the Xth Congress of the International Comparative Literature Association*. Vol. 3. New York: Garland, 1985.
Williams, Stanley T. *The Spanish Background of American Literature*. 3 vols. New Haven: Yale University Press, 1955.
Zamora, Lois Parkinson. *Narrar el apocalipsis: La visión histórica en la literatura estadunidense y latinoamericana contemporánea*. Mexico City: Fondo de Cultura Económica, 1994.

———. *The Usable Past: The Imagination of History in Recent Fiction of the Americas*. Cambridge: Cambridge University Press, 1997.
———. *Writing the Apocalypse: Historical Vision in Contemporary U.S. and Latin American Fiction*. Cambridge: Cambridge University Press, 1989.
Zamora, Lois Parkinson and Silvia Spitta, eds. "Hemispheric American Literary History." Special Issue, *Comparative Literature* 61, no. 3 (2009) 189–365.
Zapata Olivella, Manuel. *Changó, el gran putas*. Bogotá, Colombia: Oveja negra, 1983.

Chapter 2
Mistranslation and Catastrophe
Anna Brickhouse

I begin with the closing lines of Lois Parkinson Zamora's *The Usable Past: The Imagination of History in Recent Fiction of the Americas*:

> To speak of cultures without necessarily speaking of nations, to speak of history without necessarily speaking of progression, succession, or supersession.
>
> These are the beginnings of a flexible model for comparative American cultural criticism. Theorists and writers of the New World Baroque know that the "sum of knowledge" is in process, and that it accumulates according to the multiple interactions of imagined worlds and historical ones. They also recognize their shared obligation to connect those worlds. Usable pasts depend upon such connections, and such connections are arrived at only by struggling to include: cultures and communities, histories and myths, individuals and groups, genres and media. The unfinished nature of the project is obvious.[1]

It has been twenty years since Lois Parkinson Zamora issued this call for a "flexible model" of comparative American studies. Returning to her words now, I am struck less by the way these final lines of *The Usable Past* foretell her own dazzling work on the New World Baroque than by how presciently they describe and help to shape the future of a field that has emerged over the two decades since Zamora's foundational book appeared. In the heyday of ideology critique—of the hermeneutics of suspicion, of scholarly demystification of authorial concealment—Zamora swam against the current; she asked what theorists and writers might create together as resource and sustenance in a broken world. In this respect her writings from the 1990s importantly anticipated a current preoccupation in literary studies with what a post-critical idiom might look like: that is, an idiom willing to recognize "the text's status as coactor," "as something that makes a difference, that helps make things happen."[2]

When I first encountered Zamora's work, I was still a graduate student, and had yet to understand the full implications of either her methods or her compelling injunction for the Americanist field. At the time, I understood only that she was one of the few people in the world to have written about Nathaniel Hawthorne's "Rappaccini's Daughter" in the context of the wider Americas. As it happened I was obsessed by that particular story, and I knew that I had found a kindred spirit when I first read her essay on Hawthorne, Octavio Paz, and Carlos Fuentes, published in *Revista Canadiense de Estudios Hispánicos* in 1984. In preparing to write an essay in Zamora's honor, I have had the pleasure of thinking back to that formative time and contemplating my own development as a scholar and my inheritance from her exemplary comparative work.

One of things I have come to realize in this reflective process is how much I have always been an "idee fixe" sort of academic. Indeed, the first ten or so conference papers I gave at the end of my graduate studies were all on some variant of "Rappaccini's Daughter": the tale's covert entanglement with the politics of Indian removal, the tale's haunting by Africanist presences, the tale's relation to the wider Americas of the mid-nineteenth century, and so on. I might have kept going on like this indefinitely except for the sage advice of another graduate student, who very gently told me that it came across as a little weird, this obsessive and perpetual meditation on a single short story—people were starting to notice that my central text was always the same—and he suggested kindly that I should probably try to write at least one conference paper that did not take "Rappaccini" as its central subject. He was absolutely right, of course. But it is also true that an obsession with that one story is what led me out of my intellectual comfort zone and into Mexico via Octavio Paz's twentieth-century adaption of Hawthorne's story into a play. Before that, I had been a student focused exclusively on U.S. literature with no real comparative leanings. Forsaking breadth and giving up on the hope of field *mastery*—and tracking something small, something minor, but somehow important to me—was the process that yielded the most surprising findings and the most interesting stories. It was also this process that fortuitously introduced me to the comparative Americanist endeavor—a collective project that still thrills me to this day—via Zamora's transformative work.

I can see more clearly now, for example, that exploring the translation and transmission of a particular text or story across broad swathes of time may offer a kind of provisional method, one that is straightforward because narrowly circumscribed, and yet is not to be confused with studies of influence. Indeed, Zamora memorably shifted our focus from the Bloomian anxiety of influence to the hemispheric American anxieties about origins. Part of the point of following the unfolding of translation and transmission is thus to see the interaction of textual influence with change over time in all its cultural, political, linguistic, and geographic complexity. Like many other modes of inquiry, this one sits at the crossroads of literature and history, but because translation and transmission are narrowly conceived around the specificity of particular texts or stories, this method, if we can call it that, offers a way into and around the grand narratives that often organize both literature and history as fields. When a graduate student specializing in mid-nineteenth-century U.S. literature tunnels along after a story and then pops her head up after it into twentieth-century Mexico, with none of the received wisdom that comes with disciplinary training, there can be an absurd, Candide-like quality to the first observations she might make. But such moments also involve serendipity, and may yet yield something that would have remained hidden or obscured had she entered this time and place with the passport of expertise.

Here, then, is one paradox of the comparative project: while the scholar must always strive to learn deeply across fields of inquiry, there is also a potential gain in relinquishing field and discipline mastery as a self-evident value in and of itself. Early on, I was encouraged to dispense with mastery as both a discourse and a self-contained logic by reading Zamora, who presented her ideas as a play of perspectives cultivated by the writers she studies and not as the singular, bird's-eye view of the scholar who always knows more and better than the authors she reads. Similar lessons can be derived from the work of another great comparative Americanist, Doris Sommer, whose book *Proceed with Caution* asks us to cultivate a certain working notion of humility, suggesting that not every text or work of art produced by what Sommer terms "minority" subjects in the Americas exists primarily for the purpose of our decoding it with our PhD-honed skills. Some texts, Sommer argues, will push us away, but perhaps allow us to learn something important in the act of accepting that we stand outside the circle of comprehension—that we can perhaps, in fact, *know better* when we abandon the assumption that we should have the privilege to know based on a specific kind of university training. In a similar vein, Sommer's *Bilingual Aesthetics* foregrounds the potential role of *mis*translation as a register that may have important things to teach us about literary history in the Americas. Linguistic mastery is of course the assumed currency of most disciplines, and comparative literature, especially, fetishizes that which resists translation—that special word that can never be quite translated beyond its native tongue, the "untranslatable," as Emily Apter calls it. But Sommer's work shows us that struggling on with a *lack* of linguistic mastery has something to teach us, too. In no way does she advocate retreating to monolingualism, but she asks us to embrace what she calls "bilingual games": "Even embarrassing mistakes shouldn't stop you.... Always, they mark communication with ... a tear ... producing an aesthetic affect..... Don't imagine that other more dignified language games are more important."[3]

Building on both Sommer and Zamora, I have become interested over the years in what can be learned when we move away from the default model of translative mastery, and in the knowledge that can be adduced from *mis*translation itself. Perhaps one embarrassing example from my own experience will show what I mean by such knowledge. One of the literary works I wrote about in a recent book was *The First Gentleman of America: A Comedy of Conquest* (1942), a novel in English with a long bibliography of Spanish-language works at the end and, to make matters confusing, a handful of non-listed, hispanophone scholarly references sprinkled throughout the text of the novel itself. The novelist, the early twentieth-century Virginia writer James Branch Cabell, clearly wanted to be sure that readers understood the multilingual breadth of his research even if they never turned past the last page of the narrative to the bibliography at the end. Since the historical subject of Cabell's novel was the same indigenous translator at the center of the book I was then working on—*The Unsettlement of America* (2015)—I was familiar with most of the scholars he cited. But there were several quotations, taken from a chronicler whom Cabell praised as "judicious"[4] while failing to cite the title of his work, which I was surprised to find that I did not recognize. I was of course excited to stumble so fortuitously across a new source—somehow unknown to all colonial historians, and yet quoted at length by Cabell in his twelfth chapter: the rich and detailed "remarks" of a certain "Fulano Suárez."[5] Alas, I spent quite some time searching for said Señor Fulano Suárez— searching for what was essentially my own mistranslation, a misapprehension of this word *fulano* as a proper name—until I finally got suspicious and looked up *fulano* in a dictionary and found, of course, that I had been duped. The Suárez "remarks" constituted a fake source, designed to fool readers exactly like myself, while winking at potential Spanish-speaking readers who would be in on the joke that Fulano or "So-and-so" Suárez was not a real person's name. I won't claim that I learned something vital for my research here; the fake source didn't even end up in my book. But I did glean something of the novelist's orientation to his perceived readership here; I learned there was perhaps a gap between what Cabell meant and what he wanted English-speaking readers to *think* he meant. Perhaps more importantly, this bilingual game, to use Sommer's phrase, forced me, if only momentarily, out of the position of the heroic critic, the great revealer of the concealed—a position that Zamora too has long urged us to relinquish—by making me acknowledge that I had been outmaneuvered, *fulano-ed*. The experience reminded me to think in terms not of my mastery of sources, but of my potential subjection to their withholding—and it opened up for me other potential vistas of mistranslation.

More recently, I had another *fulano* sort of moment: an instance of translative impasse and failure followed by the delayed satisfaction of insight, and one both appropriate and serendipitous for a volume dedicated to Zamora. I was teaching an English translation of a 1996 novel by the late Chilean writer Roberto Bolaño: *Estrella Distante*, or *Distant Star*, a slim but dense meditation on poetry and torture during the first years of the CIA-promoted Pinochet dictatorship that began in 1972. The English edition of the novel—translated by Bolaño's first and primary Anglophone interpreter Chris Andrews—includes cover copy that informs the reader that the titular "star" of the novel is its arch-villain, Carlos Wieder: a spy and a torturer posing as an aspiring poet in 1971 Chile so that he can ferret out young, left-wing writers in their poetry seminars and disappear them in advance of the coup that will bring Pinochet to power. We never know Wieder; as the novel's "distant star," he is always just beyond the horizon, operating in many places under many names, and wherever he goes creating the conditions for neo-fascism under the guise of fostering avante-garde art. Bolaño's novel is explicitly about the politics of aesthetics, in other words, and it deploys what Zamora calls the "dissenting perspective of apocalypse."[6] Concerned with mass murder and the end of art, it plumbs what its narrator calls "trivial matters": "Like time. The greenhouse effect. The increasingly distant stars,"[7] and above all with—to borrow Zamora's words —"our ample capacities for self-destruction."[8] And it opens with a translation, an elliptical and all too abbreviated epigraph attributed to William Faulkner: "Que estrella cae sin que nadie la mire?"[9]—What star falls without anyone seeing it? In the English edition of the novel, the epigraph is a poetic, four-word question: "What star falls unseen?"[10]

But what does the question mean, whether in Spanish or English? And—an especially apt question given Zamora's groundbreaking work on the Latin American inheritances of the man Gabriel García Márquez once called his "maestro"—what Faulkner-Bolaño relation does the epigraph imagine? To answer these questions, we need, of course, the context of the original Faulkner work from which the epigraph was taken. But in my first reading of the novel, before it had even properly begun, this epigraph managed to thwart my interpretive attempts from the very outset. Not only did I not recognize the quotation, I could not find the quotation in any of the standard databases. I couldn't even find the words "star" and "unseen" in any proximity in Faulkner's works. After I spoke to a Faulkner specialist who told me that he, too, could not place the quotation in Faulkner's corpus, I began to suspect that Bolaño had made up the epigraph out of whole cloth. He alludes, after all, to the "increasingly animated ghost of Pierre Ménard."[11] Borges's famously invented "author of the *Quixote*," on the second page of the novel, and a false attribution to a fabricated source seemed in the same spirit—another Fulano Suárez kind of joke. But then the Faulkner specialist wrote back, forwarding a message from the Faulkner listserve's hive-mind, by a scholar who recognized the epigraph through layers of what turned out to be—of course, it's obvious now—translation. Bolaño had offered a quotation from Faulkner rendered into Spanish, but Andrews, as the translator, instead of returning to the Faulkner original, simply retranslated the epigraph back into English: as "What star falls unseen?" The original Faulkner text turns out to be much closer to Bolaño's Spanish: "What star is there that falls, with none to watch it?"

The question immediately recalls the old philosophical problem: If a tree falls in the forest and no one is there to hear, does it make a sound? For proponents of immaterialism such as the eighteenth-century philosopher Bishop George Berkeley, the answer is that perception is what creates existence. Bolaño, citing Faulkner, has restated the question in terms of sight—*Can a star fall with none to watch it?*—which is entirely appropriate for a novel all about visual regimes, optics, and the exercise of spectacular terror: Wieder the torturer of poets is also a photographer and visual artist who carefully documents and displays those he has disappeared. But here one might also ask, Does the original of a translation exist if no one reads it? Clearly, Chris Andrews, the Bolaño translator, did not read or know the original Faulkner text, since, in producing the posthumous translation, he simply retranslated Bolaño's Spanish back into English. Perhaps he had the same problem I did at the outset, and assumed a fabricated original, an invented relation to Faulkner on a world literary field written into existence by Bolaño alone: Bolaño has, after all, been celebrated as an exemplary figure for world literature itself.

But if world literature is generated, at least by some definitions, when works endure and gain new significance, new life, through the process of translative influence, then Bolaño's translation of Faulkner appears to operate in the reverse direction. Bolaño chose for his epigraph a Faulkner of precisely no influence, a Faulkner original to which even the English-language translator did not return. Indeed, the epigraph turns out to come from an obscure early-career Faulkner work, a book of poetry from 1924 that Faulkner wrote before he started writing the novels and stories for which he became famous: *The Marble Faun*—a title that of course recalls Hawthorne and has brought me dangerously close to falling off the Rappaccini wagon again. I am saved by the fact that the long pastoral poem by Faulkner is simply not very compelling, spoken as it is by the titular faun himself, who meditates on art and beauty, lamenting his inanimate status:

What star is there that falls, with none to watch it?
What sun is there more permanent than darkness?
What moon is there that cracks not? Ay, what laughter
What purse is there that empties not with spending?

I could see why even a Faulkner specialist hadn't identified the retranslated quotation. As Faulkner asks of the falling star, we might ask here: Does the original poet's work exist if it is never recognized after its translation and citation?

Bolaño's *Distant Star* is concerned with poetic recognition, too, though in a far darker guise: it asks if the fascist and torturer Wieder can be tracked down across the transmission and translation of his many pseudonymous verses and aesthetic manifestoes. The novel pursues the problem of finding a criminal through his art while exploring the larger intertwining of aesthetics and politics in the midst of the Cold War Americas. This is a context that Faulkner, in the 1950s, also inhabited in his capacity as a Cold War cultural ambassador, as Deborah Cohn has shown. Faulkner was sent by the State Department to Brazil, Peru, and Venezuela, where he promoted pro-U.S. sentiments in the years following the 1954 CIA-sponsored coup in Guatemala—and he did so in part by promising to effect English translations of Latin American literature back at home through the Ibero-American Novel Project established by his foundation at the University of Virginia. The project failed to yield much in the way of translation—a single novel made its way to a publisher, so delayed that its author had already died while waiting, and it soon afterward went out of print. Perhaps Bolaño decided to return this literary-ambassadorial favor with a sly wink, by translating a citation from the least known and perhaps the most non-influential of Faulkner's texts, and without naming its obscure title. *Distant Star*, set in the midst of the CIA-encouraged coup in Chile, and the aftermath of torture and disappearances, thus elaborates through its epigraph a miniature version of Faulkner's Ibero-American translation project in which, effectively, little to nothing gets transmitted.

Bolaño died the year before the English translation of *Estrella Distante* was published, but perhaps he too would have seen some glimmer of meaning in the way the retranslation of his epigraph effects a kind of mistranslation: an effacement of the original. For it is in part from Bolaño's *Distant Star* that I take the working hypothesis of a current project, one indebted to Zamora's work: that the long history of the Americas may be read in part as a series of mistranslated catastrophes, as a history *of* the mistranslation of catastrophe. I am drawing here as well on Kathleen Donegan's work on the English colonies, which offers "a new story in which crisis and catastrophe are placed at the center of the first years of English settlement in the new world."[12] In studies of Roanoke, Jamestown, Plymouth, and Barbados, Donegan shows us how the framework of catastrophe sidesteps the pitfalls of writing colonial histories as the foundations that later (teleologically, progressively) yield national histories. Stepping back a bit from the English colonies, and bringing early Americanist Donegan and the comparatist Zamora into dialogue, we can get a broader view of catastrophe as part of a centuries-long textual network in which narratives of disaster cross languages and time zones, re-emerging with new but often distorted or mistranslated meaning.

There is a moment midway through *Estrella Distante* where the narrator describes the attempt made by a handful of Chilean jurists to bring Carlos Wieder to trial for torture and murder in the midst of what the narrator calls "un terremoto de la historia," "an earthquake of history."[13] The effort to respond to this catastrophe is doomed from the start; scores of military officials defend Wieder publicly before the real trial has even begun, and the defendant himself never bothers to show up. Most telling of all is the failure of translation and transmission that occurs when the prosecution brings in its key witness: a Mapuche woman named Amalia Maluenda, who witnessed the disappearing of two sisters from the family for whom she once worked as a maid. In the intervening years since the crimes, Amalia has returned to an indigenous culture; her Spanish is halting, interspersed with Mapuche at every other word. In addition to the problem of linguistic difference is the fact that her account of the events blurs the generic boundaries of legal testimony, gathering into what the narrator describes as an epic poem that interweaves the contemporary events of the trial with a long history that includes the era of European conquest. In Amalia's account, Wieder is at times an "invader" or *conquistador*, his murders accompanied by what she calls "una música de españoles," "the music of the Spanish."[14] But neither her actual words about the twentieth-century murders nor the cataclysm of early modern colonial violence that she attempts to articulate transmit successfully to the courtroom audience. Her listeners are dumfounded, and Wieder's crimes, U.S. crimes against international law, and the foundational crimes to which Amalia tries to bear witness are soon forgotten. The trial record itself becomes a mistranslated history of catastrophe, causing the narrator to reconsider temporality not as a linear flow, like a river, but as an eruption: "como si el tiempo estuviera pasando . . . como un terremoto," "as if time were . . . but an earthquake happening nearby."[15]

Bolaño's repeated earthquake similes remind us that natural catastrophes often come to characterize both political events and alternative conceptions of history. And because his novel thinks in fascinating ways about the translation of catastrophe across languages and cultures, it suggests a kind of thought experiment on the relationship between mistranslation and catastrophe in the long history of the Americas. Homing in on the particular texts that transmit and mistranslate catastrophes across time allows us to see what Lisa Lowe has recently called the "intimacies of continents whose interconnected histories are [often] obscured"[16] by the way we organize and separate our disciplines. This premise also animates what Zamora calls the "shared obligation," on the part of scholars and writers *together*, of connecting disparate worlds in the face of a future catastrophically imperiled on many fronts. For when we understand the history of the Americas as a series of mistranslated catastrophes, as a history *of* the mistranslation of catastrophe, we are well positioned to recognize a longue durée of the spectacularizing, southernizing, and racializing of disaster, and what I hope in a future project to show is the interweaving—from the eighteenth century onward— of philosophical and economic investment in its aftermath. And perhaps, to adapt Bolaño, we might also approach the history that surrounds catastrophic events both as a river—of ideas and stories transmitted across the centuries—*and* as an earthquake: a massive rupture that exposes the ruins of the past within the present. This, I think, is a part of what Lois Parkinson Zamora was getting at in the epigraph with which I began: an alternative historicist model for comparative American studies that she has been describing for decades, and to which we will surely continue to look in our future.

NOTES

1. Zamora, *The Usable Past*, 210.
2. Felski, *The Limits of Critique*, 12.
3. Sommer, *Bilingual Aesthetics*, xii.
4. Cabell, *The First Gentleman of America*, 79.
5. Ibid., 288.
6. Zamora, *Writing the Apocalypse*, 4.
7. Bolaño, *Distant Star*, 147.
8. Zamora, *Writing the Apocalypse*, 1.
9. Bolaño, *Distant Star*, 5.
10. Ibid., 2.
11. Ibid., 1.
12. Donegan, *Seasons of Misery*, 3.
13. *Estrella distante*, 118; my translation.
14. Ibid., 120; *Distant Star*, 111.
15. Ibid., 51; ibid., 41.
16. Lowe, *The Intimacies of the Four Continents*, 20.

WORKS CITED

Bolaño, Roberto. *Distant Star,* trans. Chris Andrews. New York: New Directions Publishing, 2004.

Bolaño, Roberto. *Estrella Distante*. Barcelona: Editorial Anagrama S.A., 1996.

Cabell, James Branch. *The First Gentleman of America: A Comedy of Conquest.* New York: J.J. Little and Ives Company, 1942.

Donegan, Kathleen. *Seasons of Misery: Catastrophe and Colonial Settlement in Early America*. Philadelphia: University of Pennsylvania, 2014.

Felski, Rita. *The Limits of Critique*. Chicago: University of Chicago Press, 2015.

Lowe, Lisa. *The Intimacies of the Four Continents*. Durham: Duke University Press, 2015.

Paz, Octavio. *La hija de Rappaccini*. Mexico City: Ediciones Era, 1990.
Sommer, Doris. *Bilingual Aesthetics: A New Sentimental Education*. Durham: Duke University, Press, 2004.
Zamora, Lois Parkinson. *The Usable Past: The Imagination of History in Recent Fiction of the Americas*. Cambridge: Cambridge University Press, 1997.
———. *Writing the Apocalypse*. Cambridge: Cambridge University Press, 1989.

Chapter 3

Transamerican Friendships and American Utopias

José Carlos Mariátegui, Waldo Frank, and Victoria Ocampo

Priscilla Archibald

When the Anglo-American novelist and cultural critic Waldo Frank first wrote to a Latin American readership in 1924, he appealed to them as a friend: "We must be friends," he wrote, "not friends of the official ceremonial class, but rather friends in ideas, friends in acts, friends of a shared and creative intelligence."[1] Frank's proposal of friendship in this instance shows remarkable intuition. Referring to "a politics of friendship" as "the lost trope in anticolonial thought," the scholar Leela Gandhi examines friendship between metropolitan and postcolonial actors as a way of countering dominant ideological currents and disturbing the Manichean division between colonizer and colonized that is at the heart of imperial logic.[2] According to Gandhi, and here she is following the philosopher William James, though friendship is in no way innocent of ideology, because it involves the affective, it brings into play elements of the accidental, of happenstance and the unpredictable. This generative quality of friendship, with its unscripted potential, sheds light on Frank's role in Latin America. Frank established friendships and alliances with scores of Latin American intellectuals—from Alfonso Reyes, to José Carlos Mariátegui, to Samuel Glusberg, to Victoria Ocampo, and to Gabriela Mistral, among many others. If Latin Americans embraced Frank as they did few other North American intellectuals, they also capitalized on their friend's presence in unexpected ways. At first glance, Frank's engagement with Latin America seems not entirely inconsistent with the official pan-Americanism of the era (1910–1940) which, whether regarded as an economic, cultural, or political program, scholars generally agree was at the service of U.S. dominance in the Western hemisphere. His generalizations about Latin America and Anglo-America reinforce American stereotypes, and in the sweeping character of his messianic cultural ideology, one can't help but hear an echo of U.S. political expansionism. Yet if one examines Frank's intervention in Latin America closely, and considers not only the content of what he wrote but just what that intervention set into motion, the unilateral version of history which informs U.S. sponsored-pan-Americanism, as well as many critiques of pan-Americanism, is replaced with hemispheric histories that are inescapably polycentric. Along with New York, Buenos Aires, Mexico City, Santiago, Chile, and Havana—among other cities—were sites from which American hemispheric communication issued. If U.S. dominance in the Western hemisphere has obscured this polycentrism, it has likewise eclipsed the full significance of Frank's Latin Americanist career. By returning to the curious figure of Waldo Frank, who was the most outspoken proponent of a continental cultural imagination in the first half of the twentieth century, I wish to consider what we can learn from one particularly consequential example of a transamerican politics of friendship.

The heterodox nature of Frank's Pan-American project was plainly apparent to Latin Americans. As the Argentine woman of letters Victoria Ocampo remarked, contrasting Frank's attitude with that of many of his compatriots: "Spiritually, Waldo Frank belongs as much to Latin America as to his own America. Because of this, he and those like him are with us. But there is something in contemporary North America, a spirit of *American Citizens first*, that is important to combat. I like so many things about that country! And I dislike others."[3] Frank's extension of friendship broke down barriers that had become increasingly inflexible in the early decades of the twentieth century. Just as U.S. military excursions into Latin America had enhanced hostilities between the North and South,[4] Latin Americans welcomed Frank into their community. Peruvian writer Luís Alberto Sánchez spoke for many when he remarked: Frank "is one of ours," "he is of our race."[5]

To consider what friendship in practice meant, I will examine Frank's relationships with two key Latin American intellectuals—Peruvian Marxist, José Carlos Mariátegui and Victoria Ocampo—names which rarely appear in the same sentence, but then Frank brought together many unlikely pairs. His working philosophy revolved around the concept of the "whole," which referred ultimately to an organic social and spiritual order whose most dramatic antithesis, according to Frank, was represented by the fragmented society of the industrialized United States. Operating with the lens of this cultural ideology, Frank saw half worlds and pairs everywhere. Most famous was his prophecy of a "symphonic America," where distinct American cultures would come to operate as a harmonious whole. Frank foresaw a marriage between a spiritual Latin America and a pragmatic North America, with the former bringing spirit and the latter bringing the body, including—Frank wrote with no apparent self-consciousness—the all-important "tool."[6] But before this, Frank spied the two half worlds of Christian and Muslim Spain; his book *Virgin Spain: The Drama of a Great People* concludes with an anachronistic dialogue between Cervantes and Columbus, and in a letter to Argentine editor and writer Samuel Glusberg, he wrote about his desire to bring Mariátegui, "El Andino" to Buenos Aires, to work alongside Ocampo "la Porteña." This, he concluded, would bring about "la America Hispana que sueño y que el mundo necesita."[7] Given that Mariátegui developed a thoroughgoing critique of Peru's traditional oligarchy, while Ocampo was not only a member of Argentina's elite, but disinclined to question or even examine the legitimacy of her social privilege, it was an odd pairing indeed. It is not surprising that Frank's appeals to Ocampo that she help fund Mariátegui's move from Lima to Buenos Aires, a city which he believed was more hospitable to progressive politics, were met with silence. (Mariátegui's untimely death in 1930 meant that Frank's improbable proposal never had a chance to come to fruition.) Whatever their differences, the respective collaborations of Mariátegui and Ocampo with Frank shared important commonalities: paramount to both relationships was the construction of an American identity and an Americanist commitment, which among other things, involved re-negotiating the relationship between Europe and America.

Frank became a devoted hispanophile following a visit to Spain in 1921. In line with other U.S. intellectuals of the time, for whom pan-Hispanism and pan-Americanism were not antithetical—an idea that is foreign to much pan-Americanism which is quite specifically distinguished from or even against "the cultural unity of the former Spanish empire"[8]—Frank discovered Latin America via Spain. On a second trip to that country in 1924, he met the writer Alfonso Reyes, who was then Mexico's ambassador to Spain. The meeting would prove propitious and marked Frank's first collaboration with a Latin American intellectual. In the form of a letter to Reyes that was published in a PEN Club of Mexico newsletter, Frank wrote a short essay titled, "Mensaje a los escritores mexicanos" (Message to Mexican Writers) in which he first proposed that writers from the Spanish-speaking and English-speaking Americas join together in a project of cultural renewal. The letter was reprinted in a number of Spanish-speaking publications, catching the attention of many members of the Latin American intellectual community, including Mariátegui as well as Samuel Glusberg. Glusberg was particularly enthusiastic about Frank's humanism and adopted his idea of a hemispheric cultural identity: "Why call us Hispano, Ibero, or Latin American? All of these qualifications are but limitations... we should work toward the creation of the *good American*."[9] Glusberg was also largely responsible for facilitating the North American's initial six-month trip throughout the Latin American continent in 1929.

WALDO FRANK AND JOSÉ CARLOS MARIÁTEGUI

Two years after the publication of the PEN Club letter, Frank wrote to Mariátegui in order to thank him for the glowing review he had published about his cultural study *Our America* and novel *Rahab*. Thus began an intellectual friendship which would become increasingly intimate over the years, despite the two men having met in person only once. Arguably, the largely epistolary nature of the relationship between Frank and Mariátegui abetted both the intimacy which developed between them as well their abiding sense of the complementary nature of their respective Americanist ideologies. The highly constructed nature of epistolary communication, in which the writer creates both self and other to a degree that is less possible in face-to-face exchange, and the reader, similarly, has comparatively greater opportunity for interpretive license, allowed the two men to privilege intersections and commonalities over the seeming incompatibility between their respective methodologies and philosophies which hindsight makes so visible.[10] The single face-to-face encounter which took place between Mariátegui and Frank only deepened the solidarity which had developed over the course of their correspondence. Frank reported that the time he spent with Mariátegui was the "climax" of his 1929 trip,[11] and he dedicated his first book about Spanish America, *America Hispana*, to him. Though Frank would form close friendships with many Latin Americans, Mariátegui seemed to be the Latin American intellectual Frank most admired and with whom he felt the closest intellectual kinship.

The collaborative friendship between Frank and Mariátegui at first glance seems logical: both were prominent public intellectuals and important cultural critics and cultural facilitators. Frank founded and edited *The Seven Arts*, which, though short-lived (1916–1917), was a tremendously influential publication that brought together many of the most prominent writers, artists, and intellectuals in the United States at the time. For his part, Mariátegui founded and edited the landmark magazine *Amauta* (1926–1930), which was dedicated to politics, literature, and art, and quite explicitly, to the "science" of Marxism. Mariátegui and Frank were also important political actors. Mariátegui was the founder of the Peruvian socialist party. Sometimes referred to as a "disguised deportation" the Peruvian government awarded him a grant to spend three years in Europe (1919–1923), hoping to be rid of (or reform) an actor with a galvanizing political presence. Instead, Mariátegui returned to Peru in 1923 a committed Marxist with a well-honed understanding of political theory. For his part, Frank was involved in many of the most pressing progressive issues of the day—from the pacifism advocated in *The Seven Arts* (the unpopularity of which was largely responsible for the journal's short life span), to anti-imperialism and anti-militarism, to anti-racism, to pro labor militancy and support of women's rights. While Frank may have had serious misgivings about party politics, he was not immune from the political radicalism of the 1930s which motivated so many of his generation. He visited Russia in 1931 and wrote a book, *Dawn in Russia*, about the trip. In 1935 he was elected first president of the League of American Writers, an organization commonly considered the cultural branch of the Communist Party USA. Whatever the similarities and differences between their political commitments, Mariátegui and Frank shared a conviction that was central to their respective working philosophies and of singular note in the secularizing 1920s: both insisted on the compatibility—indeed continuity—between political and spiritual sentiment. It may surprise some to know that Mariátegui, along with Frank, admired the conservative Spanish religious writer Miguel de Unamuno.

Upon closer examination, however, the similarities between Frank and Mariátegui's work begin to disintegrate—to such an extent that the perplexity their alliance has provoked among scholars is certainly understandable. In certain respects, Spain represents ground zero in the cultural ideologies of both Frank and Mariátegui, but for opposite reasons. Frank idealized the spiritual and social "wholeness" which he believed characterized the European Middle Ages and which was progressively eroded, first with the Renaissance and further with the Enlightenment. According to Frank, that "wholeness" still existed in certain regions of Spain, and contributed to the spiritual legacy it bequeathed to Latin America. For Mariátegui, by contrast, the medieval nature of Latin America's colonizer was responsible for the backward and racist character of modern Peru. In Mariátegui's decolonizing ideology, Spanish medievalism was the historical legacy which Peru needed to overcome to become an autonomous nation.

EUROPE AND THE AMERICAS

The significant differences between Frank, the metaphysician, and Mariátegui, the materialist,[12] are evident in the positions they took in the postwar European debate between Europe's most famous pacifist, Romain Rolland, and committed communist intellectual, Henri Barbusse, about the political role of the writer.[13] Following the bitter nationalist conflicts of World War I, this issue pressed upon the hearts and minds of European intellectuals with urgency. Frank supported Rolland's promotion of an intellectual spirit unaligned with any particular political end, an attitude reflected in an ambivalence toward party politics which the North American spells out in his memoirs: "I found I could belong to no organized political or theological party, since all of them were based on untrue psychological interpretations of man's nature."[14] Mariátegui, by contrast, supported Barbusse's contention about the unavoidably political nature of all intellectual engagement. Several of the essays in Mariátegui's first book, *La escena contemporánea*, particularly those on Barbusse, on the journal *Clarté* and organization of the same name, both of which Barbusse founded, and on Trotsky, who Mariátegui praised as the leader of the Red Army and a brilliant intellectual, leave no room for doubt regarding his position on this issue.[15] Notwithstanding this difference, which was both methodological and philosophical, the two men were able to endorse one another's working philosophies with enthusiasm. Mariátegui's typical exasperation with the (bourgeois) individualistic intellectual and Frank's stated mistrust of the (dogmatic) militant intellectual were replaced with a quite different sentiment: each man saw in the other the perfect synthesis of Marxism and spirituality. Mariátegui claimed that Frank's work "demonstrates concretely and eloquently the possibility of joining historical materialism with revolutionary idealism,"[16] whereas Frank believed that Mariátegui understood the "vital mysticism of the Marxian vision."[17] Critics sometimes claim that Mariátegui took what was useful in Frank and overlooked the rest. This conclusion, however, misses the tenor of Mariátegui's writings about Frank's work and about Frank himself. The productive relationship between Mariátegui and Frank gives us an appreciation of the intellectual context of the 1920s, before once fluid ideas had been organized and reified into now accepted theories.

The epistolary nature of their exchange was also key to the intellectual solidarity which developed between them. Over the years of their correspondence, the two men had grown very close. Frank once wrote to Mariátegui, "know, dear friend, that in the deepest sense you are my brother, and you have my love (also in the deepest sense) forever."[18] Mariátegui, in turn, wrote to Frank that "you probably have few friends in Latin America as lovingly attentive to your voice and work as myself. In every page that arrives to my hands, I feel the wholeness of your presence, I encounter a note that is inalienably yours."[19] The homo-social bond which developed between Mariátegui and Frank, abetted by the highly constructed and inter-subjective nature of epistolary communication, led to a mutual practice of selective reading and outright misreading. These deliberate misreadings were nothing less than a transamerican praxis, which, at the very moment that the United States had achieved hegemony in the Western hemisphere, and Latin America's peripheral status was being consolidated in new ways, enabled the two men to mirror one another as complementary Americans.

In their writing and reading of one another, Frank and Mariátegui performed a sense of American complementarity. Their shared commitment to "the creation of a true America"—to use Waldo Frank's phrase—transformed the significance of the Rolland-Barbusse debate. That which had divided the

European intellectual community into two distinct groups, operated differently on American terrain. Far more important than the specific terms of the debate was the transition from Europe to America, and the reconciliation of the transatlantic underpinnings of each man's intellectual formation with an Americanist commitment. While Mariátegui's seminal contribution to postcolonial studies is widely recognized, his personal struggle with self-authorization as a Latin American intellectual is rarely addressed, in contrast to many creative writers. But for Mariátegui himself it was a concern of the highest priority. His first book, *La escena contemporánea*, which consists of forty-six short essays focused entirely on European figures and European themes, is regularly overlooked. The book, however, merits closer attention not only in its own right, given its impressive treatment of wide-ranging subject matter, but also because of the remarkably creative transition from this Europe-focused book to the Indo-American socialism which he developed in his classic text, *Siete ensayos de interpretacion de la realidad peruana*, comes more readily into view. *La escena contemporánea* not only demonstrates the depth of Mariátegui's knowledge of European discourses and traditions, but it also points to the burden this intellectual formation represented for the Peruvian author. Mariátegui remarked that the more thoroughly the American intellectual absorbs European culture, the more clearly does she or he perceive their rejection by that culture.[20] He wrote how when he returned to Peru after having spent three years in Europe, he was imbued with the conviction that he had a specifically American task to perform, but it was only years later when he read an essay by Frank about the role of Europe in the latter's concept of America, that he began to feel "light on my own cause."[21] Antonio Melis claims that the combination of *vanguardismo* and *Indigenismo* that characterized *Amauta* is one of the magazine's most distinguishing features.[22] Mariátegui was similarly able to balance internationalism and decolonization—a fruitful paradox which marked much of his later work. If we take Mariátegui at his word, Frank's intellectual example was of vital importance to his capacity to reconcile the regional and the cosmopolitan. Frank, Mariátegui claimed, led him to the epiphany that not every "émigré is fatally a deraciné."[23] The example of Frank, in other words, was instrumental to Mariátegui's ability to transform a European debt into an Americanist vision. Frank himself was well aware of the rigorous process of transformation Mariátegui had to undergo to fully claim an American identity and articulate an Americanist philosophy: "Mariátegui is a master" he wrote, "[who] had won in Europe a mystic sense of New World destiny."[24]

Frank was also immersed in European culture, though from an earlier age. As Mariátegui remarked, "Frank's adolescence in New York had been an enchanted revery of Europe. The mother of the future writer was a musician. Beethoven, Wagner, Schubert, Wolf, were the familiar spirits of his household. . . . The adolescent Frank questioned the philosophers of Germany and Greece. . . . When he went to Europe as a boy, he met familiar landscapes."[25] Frank had a comparatively easier time reconciling his training in European culture with an Americanist commitment. He had a platform in Europe and was a sought-after contributor to the seminal French magazine, *La nouvelle revue francaise*, undertaking his first book, *Our America* (1919), at the behest of its editors, Gaston Gallimard and Jacques Codeau. For Frank, this transatlantic partnership was perfectly consistent with "the creation of a true America." "They were a bridge between my needs," he wrote in the preface to *Our America*, "I could write a passable book for France about my country only if I wrote it also for my country, only if I wrote it to my country."[26] The advent of the United States as a power on the world stage and the dominant power in the Western hemisphere certainly contributed to Frank's sense of intellectual agency and to the ease (if compared with Mariátegui) with which Frank undertook his project of Americanization, where cultural decolonization, as it were, was inextricable from an emerging hegemony.

If, in retrospect, the contrast between Frank's messianic Americanism and Mariátegui's locally situated Indo-American socialism is only too apparent, in the 1920s, through the alchemy of friendship, these American utopias mirrored one another in a fruitful and robust reciprocity.

WALDO FRANK AND VICTORIA OCAMPO

Masculinist brotherhood, then, was key to the generative aspects of Frank and Mariátegui's alliance, integral, that is, to the unexpected mirroring which reinforced each man's American autonomy and stimulated the possibility of a polycentric Pan-American political imagination. Despite the political asymmetries between the North and the South, Frank tried to foster a horizontal transamerican discourse, something which was duly noted by his Latin American allies. As Victoria Ocampo remarked, Frank was one of the rare Europeans or North Americans who came to Argentina looking for something other than "local color."[27] Ocampo was well aware of the indifference that was regularly directed at Latin America. As Beatriz Sarlo has observed, out of her famed circle of European friends, which included Virginia Woolf, José Ortega y Gasset, Igor Stravinsky, Paul Claudet, Count Hermann Keyserling, and Jacques Lacan, among many others—only Roger Callois, who was financially dependent on Ocampo during the five years he spent in exile in Argentina during World War II, fully reciprocated her interest in "lo europeo" with an equal interest in Argentina.[28] Even Virginia Woolf, who at one point claimed to Vita Sackville-West "that she was 'in love with Victoria

Okampo'" [sic] read little of her writing, and consistently misspelled her name, alternately writing it as "O'Campo" or "Okampo."[29]

Frank, who saw himself first and foremost as an artist, was a passionate modernist and believed that the intellect and creativity possessed a unique potential to transcend a degraded capitalist order. Hence his call in "Mensaje a los escritores mexicanos" for a specifically intellectual and creative friendship where difference disappears: "We must be friends . . . of a shared and creative intelligence." While Frank dreamed of a horizontal transamerican community, in line with this modernist aesthetic, the protagonists of this community, namely the writer and artist, reflected a distinctly vertical worldview. Frank's progressive political agenda frequently took second place to his elite humanism. If Frank hesitated to unconditionally condemn the fascist forces in the Spanish Civil War because he admired aspects of the cultural traditionalism they promoted, claiming that all factions in the war possessed a degree of truth,[30] he showed fewer reservations in critiquing "shallow republican politics," insisting that democracy means not merely "all men," but also "whole men"—distinctions which, for Frank, too often proved to be at odds.[31] The contrast between Frank's artistic elitism and his progressive politics is one of the sharpest contradictions in his cultural ideology, and is part of what made his alliance with actors as different as Mariátegui and Ocampo possible. Prizing the refined sensibility she attributed to the artist and writer, Ocampo stressed the importance of acknowledging difference over and above any concern for equality.[32]

If Ocampo was both a member of and apologist for Argentina's oligarchy, her artistic and intellectual tastes were not entirely congruent with those of her class. Ocampo was drawn to simplicity, and to light, clean lines. Her unfailing eye for modernist design contrasted sharply with aristocratic tastes that were loyal to what Beatriz Sarlo calls "el bric-a-brac, la penumbra y la mala pintura."[33] Members of the oligarchy, were, as a whole, not particularly concerned with experimental modernism.[34] Thus, Ocampo's efforts to bring the great names of European Modernism to Buenos Aires (including not only writers and artists but also the composers Stravinsky and Ansermet and architects Le Corbusier and Walter Gropius) inspired little interest among upper-class sectors. Ocampo's architectural passions in particular had little purchase on the imagination of members of her class. When Le Corbusier arrived to Buenos Aires in 1929, he and Ocampo had ambitions to transform the city's architectural profile. No one, however, was willing to invest in the projects they proposed, and Le Corbusier returned to Europe disillusioned.[35] Determined to live her aesthetic principles, Ocampo did indulge her architectural passions to some degree. Imitating the designs of her modernist idol, she built a "starkly modern and functional [house] inside and out," much to the consternation of her criollo neighbors.[36]

Known as a larger-than-life personality, an arbiter of culture and style, and facilitator of the arts, Ocampo was also a prolific writer and a prolific, serious reader. She published ten volumes of essays, a four-volume autobiography, and was a regular contributor to the magazine she founded in 1931. Ocampo was also a passionate feminist. Anticipating intellectual trends by many decades, her goal, she said, was to write like a woman. Ocampo was a pioneer in many respects; in 1976 she was the first woman to become a member of the Argentine Academy of Letters.

Frank and Ocampo were both profoundly cosmopolitan actors and intellectuals. The proud provincialism of the writer Paul Valery, to cite one particularly notable example, who was famous for not wanting to leave the comforts of his native France, was not a luxury afforded to the colonial or postcolonial writer. Like Frank, Ocampo visited Europe from an early age, was educated in European cultural traditions, and was a well-known figure in European artistic and intellectual circles. However indispensable and inevitable this cosmopolitanism may have been, it came at a cost. The inherently conflictive condition of the American transatlantic intellectual was a theme present from the start of the relationship between Frank and Ocampo (as it was for Frank and Mariátegui). Describing her sense of being "exiled from Europe in America; exiled from America in Europe,"[37] Ocampo remarked how "[Waldo Frank] has experienced in the North what we have been suffering in the South."[38]

Frank believed that transamerican solidarity was the solution to the condition which Ocampo described and that the "creation of a true America," which would be the fruit of a North-South solidarity, would bring cultural redemption and spiritual enlightenment, restoring the social promise Europe once offered. To this end Frank, in collaboration with Glusberg and the Argentine writer Eduardo Mallea, had been envisioning the publication of a journal that would provide an interamerican forum. Publishing articles in English and Spanish, the journal Frank had in mind was to be called "Our America" (after José Martí's famous essay), and would promote cultural dialogue between the Americas. When he met Ocampo, he believed he had found the person to co-edit the journal alongside Glusberg. Both Ocampo and Glusberg were committed to fostering artistic talent and cultural dialogue, and just as important, Ocampo had the financial means to underwrite the journal.

This pairing of Ocampo and Glusberg proved to be a remarkable miscalculation on Frank's part, one that had important consequences for the character of the magazine he was instrumental in creating. Born into an Eastern European Jewish family that had come to Buenos Aires when he was six, Glusberg was no more of a natural ally of a traditional criollo like Ocampo than was Mariátegui. In the early decades of the twentieth century, when half of Buenos Aires' population consisted of immigrants, the most virulent racism was directed toward Eastern European Jews.[39] Glusberg's cultural priorities clashed with those of the elite *letrados* who had signed on to Ocampo's project, none of whom, unlike Glusberg, found Frank's idea of an interamerican forum with hemispheric ambitions particularly compelling. Ultimately, Glusberg did not serve as Ocampo's coeditor. Nor was he invited to be a member of the editorial board. In fact, other than its original conception, Glusberg was excluded from the magazine's planning process and operation altogether.

Though decades later, when he acknowledged how his efforts to forge an alliance between "the dynamic immigrant Jew with a prophet's America in his heart" and the "princess of good taste," had failed almost from the start,[40] Frank seemed to have arrived at an understanding of what was at stake in the exclusion of Glusberg, at the time he by all accounts missed the politics at play, understanding it primarily as to a question of personality. As the magazine project got underway, Frank advised Glusberg, warning him that he had powerful enemies in Buenos Aires who had influence over Ocampo. He commiserated with Glusberg and lamented his ultimate exclusion. Yet he also told Glusberg that he should acknowledge his own share of responsibility for the outcome, since he could be difficult, after all, and sometimes lacked the diplomacy required of an editor.[41] Carolyn Pedwell's observation that transnational empathy is not the equivalent of transnational understanding (nor a guarantee of social justice) is underscored by the dynamics which led to Glusberg's exclusion.[42] Frank had unwittingly inserted himself into a nationalist polemic that was in plain sight, thereby losing influence over the project he had initiated.

While Glusberg had anticipated working with Ocampo with enthusiasm, once things played out as they did, the politics of the situation were certainly not lost on him. He told Frank in no uncertain terms that Ocampo would be the last person to promote the totalizing project.[43] And indeed, he was right. As it turned out, the publication which Ocampo successfully directed for over four decades was called *Sur* rather than "Nuestra America," named and modeled after the Spanish *Revista Occidente*, which was edited by Ocampo's friend, the conservative Spanish social critic, José Ortega y Gasset. *Sur*'s articles were published in Spanish and while the magazine did include Spanish translations of North American authors, its orientation was far more transatlantic than transamerican. Ocampo's editorial instincts were very much in line with her class interests. As an upper-class Argentine from Buenos Aires, whose education took place largely in French and English, Ocampo identified more readily with Paris and London than with Mexico City or New York. In the context of the decolonizing nationalisms that helped usher in modernity in Latin America, Ocampo's position was only too clear: "Turn one's back on Europe! Don't you sense the infinite absurdity of that phrase?"[44]

Judged by many as "extranjerizante," a magazine catering to foreign eyes and minds, *Sur* was critiqued from its very first issue. That issue, which appeared in 1931, boasted an impressive roster of international contributors which included Frank and Ocampo, Drieu La Rochelle, Jules Supervielle, Alfonso Reyes, Eugenio d'Ors, Ricardo Guiraldes, Ernest Ansermet, Walter Gropius, and Jorge Luis Borges, among others, as well as expensive and eye-catching reprints of photographs and paintings of distinctly American scenes. Not only *Sur* but Ocampo herself became focal points where conflicting definitions of America and Americanness vied for dominance. The Peruvian Luís Alberto Sánchez referred to Ocampo as a "bad American,"[45] Glusberg proposed launching a movement that would directly counter *Sur's* influence,[46] while Borges claimed that Ocampo was that most Argentinian of women.[47] Frank joined in the chorus when in a letter to Ocampo he wrote: "Victoria, you are, in effect, American. And more than Victoria Ocampo knows. But I know it."[48] In the case of Ocampo, however, no amount of heavy-handed reading or misreading could will her into the type of American Frank wanted her to be. Stung by Frank's disapproval, Ocampo responded that he had chosen "a person, and not a puppet [to edit *Sur*] and that this person would work according to her own concept of literature."[49] Ocampo would insist that she too had a concept of America. Her Latin America was multilingual and irremediably cosmopolitan (as, of course, was Frank). Equal parts European and American, this cosmopolitanism was not only integral to the American story and Ocampo's autobiography, but it was, she claimed, inscribed on her body: "Mon cerveau est en Europe" she wrote "et mon coeur en Amérique."[50]

When Frank lamented that Ocampo "overvalue[d] perhaps . . . Tagore, Virginia Woolf, T.E. Lawrence, and the salons of London and Paris"[51] he unknowingly identifies the nationalist project informing Ocampo's editorial choices. As Gorica Majstorovic has observed, nineteenth-century Argentine republicans, Ocampo's powerful forefathers, "fuse(d) elite culture with selected versions of internationalism," identifying Argentina with the cultures of France and Britain, and in this way, elevated their country to equal standing with Spain.[52] The culture of Buenos Aires, particularly that of the upper classes, conformed to this international ideology. At the turn of the century, it was common for upper-class Argentine families to spend several months of the year in Paris. Argentines often spoke flawless French, and were well-versed in French literature, music, and art. Like many of Argentina's elite, Ocampo's education reflected this cultural ideology. Educated in English and French, she was fully trilingual. Over time Ocampo would write in Spanish, but she originally wrote in French—her early articles were translated by others.

Ocampo once remarked to Frank, reflecting on *Sur*: "Everything has been possible thanks to your help. [*Sur*] will be the constant place of our encounter."⁵³ The incongruities which this "place" brings into sharp relief not only point to a question of different class and national identities, and different cultural priorities, but they also illustrate the role of gender in the production of American heterogeneities. As others have observed, whether as Director of *Sur*, patron of the Arts, or salon leader, Ocampo transformed the cultural cosmopolitanism granted to her by virtue of her class, from the passive attribute it was intended to be into an active instrument with which she forged a public female subjectivity. Evoking a transamerican historical episode, Sylvia Molloy provides an interesting gloss on the way that culture both displaced and mimicked the political in Ocampo's project. Ocampo, she writes, "converts civic duty into a cultural mission. In this mission she conceives of herself as a prominent figure, comparable to her grandfather, who one hundred years earlier traveled to Washington in order to gain U.S. recognition of Argentine independence."⁵⁴ Reinforcing the authority of elite patriarchy on behalf of female subjectivity and a feminine power is, of course, a considerable contradiction, one which Ocampo never fully resolved.⁵⁵

If Ocampo's cultural and class allegiances made her disinclined to identify with or simply identify many aspects of the modern Argentine nation (there were those such as Ricardo Piglia who claimed that *Sur* was decades out of date⁵⁶), Frank's hermeneutic rigidity was likewise a distinct privilege of power. Frank knew what he would find in Latin America before he arrived there, namely Anglo-America's other half. Nothing he encountered once he did arrive contradicted his working philosophy. On the contrary, it confirmed it. Frank's insistence on casting Latin America as the antidote to an alienated and industrialized North ultimately limited the type of influence he would have on literary culture. As an advisor for Doubleday and Farrar-Straus, Frank selected regionalist titles to be translated for a North American audience, overlooking the writers (such as Borges, Vallejo, and Arlt, among others) who were not only the counterparts to U.S. experimental modernists—a group to which Frank himself belonged—but were those who would gain a secure place in the Latin American literary canon as well as an international readership.⁵⁷ It is curious that the editorial orientation Ocampo established in the pages of *Sur* came as a surprise to Frank since she had always been forthcoming about her disinterest in literary regionalism and didn't hesitate to tell Frank that his dream of a tellurian Latin American essence was precisely that an "impossible dream."⁵⁸ Frank seemed so convinced of the inexorable inevitability of his hemispheric prophecy that it was impossible for him to apprehend that, like all discursive constructions, it was subject to winds of historical contingency.

Frank's inclination to traffic in American stereotypes which subordinated a Latin American essence to North American agency is among the reasons why the popularity he enjoyed in Latin America has proven so baffling to many

North American scholars. If he has received some attention over the past fifteen years or so from scholars working in the field of American Hemispheric Studies,[59] his singular importance to this field is rarely acknowledged. (Sebastiaan Faber's treatment of Frank is an important exception.) Frank's status in the 1930s and 1940s as an "expert" in Latin America is regularly overlooked, he is often left out of Latin American intellectual histories,[60] and has even been the recipient of unnecessary and unhelpful ad-hominen attacks (decades after his death in the 1960s) such as that by one historian who described him as "the possessor of a portentous, overblown writing style well suited to his inflated vision of himself."[61]

While history may have a difficult time accounting for Frank, whether regarding his intellectual standing in the early decades of the twentieth century in general or his popularity among Latin Americans in particular, as an editorial written during Frank's visit in 1929 indicates, Frank was not just popular in Latin America. He was extraordinarily popular, especially among the discriminating audiences of Buenos Aires: "Even those in Buenos Aires who knew best the work of Waldo Frank, the remarkable originality of this thought, could not foretell the unique success of his lectures in the leading universities of Argentina. Neither Ortega y Gasset nor Keyserling—both preceded by an older renown—had triumph as complete as Waldo Frank in Buenos Aires."[62]

Frank's appeal had not diminished in the forties when he returned to Latin America with the express purpose of persuading Argentina to join the Allies in World War II (a rare instance when his political position aligned with that of the U.S. government). Arriving in Brazil, he was not only deluged at the airport by journalists and cultural representatives but also informed by a minister from the Foreign Office that he was a "guest of Brazil."[63] Frank was granted a quasi-official status throughout Latin America. In addition to being hosted by writers' organizations, universities, and cultural institutions in 1942, official invitations to speak came from the governments of numerous countries; the president of Colombia called him personally.[64]

If the truth be told, Frank certainly *was* interested in "local color." Yet he was even more interested in conversation, and that is surely what informed Ocampo's initial impressions of him. Latin Americans were particularly impressed by his determination to learn Spanish: "For the first time a North American spoke to us in Spanish" Ocampo wrote, "for the first time, also, a North American writer took us seriously."[65] Frank's relationship with Latin Americans began with an invitation to Spanish-speaking writers and artists to participate in a dialogue. Frank's "expertise" grew out of this transamerican dialogue. When Frank arrived in Latin America, he told his audiences that "I have come to learn."[66] Though admittedly, it is not always clear just what Frank learned in Latin America, or exactly how his encounter with the cultural differences of the Spanish-speaking Americas impacted his cultural ideology, the development of his discourse was inseparable from Latin American agency. Traveling from the metropolis to the periphery, adopting Spanish as the lingua franca of his visit, and engaging his Latin American interlocutors as agents of knowledge rather than objects of a knowing gaze, Frank reversed the colonialist logic which permeated most Anglo-Latin relationships. However centered Frank's cultural ideology may have been, as an examination of his relationship with both Mariátegui and Ocampo suggests, Frank nevertheless played a generative role in Latin America, often in unexpected ways and in ways that encourage us to decenter our perspective.

AMERICAN UTOPIAS

If Ocampo today is among Argentina's most celebrated women, and if Mariátegui's importance to progressive politics and scholarship in Peru, in Latin America and in Latin American studies more broadly, cannot be overstated, Frank's unwieldy metaphysics do not translate well into contemporary intellectual forums. Yet Frank's sense of a distinctly American promise, one that would follow upon the unification of North and South, and his dream that the new world would truly be a "new world" rather than "Europe's grave," perhaps belongs as much to the future as to the past. It finds an echo in the work of Aníbal Quijano and Immanuel Wallerstein, two contemporary social scientists whose collaboration itself represents an important transamerican alliance, and who on the 500th year anniversary of the Americas wrote about American utopianism, with a prophetic spirit and poetic cadence worthy of Frank himself:

> But today, if one listens to the sounds, the images, the symbols, and the utopias of the Americas, one must acknowledge the maturation of an autonomous social pattern, the presence of a process of reinvention of culture in the Americas. This is what we are calling the Americanization of the Americas, which is sustained by the crisis of the European pattern . . . . Sooner or later, these American utopias will be joined together to create and offer to the world a specifically all-American utopia.[67]

While the "symphonic" forces of the Americas may have been more contrapuntal and even discordant than Waldo Frank, with his instinct for synthesis and horror of fragmentation, permitted himself to imagine, it is worthwhile revisiting his hemispheric project, and the practice of friendship which animated it. Today, as the Americas confront the historical legacies of colonialism and the transatlantic slave-trade with a renewed urgency, Waldo Frank's sense of an American becoming seems uncannily prescient.

NOTES

1. Frank, "Mensaje," 305.
2. Gandhi, *Affective Communities*, 14.
3. See Hermes Villordo, *El grupo sur*, 25. My translation.
4. The U.S. invasions of Nicaragua and the Dominican Republic were fresh in the minds of Latin Americans at the time of Frank's visit.
5. Rostagno, "Waldo Frank's Crusade," 66.
6. See Frank, *America Hispana*, 10.
7. Tarcus, *Mariátegui en Argentina*, 182.
8. Faber, "Learning from the Latins," 260.
9. See Tarcus, 125. My translation.
10. For an excellent analysis of the formal properties of epistolary communication see: Margaretta Jolly and Liz Stanley, "Letters as/not a genre."
11. Tarcus, 189.
12. While it is fair to describe Mariátegui as a materialist, he was certainly an unconventional one, believing as he did that every true materialist is likewise an idealist. In "Mística revolucionaria," Michael Löwy refers to the "surprising dialectic between materialism and idealism" at the heart of Mariátegui's work and vision (58).
13. For a study of the Rolland-Barbusse debate, see Ollivier-Mellios "L'Art, la Pensée, la Politique" and Fischer, *Romain Rolland*, 79–111.
14. Frank, *Memoirs*, 145.
15. See Mariátegui, *La escena contemporánea*.
16. Mariátegui, *El alma matinal*, 187.
17. Frank, *America Hispana*, 174.
18. Melis, *Mariátegui: Correspondencia*, 189.
19. See Tarcus, 195.
20. See Benardete, *Waldo Frank in America Hispana*, 67.
21. See Ibid.
22. See Archibald, *Imagining Modernity in the Andes*.
23. See Benardete, 46. My translation.
24. Frank, *America Hispana*, 166–70.
25. Mariátegui, "Itinerary of Waldo Frank," 68.
26. Frank, *Our America*, xi.
27. Rodriguez Aycaguer, *Visitas misionales*, 43.
28. Sarlo, *La máquina cultural*, 144.
29. Parrott, "Friendship, Letters and Butterflies," 1–2.
30. Faber, 286.
31. Frank, *Virgin Spain*, 396.
32. Majstorovic, "Cosmopolitanism and the Nation," 53.
33. Sarlo, 168.
34. Ibid.
35. Ibid., 174–78.
36. Meyer, *Victoria Ocampo*, 96.

37. Majstorovic, "An American Place," 176.
38. Meyer, 106.
39. Chasteen, *Born in Blood and Fire*, 217–19.
40. Frank, *Memoirs*, 171.
41. Tarcus, 214–15.
42. Pedwell, "Introduction," in *Affective Relation*, 1–43.
43. Tarcus, 213.
44. Cited in Rodriquez Aycaguer, 46.
45. Cited in Rostagno, 66.
46. Ibid., 67.
47. Cited in McNeese, *Jorge Luis Borges*, 57.
48. Cited in Iglesias, *La violencia del azar*, 167. My translation.
49. Cited in Iglesias, 170. My translation.
50. Cited in Rodriguez Aycaguer, 55.
51. Cited in ibid., 61. My translation.
52. Majstorovic, "Cosmopolitanism and the Nation," 50.
53. Cited in Rodriguez Aycaguer, 53. My translation.
54. See Rodriguez Aycaguer, 47. My translation.
55. See Greenberg, "A Question of Blood." In this essay, Greenberg argues that the contradiction between Ocampo's class allegiance and her feminist principles was a central and vexing issue at the heart of her work and life.
56. Majstorovic, ibid., 55.
57. Rostagno, 63.
58. See ibid, 64.
59. In addition to Faber, see Lawrence, *Anxieties of Experience* and Rogers, *Modernism and the New Spain*.
60. In U*nder Northern Eyes*, Mark Berger's well-known examination of the history of Latin American Studies, there is no mention of Frank. Granted, Berger's analysis of early Latin Americanist discourse is focused on the close relationship between academia and government and Frank was adamant about his distance from both. Still, considering his prominence in the Anglo-American intellectual community and his status as an expert on Latin America, he might have merited a footnote, if only as an example of alternative discourses. Similarly, in Ricardo Salvatore's excellent book about the founders of Latin American Studies, *Disciplinary Conquest*, there is only a one sentence reference to Frank. It is not clear how Frank fits within the history of Latin American Studies.
61. Pike, 250. Two critiques of Frank—in Pike's *The United States and Latin America* and in Ogorzaly's *Waldo Frank*—point to the challenge he poses for intellectual history. In one swift sentence, Pike dismisses both Frank, the writer, and Frank, the man. For his part, Ogorzaly claims that Frank's popularity in the Latin America had to do with the fact that he told the Latin American intelligentsia, whose elitist cultural ideologies privileged the intellectual and artist, what they wanted to hear (Ogorzaly, 9). This is an idea that is reiterated by Stein and Alarcón in their commentary on the Frank-Mariátegui correspondence ("José Carlos Mariátegui y Waldo

Frank"). The problem with Pike and Ogorzaly's evaluations of Frank is not simply that they are unkind to Frank, who is credited with tailoring his message to whatever an audience might wish to hear, but in dismissing Frank so categorically, they also dismiss the local Latin American intelligentsia who is thought to have been either duped by him or complicit with his cultural elitism—either scenario being unlikely in the case of so astute an interlocutor as Mariátegui, to cite only one example. Faber points to the condescension implicit to these conclusions, with both scholars reaffirming the problematic relationship between North American-trained Latin Americanists and a local Latin American intelligentsia, where the former discount the authority of the latter, who for their part discredit the so-called knowledge produced in the U.S. academy (Faber, 261). In their respective critiques, both Pike and Ogorzaly reverse the promise that Frank brought to Anglo-Latin relations.

62. Benardete, 223. My translation.
63. Frank, *South American Journey*, 23.
64. Ibid, 84.
65. cited in Sitman, "(Re) Discovering America in Buenos Aires," 117.
66. Cited in Faber, 80.
67. Quijano and Wallerstein, "Americanity as a Concept," 556–57.

WORKS CITED

Benardete, Mair José, ed. *Waldo Frank in America Hispana*. New York: Instituto de las Españas, 1930.
Berger, Mark. *Under Northern Eyes: Latin American Studies and U.S. Hegemony in the Americas*. 1898–1990. Bloomington: Indiana University Press, 1995.
Chasteen, John Charles. *Born in Blood and Fire: A Concise History of Latin America*. New York: Norton, 2001.
Faber, Sebastiaan. "Learning from the Latins: Waldo Frank's Progressive Pan-Americanism." *CR: New Centennial Review* 3, no. 1 (2003): 257–95. Print.
Fischer, David James. *Romain Rolland and the Politics of Intellectual Engagement*. Berkeley: University of California Press, 1988.
Flores Galindo, Alberto. *La agonía de Mariátegui: La polemica con la Komintern*. Lima: Desco, 1980.
Frank, Waldo. "The Address of Waldo Frank." In *Waldo Frank in America Hispana*, edited by Mair José Benardete, 29–37. New York: Instituto de las Españas, 1930.
———. *America Hispana*. New York: Charles Scribner's Sons, 1931.
———. *Dawn in Russia: The Record of a Journey*. New York: Charles Scribner's Sons, 1931.
———. *Memoirs of Waldo Frank*. Edited by Alan Trachtenberg. Amherst: University of Massachussetts Press, 1972.
———. "Mensaje de Waldo Frank a los escritores mexicanos," *Reportorio Americano* 8 (August 1924): 305–06.
———. *Our America*. New York: Boni & Liveright, 1919.
———. *South American Journey*. New York: Duell, Sloan and Pearce, 1943.

———. *The Re-discovery of America*. New York: Charles Scriber's Sons, 1929.
———. *Virgin Spain: Scenes from the Spiritual Drama of a Great People*. New York: Boni & Liveright, 1926.
Gandhi, Leela. *Affective Communities: Anti-Colonial Thought, Fin-de-Siecle Radicalism, and the Politics of Friendship*. Durham: Duke University Press, 2006.
Greenberg, Janet. "A Question of Blood: The Conflict of Sex and Class in the *Autobiografía* of Victoria Ocampo." In *Women, Culture, and Politics in Latin America*. Edited by Emilie Bergmann, 130–50. Berkeley: University of California Press, 1990.
Hermes Villordo, Oscar. *El grupo sur: Una biografía colectiva*. Buenos Aires: Planeta Argentina, 1994.
Iglesias, Cristina. *La violencia del azar*. Buenos Aires: Fondo de cultura económica, 2003.
Jolly, Margaretta and Liz Stanley. "Letters as/not a Genre." *Life Writing* 2, no. 2 (2007): 91–118.
King, John. S*ur: A Study of the Argentine Literary Journal and its Role in the Development of a Culture, 1931–1970*. Cambridge: Cambridge Iberian and Latin American Studies, 1986.
Lawrence, Jeffrey. *Anxieties of Experience: The Literatures of the Americas from Whitman to Bolaño*. Oxford: Oxford University Press, 2018.
Löwy, Michael. "Mística revolucionaria: José Carlos Mariátegui y la religion." *Utopía y Praxis Latinoamericana* 10 (2005): 49–59.
Majstorovic, Gorica. "An American Place: Victoria Ocampo's Editorial Politics, the Foundation of *Sur*, and Hemispheric Alliances." *Arizona Journal of Hispanic Cultural Studies* 9 (2005): 171–80.
———. "Cosmopolitanism and the Nation: Reading Asymmetries of Power in Victoria Ocampo's 'Babel.'" *Contracorriente* 3 (2006): 47–64.
Mariátegui, José Carlos. "Arte, revolución y decadencia." *Amauta* 1, no. 1 (1926): 3–4.
———. *El alma matinal y otras estaciones del hombre de hoy*. Lima: Amauta, 1970.
———. *La escena contemporanea*. Lima: Ediciones Minerva, 1925.
———. "Presentación de *Amauta*," *Amauta* 1 no. 1 (1926): 1–2.
———. *Siete ensayos de interpretación de la realidad peruana*. Lima: Amauta, 1928.
———. "Itinerary of Waldo Frank," in Bernadete, *Waldo Frank in America Hispana*, 66–71.
McNeese, Tim. *Jorge Luis Borges*. New York: Infobase, 2008.
Melis, Antonio. *José Carlos Mariátegui: Correspondencia (1915–1930)*. Lima: Biblioteca Amauta, 1984.
Meyer, Doris. V*ictoria Ocampo: Against the Wind and Tide*. New York: George Braziller, 1979.
Milne, Esther. *Letters, Postcards, Email: Technologies of Presence*. New York: Routledge, 2010.
Mumford, Lewis. "Introduction." *Memoirs of Waldo Frank*. Amherst: The University of Massachusetts Press, 1973.

Ogorzaly, Michael. *Waldo Frank: Prophet of Hispanic Regeneration*. Lewisburg: Bucknell, 1994.
Ollivier-Mellios, Anne. "L'Art, la Pensée, la Politique: Un débat entre intellectuels francais et américaines 1919–1922." *Revue francaise d'études américaines* 76, no.1 (1998): 104–19.
Parrott, Fiona G. "Friendship, Letters and Butterflies: Victoria Ocampo and Virginia Woolf." *STAR (Scotland's Transatlantic Relations) Project*. http://www.star.ac.uk (April 2004): 1–7.
Pedwell, Carolyn, *Affective Relations: The Transnational Politics of Empathy*. New York: Palgrave MacMillian, 2014.
Pike, Frederic. *The United States and Latin America: Myths, Stereotypes of Civilization and Nature*. Austin: University of Texas Press, 1992.
Quijano, Aníbal. *Introducción a Mariátegui*. México: México Ediciones Era, 1980.
Quijano, Aníbal and Immanuel Wallerstein, "Americanity as a Concept, or the Americas in the Modern World System." *International Journal of Social Sciences* 134 (November 1992): 549–57.
Rodriguez Aycaguer, Miguel. *Visitas misionales: Waldo Frank en Argentina*. Buenos Aires: Impresiones Buenos Aires, 2007.
Rogers, Gayle. *Modernism and the New Spain*. Oxford: Oxford, 2012.
Rostagno, Irene. "Waldo Frank's Crusade for Latin American Literature." *The Americas* 46 (July 1989): 41–69.
Salvatore, Ricardo D. *Disciplinary Conquest: U.S. Scholars in South America, 1900–1945*. Durham: Duke University Press, 2016.
Sarlo, Beatriz. *La máquina cultural: Maestras, traductores y vanguardistas*. Buenos Aires: Editorial Planeta Argentina, 1998.
Sitman, Rosalie. "(Re) Discovering America in Buenos Aires: The Cultural Entrepreneurship of Waldo Frank, Samuel Glusberg and Victoria Ocampo." *Revista Pléyade* 5 (January-June 2015): 113–36.
Stanley, Liz. "The Epistolarium: On Theorizing Letters and Correspondences." *Auto/Biography* 12 (2004): 201–35.
Stein, William W. and Renato Alarcón. "José Carlos Mariátegui y Waldo Frank: dos amigos." *Anuario Mariáteguiano* 1, no. 1 (1989): 161–184.
Tarcus, Horacio. *Mariátegui en Argentina o las políticas culturales de Samuel Glusberg*. Buenos Aires: El cielo por asalto, 2001.

Chapter 4

Dark Meadows of Gnosis

Robert Duncan and José Lezama Lima's Inter-American Mythopoetics

Christopher Winks

The German Romantic poet Friedrich Hölderlin's piercing question in his elegy "Brot und Wein" ("Bread and Wine")—"Wozu Dichter in dürftiger Zeit?" ("What are poets for in a destitute time?")—reflected his disillusionment with the outcome of the French Revolution, which had aroused so many transformative hopes in his generation of German students, among whom were Hegel and Schelling. The shaping historical context of this phrase is something Martin Heidegger, one of Hölderlin's most perceptive (because poetically attuned) twentieth-century readers, chooses to ignore, as indeed he ignores in his work all historical context beyond a few generalities. Yet today's historically minded reader, contemplating the disaster of the present, may well find a confirmation of her hopes and fears in the philosopher's counsel to "think of the world's night as a destiny that takes place this side of pessimism and optimism. Perhaps the world's time is now approaching its midnight. Perhaps the world's time is now becoming the completely destitute time. But also perhaps not, not yet, not even yet, despite the immeasurable need, despite all suffering, despite nameless sorrow, despite the growing and spreading peacelessness, despite the mounting confusion."[1] For Heidegger, it is in the space of that "perhaps" and that "not yet" that poets can find their realm of address; amid destitution, the task of poets becomes "to gather in poetry the nature of poetry. Where that happens we may assume poets to exist who are on the way to the destiny of the world's age. We others must learn to listen to what *these* poets say."[2]

Admittedly, Heidegger showed scant interest in his contemporary world of poetry beyond a select few writers in the German language, and I am sure we are aware of what his own conception of what "the destiny of the world's age" came to mean for him several years after he gave the first version of the lecture "What Are Poets For?" in 1926. But bracketing these considerations, and acknowledging, for the sake of the present argument, the validity of his warning not to "deceive ourselves through reckoning time merely in terms of that which is by dissecting that which is,"[3] it is possible to develop and repurpose Heidegger's thoughts by means of Cuban poet José Lezama Lima's concept of the "imaginary eras." In a 1964 interview with Armando Alvarez Bravo, Lezama defined these eras as "dominated by an image" that leaps over historical causalities and proclaims the unconditioned nature of the poetic image, such that "a culture may give greater depth to concepts taken from another culture."[4] In its refusal of a deterministic causality, this concept resonates with Ezra Pound's declaration that "all ages are contemporaneous."[5] And keeping in mind as well Heidegger's citation of Rainer Maria Rilke's epistolary complaint of the "empty, indifferent things, sham things, *dummies of life*"[6] invading Europe from America, it might at this juncture be useful to borrow an idea from Heidegger's near-contemporary Spengler and, as did many Latin American and Caribbean thinkers (from C. L. R. James to Alejo Carpentier and Aimé Césaire, among others) upon their first encounter with *The Decline of the West*, read it against the grain of its author's conservative intention. Specifically, to acknowledge such a decline (particularly evident, if not indeed aggravated, in present times) could well betoken a moving of the cultural center and the advent of a new sensibility in the American hemisphere. Indeed, such an awakening was heralded many years before Spengler by José Martí, who extolled "our America" as a potential bulwark against precisely that cheapening of human creativity often violently imposed by the imperial colossus of the North and pungently anatomized by Lezama in his poem "Thoughts in Havana": "They have some show windows and wear some shoes. / In those show windows they alternate the stuffed mannequin with the stuffed ossifrage."[7]

Likewise, the cosmopolitan modernist movement in U.S. poetry ushered in by Martí's near-contemporary Walt Whitman (whose galvanic effect on Latin American poetry is well known) and furthered by, among others, Gertrude Stein, Pound, H.D., and William Carlos Williams, acted as an exemplary counterstatement to the show windows and stuffed mannequins of official U.S. culture; it was these sources that would later—in the 1950s—inspire the renovating impulses of the so-called "New American Poetry" as it waged a battle against the ongoing academization of U.S. poetry. In his concept of the "symposium of the whole," one of these "New American Poets," Robert Duncan, called for a poetics that would incorporate "the female, the lumpenproletariat, the foreign; the animal and vegetative; the unconscious and the unknown; the criminal and failure—all that has been outcast and vagabond [...] into the creation of what we consider we are."[8] This amplifies Martinican poet Aimé Césaire's affirmation, in his lecture "Poetry and Knowledge": "Within us, all the ages of mankind. Within us, all mankind. Within us, animal, vegetable, mineral. Mankind is not only mankind. It is *universe*."[9] In short, poetry is at once a reflection and an *activation* of totalities.

In this same chapter of *The H.D. Book*, Duncan remarked that

> the drama of our time is the coming of all men into one fate, "the dream of everyone, everywhere." The fate or dream is the fate of more than mankind. All things have come now into their comparisons. But these comparisons are the correspondences that haunted Paracelsus, who saw also that the key to man's nature was hidden in the larger nature.[10]

And Lezama tranquilly, without the slightest hint of hyperbole, affirmed in the interview with Alvarez Bravo: "We both serve poetry and all those who do the same will agree with me when I say that in the end poetry will unify everything; it is already beginning to do so."[11] Juxtaposing these statements brings out a kinship between Duncan and Lezama as creators of complementary and, I would argue, compatible poetic systems, American in their openness to emanations from a breadth (and breath) of traditions past and present, vivified by a mythopoetics oriented toward a transformative comprehension of what Lezama calls "the eternally enigmatic other side of things."[12] Myth, as Duncan states in his seminal essay: "The Truth and Life of Myth," "gives life-form, and men living in that myth live in its history, in its living changes and permutations, not its petrifactions [. . .] every part of man's story has been re-informed by the creative genius of his own present moment."[13] A mythopoetics, then, that is not obscurantist regression but a process of knowing, of "telling the story that cannot be told," a gnosis wherein "I get the drift I do not know / The Word moves me."[14] Compare Heidegger: "We never come to thoughts. They come to us."[15] For his part, Lezama speaks in the interview with Alvarez Bravo of the "image [as] the reality of the invisible world," invoking its "infinite possibility."[16] In an essay titled "Introducción a la Esferaimagen" (Introduction to the Sphereimage) Lezama terms myth "a participated image," whereas an image is "a myth beginning its adventure, which particularizes itself in order to shine forth anew."[17] This resonates with Lezama's first published work, the 1937 *Muerte de Narciso*, in which the death of the mythic figure marks the effective "birth" of the poet, who continues his work under the floral protection of Narcissus, also a tutelary figure of Duncan's inspiration, who identifies the dead youth as "myth and mystery of what we mean to be."[18]

The centrality of Narcissus to both Duncan and Lezama marks them as theorists and practitioners of a poetic "gay science" in more than one sense. Near-contemporaries born nine years apart, both were largely self-taught "magpies" in Duncan's sense ("Poets are like magpies: they grab at anything bright and take it back to their nest, and they'll use it sooner or later"[19]), drawing upon (and, one could say, queering) a vast range of heterogeneous readings. Their poetic work was also shadowed—and lit—by illness; the critic Peter O'Leary has written extensively and persuasively of Duncan's work as a kind of pharmakon, as both psychotic break and healing balm, whereas Lezama's lifelong struggles with asthma are mirrored in the swell and heave of his poetic line, and are dramatically voiced in his recordings, where each reading tends to end on an inhalation that turns the final vocable into an upward slide.

Finally, both were poets in destitute times: Lezama's poems and essays emerged in the late 1930s and early 1940s, a time when the Republic of Cuba, transitioning toward a nominally democratic regime, showed itself to be incapable of and unwilling to shake off North American influence. *Muerte de Narciso* appeared—to general indifference, and on the part of the official cultural philistines, derisive hostility—when Fulgencio Batista was moving toward his decades-long predominance in Cuban political life, and Lezama's major collection *Enemigo rumor* ("Inimical Murmur"), from which is drawn the poem discussed in this essay, "Una oscura pradera me convida" ("A Dark Meadow Invites Me"), appeared in 1941. Through the little magazines he edited—*Verbum, Nadie parecía, Espuela de Plata*, and most significantly *Orígenes*—Lezama along with his collaborators sought to contribute to a cultural and spiritual awakening of Cuban intellectual life, and beyond that, the country as a whole. For his part, Duncan achieved notoriety in 1944 with a personally and politically revelatory essay "The Homosexual in Society," which led John Crowe Ransom of the *Kenyon Review* to pull several of his poems from publication. During the 1940s and 1950s, he published in various small presses and journals. As if to herald the creatively insurgent times to follow, his first collection, *The Opening of the Field*, appeared in 1960, though many of the poems included therein had been written several years earlier. "Often I Am Permitted to Return to a Meadow," the opening poem of the collection and the one presently under analysis, appeared in 1953, in the depths of the bleak McCarthy years.

A meadow serves as the binding metaphor in both poems, which are narrated in the first person. To establish this point, let me offer the following reflection by Gaston Bachelard in *Poetics of Space*:

> Each one of us . . . should speak of his roads, his crossroads, his roadside benches; each one of us should make a surveyor's map of his lost fields and meadows. [. . .] Thus we cover the universe with drawings we have lived. These drawings need not be exact. They need only to be tonalized on the mode of our inner space.[20]

In his *Dictionary of Symbols*, Juan Eduardo Cirlot cites a related observation by Bachelard that "the meadow, being nourished by the waters of a river, is in itself a subject of sadness, and that, in the true meadow of the soul, only asphodels grow. The winds find no melodious trees in the meadow—only the silent waves of uniform grass."[21] Accentuating the melancholic, somber cast of the metaphor, the asphodel is death's flower and conjures up the ancient myth of the Elysian Fields where the blessed heroes wander after death. At the same time, a meadow is a clearing, a way into what Heidegger, borrowing and extending a concept of Rainer Maria Rilke's, calls the Open, intimately linked to the act of creation: "What poetry, as illuminating projection, unfolds of unconcealedness and projects ahead into the design of the figure, is the Open which poetry lets happen, and indeed in such a way that only now, in the midst of beings, the Open brings beings to shine and ring out."[22] If, for Heidegger, Truth itself is a clearing, both Duncan and Lezama in their poems follow the path of their poetic master Dante and enact a kind of pilgrimage into the Open, which "invites" Lezama and "permits" Duncan's return. This passage brings them into an evocation of Being shadowed over by Death even as it marks what Lezama's close friend and interlocutor, the Spanish philosopher (and reader of Heidegger) María Zambrano identifies in her unclassifiable poetic-philosophical work *Claros del bosque* ("Clearings in the Forest") as a Dantean *incipit vita nova*, a moment of revelation on the threshold of a domain where "everything alludes, everything is allusion and everything is oblique, the very light that manifests itself as a reflection appears obliquely, but not smoothly like a sword."[23] On a formal level, both poems are composed of twenty-three lines (not counting the titles)—Duncan's is divided into nine stanzas of uneven (2-3-2-3-3-3-2-3-2) lineation, whereas Lezama's is continuous. In short, Lezama's poem is an unfolding, whereas Duncan's is irregular, even hesitant, marked by caesuric gaps. I reproduce Duncan's poem here for ease of reference.[24]

Often I Am Permitted to Return to a Meadow

as if it were a scene made-up by the mind,
that is not mine, but is a made place,

that is mine, it is so near to the heart,
an eternal pasture folded in all thought
so that there is a hall therein

that is a made place, created by light
wherefrom the shadows that are forms fall.

Wherefrom fall all architectures I am
I say are likenesses of the First Beloved
whose flowers are flames lit to the Lady.

She it is Queen Under The Hill
whose hosts are a disturbance of words within words
that is a field folded.

It is only a dream of the grass blowing
east against the source of the sun
in an hour before the sun's going down

whose secret we see in a children's game
of ring a round of roses told.

Often I am permitted to return to a meadow
as if it were a given property of the mind
that certain bounds hold against chaos,

that is a place of first permission,
everlasting omen of what is.

    The title flows directly into the poem. Initially, the poet appears as a passive recipient of permission, but at the same time he has been to that meadow before: to this primal image, the as-yet-unnamed force "permits" him to return. Unlike Zambrano's imagined discoverer of the clearing in the forest, he does not turn away from the meadow for fear of entering into an ecstatic state. But the meadow is endowed with a second nature—Lezama would have called it "supernature," something unconditioned and unconditional—as a subjunctive "as if." Punning on "mind" and "mine," the poet introduces an ambiguity: is the "made place" that he identifies as "mine" the creation of a mind that is not his, or when it is made, is he not "in his" mind but in a state of ecstatic receptivity to the Word through which the scene is made manifest? Zambrano, in speaking of "the clearing in the forest"—and a meadow is certainly one such clearing, in which sky and earth mirror each other—describes it as a "center in which it is not always possible to enter [. . .] it is another kingdom that a soul inhabits and watches over. [. . .] The immediate lesson of clearings in the forest is this: one does not have to go in search of them, nor seek anything from them."[25] The permission extended the poetic I must come from one such soul or *genius loci*, and Duncan affirms that the "made" place (recall that the original Greek meaning of *poiein* was "to make") is "so near to the heart" as to in effect be "mine." Playing on the dual meaning of "fold" as both the dwelling place to which those (invisible in the poem) animals who through grazing make the meadow into a "pasture" must return at close of day and as an act of bending or creasing or blending, Duncan metamorphoses it into a second "made place," a hall engendered by a primeval divine light. The provenance of this light is Gnostic and Neo-Platonic, in that the "shadows that are forms" emanating from it are removed from their *fons et origo* and are thus mere semblances of the ideal form. The use of the verb "fall" in this context bears unmistakable resonance with the "fall" of Man—caused, according to the Gnostics, by the false demiurge that created the world of deceptive shadows.

The opening line of the fourth stanza repeats the "wherefrom" of the last line of the third, but since a period separates the former from the latter, it is not necessarily the case that the source of the second "wherefrom" is the shaping light. It could very well be the poetic I, and the "architectures" that fall (note the rhyme with the second stanza's "hall") could be the poet placing himself in the role of Maker and Destroyer. By suggestively—in syntactic terms, perplexingly, almost as if it were a stammer—following "I am" with "I say," the poet links Being with Saying (consider Heidegger's "Man speaks only as he responds to language"[26]). And if architectures are made to fall, it is because they conceal the fact that, again in Heidegger's words, "poetry [is not] building in the sense of raising and fitting buildings. But poetry, as the authentic gauging of the dimension of dwelling, is the primal form of building."[27] The gnomic quality of the stanza is accentuated by the uncertainty as to whether the "architectures" or the "I am I say" are the "likenesses of the First Beloved." Do the edifices fall away in the face of this Lady's splendor, as Dante's words in *Paradiso* failed before the final apotheosis of Beatrice and the divine presence, or are the poet's very being-and-saying—tentative as they might be—instantiations of that Lady's puissance? The following stanza would appear to confirm the second interpretation, as those "hosts" or attendants of the Lady as "Queen Under The Hill" (the Venusberg of Teutonic legend, given new life in the nineteenth century by Wagner's opera *Tannhäuser* and Aubrey Beardsley's unfinished erotic tale), are a "disturbance of words within words," which is precisely what the poetic impulse brings about, what Walt Whitman called the "something [that] startles me where I thought I was safest."[28] And if such a disturbance is a "field folded," a meadow brought into inmost dwelling, the Queen could also be an avatar of Kore/Persephone, abducted by Hades while gathering flowers in a field and transformed into a subterranean ruler over the dead, re-emerging in spring to cause those flowers to blossom anew.

The overtones of death become more audible in the following two stanzas: the dream imaged in and by the field is of the "grass blowing / east against the source of the sun" in the hour before sunset, evoking the Book of Peter's gloss on a quote from the prophetic Book of Isaiah: "For all flesh *is* as grass, and all the glory of man as the flower of grass. The grass withereth, and the flower thereof falleth away."[29] Recall as well Cirlot's paraphrasing of Bachelard's "silent waves of uniform grass." And the secret of this windblown grass is to be found in the children's round game of Ring Around the Roses, whose origins lie in the medieval plague, and which culminates in a symbolic collective death—another fall—following the invocation of "ashes." The Lady, then, is a figure of both Eros and Thanatos.

The final two stanzas of the poem act as a kind of musical coda, repeating the title verse, only now the meadow has metamorphosed from being like unto a "scene made up by the mind" to a putative "given property of the mind / that certain bounds hold against chaos." "Given" carries both the sense of a bestowal and a postulate, and the ambiguity of the relative pronoun "that" could refer either to the mind or its given property. The indefinite quality of the "certain" adds subtly to the mystery. What is not in question is the chaos against which those bounds act to safeguard the mind and/or its meadow/property. The matter of who or what is extending the poet his permission to return again imposes itself. If we can imagine the meadow as encircled by forests in the way Zambrano would like us to think of it (and as Duncan's life-partner Jess depicts in his illustration for *The Opening of the Field*[30]), then the "place of first permission" would mark a momentary exit from the Dantean "dark wood" and an entry into what Zambrano calls

> a glorious moment of lucidity which is beyond consciousness and which floods it. It, consciousness, thus becomes enlivened, clarified, truly fecundated by this moment. [. . .] A method emerging from a complete "incipit vita nova" that awakens and takes charge of all areas of life.[31]

The concluding paradox of the poem's final line, "the everlasting omen of what is"—for are not omens portents of the future, not of the present, and do they not emerge in and for only a moment, to be interpreted later by soothsayers?—could point to this Dantean *incipit*, wherein the "field" would be that of the poem itself. (Duncan was inspired by Charles Olson's concept of "composition by field" as a poetic method.) Zambrano says that "if nothing is sought, the gift [of the clearing] will be unpredictable, unlimited."[32] Poetry then becomes that "given property of the mind" to which the meadow is compared, and each poem a permission of the Muse, a token and sign of a *vita nova*.

In a brief prefatory remark to a 1968 recording of "Una oscura pradera," Lezama connects the poem with his vocation and emphasizes its "secret nostalgia" whose "implicit content is an evocation of death, of Non-Being."[33] Here follows the poem, in its original Spanish[34] and in my own translation:

Una Oscura Pradera Me Convida

Una oscura pradera me convida,
sus manteles estables y ceñidos,
giran en mí, en mi balcón se aduermen.
Dominan su extensión, su indefinida
cúpula de alabastro se recrea.
Sobre las aguas del espejo,
breve la voz en mitad de cien caminos,
mi memoria prepara su sorpresa:
gamo en el cielo, rocío, llamarada.
Sin sentir que me llaman
penetro en la pradera despacioso,
ufano en nuevo laberinto derretido.
Allí se ven, ilustres restos,
cien cabezas, cornetas, mil funciones
abren su cielo, su girasol callando.
Extraña la sorpresa en este cielo,
donde sin querer vuelven pisadas
y suenan las voces en su centro henchido.
Una oscura pradera va pasando.
Entre los dos, viento o fino papel,
el viento, herido viento de esta muerte
mágica, una y despedida.
Un pájaro y otro ya no tiemblan.

(A Dark Meadow Invites Me

A dark meadow invites me,
its steady, close-fitting tablecloths,
revolve in me, fall asleep on my balcony.
They rule its reaches, its indefinite
alabaster dome recreates itself.
On the waters of a mirror,
the voice cut short in the middle of a hundred paths,
my memory prepares its surprise:
fallow deer in the sky, dew, sudden flare.
Without sensing they're calling me

I slowly penetrate the meadow,
proud in a new melted labyrinth.
There to be seen, illustrious remains,
a hundred heads, bugles, a thousand shows
open their sky, silencing their sunflower.
Strange the surprise in that sky,
where unwillingly footfalls return
and the voices sound in its swollen center.
A dark meadow passes by.
Between the two, wind or fine paper,
the wind, wounded wind
of this single death, magic and dismissed.
One bird, another bird, no longer tremble.)

Like Duncan's poem, "Una oscura pradera. . ." evokes the liminal space between Eros and Thanatos as the realm in which the poet comes into possession of, or is possessed by, his gift. While unlike "Often. . ." this poem does not serve as an introit, coming fourth in *Enemigo rumor*'s opening sequence *Filosofía del clavel* ("Philosophy of the Carnation"), it is significant that it is the first in which the poetic I is (at least in the opening half) prominent. But as distinct from Duncan's poem, what is at play here is precisely that "super-nature" which Lezama regularly described as one of the cornerstones of his poetic system: "man replies to the determinism of nature with the total freedom of the image. [. . .] nature, when enlarged by the image man provides, attains to the new realm of supernature."[35] So while the dark Elysian meadow beckoning the poet to enter seems at first to be an avatar of Duncan's meadow after the sun has gone down, its condition as a natural phenomenon is in the end no less artificial, no less "a made place" than Duncan's. In keeping with the constant metamorphic unfolding of Lezama's poetry, where nothing is stable, always in motion toward the unconditioned image, the focus shifts in the second line to the "tablecloths" covering the meadow, which connect to the "invitation" the poet receives and briefly conjure up the image of a banquet, swiftly dispelled when these tablecloths are said to "revolve" in the poet and are endowed with the animate quality of sleep. Perhaps these versatile tablecloths, at once covering the meadow, whirling within the poet, and slumbering on the balcony (a manmade creation suspended between earth and sky and jutting out from a dwelling), could be an instantiation of what Lezama calls in "Confluences": "a germ that sprang from a union of the most distant stars with the most hidden things inside us."[36] The function of a tablecloth is to cover a bare surface, or to turn a simple table in a place of worship into a sanctified space; in this case, it is a means, along with the "alabaster dome," through which the meadow's reaches are converted into supernature. A dome also encloses and sacralizes, and one of alabaster's properties is the ability to draw salvific energies to the individual, in this case by offering the poet a model of the self-recreation through which the poetic image moves, and through that a paradigm of his vocation.

The image of the liquefying mirror is a common trope in the baroque and neobaroque repertoire, but in the context of the dark meadow, it is equally possible to read it through María Zambrano's perception of the clearing as a "mirror that trembles, a flickering light that scarcely allows something to be outlined only to have it dissolve. And everything alludes, everything is allusion and everything is oblique." Such is the "surprise" that the poet's Mnemosyne prepares, at the moment speech falls silent at the crossroads, which as Lezama once jocularly pointed out, is the greatest delight of the centipede. Lezama observes in *La expresión americana*: "Memory is a deed of the spirit, but memory is a plasma of the soul, it is always creative, spermatic, because we memorize from the root of the species."[37] Poetic activity, mobilizing as it does the unconditioned—liberated—image, must also surrender to silence in order the better to hear deeper, primordial sounds. The succession of images that unexpectedly emerge from memory: the *gamo* or fallow deer was often kept as a quarry by monarchs and allowed to graze in the royal gardens, and its celestial apotheosis here both proclaims its own regal status and establishes an equivalency between sky and meadow. Dew was an image dear to Lezama, in that it is a celestial blessing of the earth; and the flare speaks to *lo súbito*, a sudden irruption or disruption of the habitual. These images, whose summoning power is subliminally sensed, impel the poet-pilgrim to "penetrate" (a word that recurs throughout Lezama's oeuvre, and whose erotic as well as gnostic implications need no amplification) the precincts of the meadow, which the poet's presence transforms into a "new melted labyrinth," thus ringing an oxymoronic change on another standard baroque image. "Melted" connotes liquefaction, and indeed meadows, as Bachelard reminds us, are mantles of greenery (might we discern a pun here between the dark meadow's tablecloths—*manteles*—and Bachelard's *manteaux*?).

The poet walks proudly amid this landscape of ruins, which recalls a metaphysical painting by Giorgio de Chirico or Carlo Carrà in its assemblage of fragments from dead civilizations and battles. Or, as Ramón Xirau points out in his acute analysis of this poem,[38] it might conjure up autobiographical recollections of the poet's childhood in a military camp, which would speak to the "nostalgia" Lezama cites as an emotional element in the poem. Yet it is precisely the appearance of the labyrinth—significantly, at the halfway point of the poem—that marks the disappearance of the poetic I from the poem; having once entered the meadow, he is one with it and its variegated metamorphoses. His proud bearing is an instance of what Heidegger, following Rilke, calls "unshieldedness[, which] can keep us safe only when the parting against the Open is inverted, so that it turns toward the Open—and into it."[39] The "thousand shows," a panoply of wonders or starry firmament besting the hundred paths and heads, are sufficiently spectacular in their nocturnal splendor as to silence the sunflower that habitually turns toward the sun with the same slowness, perhaps, as the meadow's tablecloths once revolved within the poet.

The "surprise" earlier prepared by the poet's memory has now become a dweller in the sky of a thousand shows. "The duration of poetry sows its seeds by a resurgence in the stars," remarks Lezama in "Confluences."[40] As above, so below: sky and meadow are both of the Open and form a communicating vessel, and this accentuates the uncanniness of the footfalls returning, like Duncan, to the sky-meadow, and the unborn voices issuing from the sky-womb whose water is about to break upon the world. Then, Lezama reprises the opening image of the "dark meadow," just as Duncan reiterates the opening line of the poem, but now it is endowed with motion. Or is it the poet who moves past it into an unknown realm, the hypertelic space of non-Being that Lezama mentions in his brief spoken commentary on the poem? Though wind and fine paper can be brought together in a fan, Lezama lingers on the wind—the *flatus Dei* which Tertullian, a theologian Lezama was fond of quoting, defined as that divine breath which makes man into God's image. His use of the adjective "wounded" to qualify the repetition of "wind" unavoidably recalls his own lifelong struggles with asthma, poignantly gestured toward in his statement, "by breathing more deeply we find a universal rhythm."[41] Here the poet foresees his own death, which is ever and always "single," our own, and "magic and dismissed" (the Spanish *despedida* also means "farewell").

The final line recalls the concluding movement of Gustav Mahler's Symphony No. 2—before the hushed entry of the last chorus, which, gradually growing in strength and volume, will proclaim the soul's resurrection (the symphony's subtitle), a flute tremulously utters bird-calls amid a background of distant brass fanfares, as if it were a final breath of life. The image of resurrection is especially appropriate here because it supersedes the apparent closure of the poem, and speaks to one of Lezama's central preoccupations. In speaking of the image as a body of infinite possibilities, Lezama terms resurrection the greatest such possibility. This counters Heidegger's notion of being-toward-death—formulated, as Xirau reminds us, early in his philosophical trajectory and not specifically engaged in his later writings on poetry—with "a concept of poetry that establishes the prodigious causality of being-for-resurrection, of being that triumphs over death and over the Saturnian realm."[42] In this connection, it is worth pointing out that Lezama, although a professed Catholic, never went to confession, and astonished his friend and colleague, the priest Angel Gaztelu, by blithely affirming the non-existence of Hell, in which case, the promised resurrection would be for all.

After some pressure on Gaztelu's part, Lezama finally admitted that Hell did in fact exist, but it was uninhabited and likely always had been. The poem, then, is precisely the space of resurrection, in which the word triumphs over death and all other contingencies.

As well, the erotic undertones of the poem emerge in the equivocal meaning of "pájaro" and the cause of both the one bird and another's trembling and its cessation. "Pájaro" is a slang word for "penis" (and, in a somewhat derogatory sense, homosexual). Lest this be considered a case of over-analyzing, it suffices to turn to Lezama's interview with Alvarez Bravo, where he expounds with great delight on the various meanings and permutations of the German word "Vogel" (bird) as an example of *lo súbito*: "[a student of German] encounters the unconditional *vögeln*, which gives him the meaning of the bird penetrating into the cage, that is, copulation."[43] If the significance of the word "penetration" in the poem is recalled, the dark meadow can be seen in a different, more eroticized light—a reading that arguably is not wholly unrelated to my own, given the close affinity between Eros and death that haunts both this poem and Duncan's. Yet Lezama's poem, however shadowed over by images of non-being, is far less fraught, more tranquilly assured and suffused with a kind of inner benediction, than Duncan's agonistic struggles with the chaos that perpetually lurks outside the "given properties of the mind."

Heidegger quotes Hölderlin's poetic observation in "Brot und Wein," "Each of us goes toward and reaches the place that he can," in the context of putting forth the requirement of poets in destitute times to "attend, singing, to the trace of the fugitive gods" and to "gather in poetry the nature of poetry."[44] In connection with the two pilgrim poets under discussion here, Heidegger's words carry unmistakable relevance: Lezama's pagan Catholicism and joyful knowledge and Duncan's syncretic myth-and-soul-making, are both poetic systems of ingathering that not only seek out the traces of the fugitive gods but re-animate them in the realm of that language which, in Heideggerian terms, speaks. And beyond simple consolation in destitute times, they call on the reader to arrive at the place of her own *incipit vita nova*, to make a "disturbance of words within words" and to reinvest the world with new meanings drawn from the totality of human imagination.

NOTES

1. Heidegger, "What Are Poets For?" in *Poetry, Language, Thought*, 89–142, 93.
2. Ibid., 94.
3. Ibid.
4. Álvarez Bravo, "Interview with José Lezama Lima," 176.

5. Pound, *The Spirit of Romance*, 6.
6. Rilke, *Briefe aus Mazot*, 333 f.; cited in Heidegger, "What Are Poets For?," 113.
7. Lezama Lima, "Thoughts in Havana," 61.
8. Duncan, *The H.D. Book*, 154.
9. Césaire, "Poetry and Knowledge," in *Lyric and Dramatic Poetry*, xlii–lvi, xlviii.
10. Duncan, *The H.D. Book*, 153.
11. Álvarez Bravo, 183.
12. Ibid., 174.
13. Duncan, "The Truth and Life of Myth," in *Collected Essays and Other Prose*, 139–194, 172.
14. Duncan, "God-Spell," in *The Collected Later Poems and Plays*, 412.
15. Heidegger, "The Thinker as Poet," in *Poetry, Language, Thought*, 1–14, 6.
16. Alvarez Bravo, 177.
17. Lezama Lima, "Introducción a la esferaimagen," 286; my translation.
18. Duncan, "Star, Child, Tree," cited in Peter O'Leary, *Gnostic Contagion: Robert Duncan and the Poetry of Illness* (Middletown, CT: Wesleyan University Press, 2002), 134.
19. Oral quotation, cited by David Meltzer in an interview, in *San Francisco Beat*, 188–215, 197.
20. Bachelard, *The Poetics of Space*, 11–12.
21. Cirlot, *A Dictionary of Symbols*, 262.
22. Heidegger, "The Origin of the Work of Art," in *Poetry, Language, Thought*, 17–87, 72.
23. Zambrano, *Claros del bosque*, 12; my translation.
24. See Duncan, *Collected Later Poems and Plays*, 3.
25. Zambrano, 11.
26. Heidegger, "Language," in *Poetry, Language, Thought*, 187–210, 210.
27. Heidegger, "'…Poetically, Man Dwells…,'" in *Poetry, Language, Thought*, 211–29, 227.
28. Whitman, "This Compost," in *Complete Poetry and Selected Prose*, 260–261, 260.
29. 1 Peter 1: 24, in *The Holy Bible*, 1013.
30. Reproduced as the frontispiece of Duncan, *The Opening of the Field*.
31. Zambrano, 14–15.
32. Ibid., 11.
33. Transcribed from a second-generation cassette recording; accessible on Youtube https://www.youtube.com/watch?v=dasf4bPepUU.
34. Lezama Lima, "Una oscura pradera me convida," in *Poesía completa*, 29–30.
35. Lezama Lima, "Confluences," trans. James Irby, in Eshleman, *A Sulfur Anthology* 351–366, 354.
36. Ibid., 353.
37. Lezama Lima, "Mitos y cansancio clásico," in *La expresión americana*, in *Obras completas, Tomo II*, 279–301, 287–288; my translation.

38. See Xirau, "Lezama Lima o de la fé poética," in *Entre la poesía y el conocimiento*, 470–489; in particular 479–481.
39. Heidegger, "What Are Poets For?" 121.
40. Lezama Lima, "Confluences," 363.
41. Ibid., 353.
42. Álvarez Bravo, 177.
43. Ibid., 179.
44. Heidegger, "What Are Poets For?" 94.

WORKS CITED

Álvarez Bravo, Armando. "Interview with José Lezama Lima." Translated by James Irby. *Sulfur* 24 (Spring 1989): 172–185.
Bachelard, Gaston. *The Poetics of Space*. Translated by Maria Jolas. Boston: Beacon Press, 1994.
Césaire, Aimé. *Lyric and Dramatic Poetry, 1946–82*. Translated by Clayton Eshleman and Annette Smith. Charlottesville: University of Virginia Press, 1990.
Cirlot, Juan Eduardo. *A Dictionary of Symbols*. 2nd ed. Translated by Jack Sage. London: Routledge, 2002.
Duncan, Robert. *Collected Essays and Other Prose*. Edited by James Maynard. Berkeley: University of California Press, 2014.
———. *The Collected Later Poems and Plays*. Edited by Peter Quartermain. Berkeley: University of California Press, 2014.
———. *The H.D. Book*. Edited by Michael Boughn and Victor Coleman. Berkeley: University of California Press, 2011.
———. *The Opening of the Field*. New York: New Directions, 1973.
Eshleman, Clayton, ed. *A Sulfur Anthology*. Middletown, CT: Wesleyan University Press, 2015.
González Cruz, Iván, ed. *La posibilidad infinita: Archivo de José Lezama Lima*. Madrid: Verbum, 2000.
Heidegger, Martin. *Poetry, Language, Thought*. Translated by Albert Hofstadter. New York: Harper & Row, 1973.
Holy Bible. London/New York/Toronto: Oxford University Press, n.d.
Lezama Lima, José. "Introducción a la esferaimagen." In *La posibilidad infinita: Archivo de José Lezamaima*, edited by Iván González Cruz, 286–289. Madrid: Verbum, 2000.
———. *Obras Completas, Tomo II*. Mexico City: Aguilar, 1977.
———. *Poesía completa*. Edited by César López. Mexico City: Sexto Piso, 2016.
———. "Thoughts in Havana." Translated by James Irby. In *The Whole Island: Six Decades of Cuban Poetry*, edited by Mark Weiss, 59–71. Berkeley: University of California Press, 2009.
Meltzer, David, ed. *San Francisco Beat: Talking with the Poets*. San Francisco: City Lights, 2001.

O'Leary, Peter. *Gnostic Contagion: Robert Duncan and the Poetry of Illness.* Middletown, CT: Wesleyan University Press, 2002.
Pound, Ezra. *The Spirit of Romance.* New York: New Directions, 1968.
Weiss, Mark, ed. *The Whole Island: Six Decades of Cuban Poetry.* Berkeley: University of California Press, 2009.
Whitman, Walt. *Complete Poetry and Selected Prose.* Edited by James E. Miller, Jr. Boston: Houghton Mifflin, 1959.
Xirau, Ramón. *Entre la poesía y el conocimiento.* Mexico City: Fondo de Cultura Económica, 2004.
Zambrano, María. *Claros del bosque.* Barcelona: Seix Barral, 1993.

Part II
BAROQUES

Chapter 5

La Santa Muerte
Necroaesthetics and the Folk Baroque
Silvia Spitta

As I write this essay in honor of Lois Zamora Parkinson's important writings on magical realism and the New World Baroque and to celebrate her seminal contributions across several fields (English, Comparative Literature, Latin American Studies, Art History), a *calaca catrina* lords it over my desk. Made by Joel García, a well-known Mexican papier-mâché artist, she is lanky, wears high heels, sports a short mauve dress, pearl necklace, gaudy earrings, and a feathered boa. From under the calaca's trademark large floppy hat, she greets me every morning with her generous wide-mouthed laugh and smiling gaping black eye sockets. Cigarette in hand, she is sexy, and seems either about to walk away from death, or conversely, to embrace death with such a lust for life that she literally overcomes it. Her energy is exuberant and contagious, her effect on me always a benign reminder to grasp the day.

Anyone who has been to Mexico on Day of the Dead and has seen the myriad altars lovingly erected all over the country on November 1 and 2 will immediately recognize in these sensuous exhibits the rich blending between Catholic and pre-Hispanic belief systems. They will become aware of modern Mexico's profound and continued reverence for the multiple entanglements between life and death that the culture has inherited from pre-Hispanic times. Historical anthropologist Claudio Lomnitz famously pointed out that death is Mexico's "tutelary sign" since it is not only omnipresent but also the oldest cult.[1] Faced with the omnipresence of death in life, then, the visitor coming from the United States or Europe to Mexico will at first be taken aback by the country's seeming obsession with death and the exuberant folk Baroque manifestations thereof. But the flamboyant representations and overflowing altars soon, almost despite themselves, draw visitors in with their sheer sensual beauty and bring our own culture's repression of death into sharp relief. The relegation of the dying to hospitals and hospices and the dead to cemeteries beyond the "city walls"—that is, the heterotopias described by Foucault—suddenly come into sharp focus. In contrast, in Mexico, on November 1 and 2, the dead become center stage for two days and the overflowing altars laden with flowers and pictures of and gifts to the departed are everywhere. Wildly decorated skulls made of sugar await to be eaten as a form of secular communion amid the profusion of marigolds or *cempasuchil*—commonly known as "flowers of the dead."

The renowned altar at the Dolores Olmedo Museum, to which Lois once took me, is simply overwhelming in its abundance and sheer beauty (figures 5.1 and 5.2).

Filling a large room, *calacas* are organized into tableaux that represent key figures and events in Mexican history—particularly of the Mexican Revolution. History parades triumphantly before the visitor, making the past present. A constant stream of visitors and masses of school children march in front of this stunning theater of the dead, which is crowned by the portrait of the famous patroness of the arts. The entire setting provides a powerful lesson in philanthropy and history; more importantly perhaps, it symbolically unites all by underpinning a common political national imaginary.

In contradistinction to the cult of death and reminding us of characterizations of the Baroque's *horror vacui* (which is the era's aesthetic of excess and exaggeration), "Tree of Life" or "árbol de la vida" ceramics which celebrate

Figure 5.1 Calaveras, Altar, Museo Dolores Olmedo, Mexico City, Mexico. *Source*: Photo Silvia Spitta

La Santa Muerte 77

Figure 5.2 Detail, Altar, Museo Dolores Olmedo, Mexico City, Mexico. *Source*: Photo Silvia Spitta

life, are equally omnipresent in Mexico every day of the year, and also distinguished by their sheer overabundance. Dating back to Olmec times, they literally overwhelm sight and the viewer's capacity to distinguish any one object or scene among the myriad objects and scenes represented.[2] Both the altars to Day of the Dead and the Trees of Life, then, not only remit us to the dance between both, but they also remind the visitor that the Baroque, despite its waning as the political and aesthetic manifestation of the seventeenth century, nevertheless continues to underlie everyday artistic sensibilities across Latin America—indeed, that the Baroque survives as a *folk* Baroque. That is, as a dramatic and oftentimes beautiful artistic sensitivity and sensibility that permeates popular culture (as in the untranslatable *cultura popular*). But it also survives in other, equally flamboyant, but perhaps deadlier scenarios.

Indeed, Day of the Dead not only gives the dead their day among us, but the altars also represent the Aztec's veneration of the god Mictlantecuhtli and his wife Mictecacíhuatl, Lords of the Land of the Dead. Venerated across Mesoamerica, all souls were held to come face to face with them on their journey to the *inframundo*. Significantly, as I will elaborate below in my analysis of the emergence of the cult of Santa Muerte, and the profound implication of this cult with the devastating effects of neoliberalism and the (narco) state, the only ones who would be spared this encounter with them were those who suffered a *violent death*.[3] This darker, less visible counterpart to the celebration of life and death on November 1 and 2 became evident to me in the early 2000s when I visited Mexico City and wandered around the city photographing different altars. One in particular literally stopped me in my tracks. Unlike all the other colorful and exuberant altars, it seemed to be purposefully shocking and grotesque. Several dismembered dolls, hair disheveled, shoes and legs strewn about the floor amid wilted flowers, were laid out on a dirty blanket composing an altar in the street. It could easily have been ignored as so much trash, were it not for the candles amid the broken dolls' bodies (figure 5.3).

Trying to account for the horror she felt upon seeing life-size statues of decapitated martyrs holding their heads in their hands in the Chapel de Santo Cristo (Tlacolula de Matamoros, Oaxaca), Lois Zamora surmises that for the faithful at the time, this experience might have been altogether different. She argues that *horror vacui* is not only a baroque conceit, but rather that it became so central to the era's aesthetic because it responded to the "Ignatian insight that metaphysical wholeness may reside in objects, including human body parts."[4] Thus, the gruesome and shocking representations of torture and suffering likely would have been viewed by the faithful at the time as a wonderful sign of God's omnipresence. This insight, of course, also drove the (grotesque) worldwide practice of dismembering the bodies of dead saints to provide churches with relics upon which to "ground" their authority. Zamora's appeal to Ignatian beliefs, to explain her shock at her shock, would imply that a certain normalization of torture and dismemberment was at work in the culture at large—which, of course, was the case if we remember that the Inquisition's terror machinery existed alongside (and perhaps underlay) the Baroque's Counter Reformation aesthetic impulse. Indeed, critics of the Baroque—dismissed as "detractors"—importantly argue that the Baroque functions "not only as an aesthetic of plenitude, exaggeration and excess, but as a historical medium of cultural teratology." That is, the Baroque is *both* an aesthetic of plenitude and exuberance *and one of monstrosity and horror*. Indeed, the "interest in visual excess, corporeal extremes, abjection and martyrdom" as well as "sensual and erotic imagery" was actively promoted by the Catholic Church from 1585 (and Pope Sixtus V) to 1667. The works

Figure 5.3 Street Altar, Mexico City, Mexico. *Source*: Photo Silvia Spitta

of Bernini, Pietro da Cortona, Domenico Fontana, and many others clearly play with this dynamic.⁵ And we must not forget the deep connection between sensuality and death in baroque drama.

The sight of decapitations and other gruesome acts, then, must have been normalized in one way or another; indeed, for the faithful during the Baroque, the sight of beheadings (and thus the representation of beheaded martyrs) might have been quite a familiar sight both in day-to-day life and in religious art. Similarly, I realize that the altar I stumbled upon in the streets of Mexico City that so shocked me, may have been an index of the violence that the country was already experiencing, but which would only become fully evident a decade later. In the early 2000s it seemed to allude very directly to the extreme forms of violence affecting women far away at the U.S.-Mexico border—in particular, Ciudad Juárez. The neologism *femicides* was created to refer to the particularly aggressive sexual forms these murders took and the horrific ways in which young, mestizo women who had left their families in search of work and independence in the maquiladoras had been raped, tortured, dismembered, and thrown out as so much trash. An intriguing little book entitled *Trash,* edited by John Knechtel and published by MIT in 2007, collects reflections and artistic works around garbage. The most arresting among them include trash flâneur Lisa Rochon's photographs of Toronto streets where the homeless are often confused with the trash that litters alleyways, and Gay Hawkins's photographs entitled, "Sad chairs," of abandoned chairs across the city, which force the viewer to wonder what happens when wasted things hang around refusing to go away. Heather Roger argues that trash is the outcome of our economic system and that "the biggest beneficiaries of a trash-rich market are those at the top. Garbage is the detritus of a system that unscrupulously exploits not only nature, but also human life and labor."[6] Included in this volume, with no explanation or apology whatsoever, were the testimonies of mothers of murdered victims in Ciudad Juárez. They all, in one way or another, repeatedly emphasized how the poor are treated as trash, how their dismembered daughters were treated as trash by the murderers, but perhaps even more tellingly, by the Mexican authorities and the media alike. The testimonies of the mothers of daughters who had been the victims of this widespread femicidal macho fury, highlight the deeply unsettling notion of neoliberalism on the border as a system run amok, where human beings, particularly young, indigenous-looking, and poor women, many of them employed in the maquiladora industries doing piecemeal work, are in turn sexually "disassembled:" hacked apart and strewn on garbage dumps in the city as so much waste.[7] The same year I encountered the gruesome trash "altar" on the street in Mexico City, another altar at the Museo de Artes Populares both commemorated and denounced the deaths of the women murdered in Juárez. Writing this as I do in 2021, these earlier altars that I encountered years ago were strangely premonitory of the femicidal fury that has befallen Mexico since then. Once allegedly limited to the border (seen as a lawless no one's land by narcos and maquilas alike), this fury has spread like wildfire since then reminding us once again, of how cheap the idea "this cannot happen here or to me" is—indeed, that while gruesome events may happen far from sight initially, they do and will overcome the center eventually.

After 1993, when the first murders were detected and a clear pattern began to emerge, the authorities' and media's sexism became blatantly evident when blaming the victims passed as "reporting." In news article after news article, the young victims were accused of having dressed provocatively, of leading the easy life, of being so many whores "looking for it." Under the impact of the outrage of women activists on the border and worldwide critique, the deeply misogynist reporting that passed as "news" was unveiled and the term *femicide* was put into circulation. This early discourse around the murders has now given way to a more complex critique of the forces at work conjoining globalization, the interests of the Juárez oligarchy, narcotics trafficking, the Mexican and Russian cartels, and last but by no means least: Mexican men's deep misogyny. These, like an Ariadne's thread, reach deep into the heart of Mexico's ruling elites. Important in this respect is journalist Sergio González Rodríguez's moving report on the murders titled *Huesos en el desierto* (Bones in the Desert) (2002) (echoed in Bolaño's *2666*) in which the author González Rodríguez reflects that his report could be used as a blueprint for committing the perfect crime: you only have to imagine a city where men are free to rape, torture, and murder women; where the police force is ready to cover up the crimes and/or serve as accomplices to the crimes and blame the victims and then threaten anyone who dares to question their actions; and a government that looks the other way. His conclusion that these crimes would constitute a true horror story were it not for the fact that they are real and not at all speculative is chilling, as is the fact that before his death in 2017 things had only gotten much worse and the killing machine had been recognized at work everywhere in Mexico and affected everyone.[8] All talk of the "democratic turn" in the country in the 2000s when the PAN came in to power after seventy years of PRI dominance, was profoundly contradicted by this state of affairs.[9] The simultaneous dismantling of the post-revolutionary safeguards for distributing wealth combined with neoliberal corporate attacks of the age-old *ejido* system and the unions has had the effect that between 1982 and 1996 wages in Mexico dropped precipitously—sometimes by up to 74 percent[10] creating a "reserve army of young unemployed or underemployed men, some of whom found work with the traffickers."[11] The "psychic strains of violence" as Roush would have it are what is stimulating the cult to Santa Muerte to grow.[12] Indeed, already in the 1990s the older representation of death as a "purely skeletal image with no facial expression" that connects to the notion of death as indifferent and neutral, was replaced by the more grotesque versions that predominate today such as Santa Muerte who now looks at us "with a gleefully malicious face" and sometimes even glowing red psychedelic eyes.[13]

    The broken doll altar that I encountered on the street in Mexico City and that has led to this reflection, sadly, was either was the gruesome creation of a sick mind, but more likely, an index that pointed directly to the femicide machine. Indeed, a few years later (2010), I experienced a similar shock when I began to see representations of Santa Muerte *suddenly*, evident all over the city. First seen along the U.S.-Mexico border in 2002 in the home in Tamaulipas of a prominent narco, Gilberto García Mena, el "June" of the Gulf Cartel,[14] she gained prominence in Mexico City in the marginal neighborhood of Tepito shortly thereafter. She has come to be known across the country and well beyond it as la Niña Blanca (White Girl), la Huesuda (Bony Lady), la Flaquita (Skinny Lady), la Santísima Muerte (Our Lady of the Holy Death), among others. She is typically represented as a grotesque skeleton dressed in a robe and holding a scythe or a globe. Indeed, signaling the shattering violence across Mexico, Santa Muerte is fast replacing the Virgin of Guadalupe, who has become whitened and absorbed as a state religion, taking her place as *the* patroness not only of the poor and indigenous but also of gays, transgender, transsexuals, prostitutes, prisoners, smugglers, police officers, bar owners, and even narcos. Indeed, she is and now, along with Jesus Malverde, inextricably associated with narcotrafficking.[15] With nowhere else turn—and least of all the police or the Mexican state—millions today have turned to praying to la Huesuda to protect them against assaults, drugs, prison sentences, and gun deaths.

More importantly and adding yet another twist to the symbolic transfiguration of the Virgin's role as "mother" and protectress of the vulnerable, Santa Muerte's followers believe she protects people against *violent death* —called a "muerte artera"—which is defined as a cruel, malicious (and even vicious) death. Adding a gruesome twist to this search for protection, many who have turned to Santa Muerte notoriously *also* pray for her to avenge them. Indeed, Santa Muerte's "reparative" function has been coupled to her ability to instill fear.[16] Fear of a violent death, una muerte artera—is at the heart of the narcos' strategy of controlling the population by loudly broadcasting their desire to hurt or do damage to someone as revenge. They do this by means of various highly visible and theatrical gestures as when they use the bodies of tortured and decapitated people as "messengers of terror"[17] or when they hang *narcomantas* as billboards on which they broadcast a message (*narcomensaje*), or, having learned from Al Qaeda's videotaped executions (beginning with that of Nicholas Berg in 2004) and those of Daesch/ISIS, they film torture and decapitation scenes and post them online as *narcovideos*. While the Mexican government supposedly deletes these postings as soon as they appear, they are immediately reposted on sites such as the *Blog del Narco* which has a section devoted to "gruesome killings." In tune with these macabre theatrics, a narcoslang has emerged with words that describe the ways narcos "disappear" and dehumanize their victims. Words such as *enteipado* (a face covered by tape), *empozolado* (a body disintegrated in acid), *zarandeado* (a body burned), and so on all erase the bodies, faces, and identities of victims.[18] As Jean-Louis Comolli ventures to surmise in his study of Daesch/ISIS's videos and their relation to cinema and death, people's fascination with both (cinema and the live videotaping of death) is widespread and not altogether devoid of a certain erotic dimension. In fact, he argues that the filming of torture and mutilation done for the "benefit" of the public turns spectators into voyeurs. Despite their disgust and repulsion, they are drawn into the macabre spectacle and participate in the erotic moment ("participent du moment érotique").[19] In this, the cult of Santa Muerte is quite different from most other religious cults, which are focused on goodness, forgiveness, and perfecting the world. Indeed, as Jacqueline Hidalgo has argued, when responding to an early version of this essay in which I was trying to work out how to teach my students at Dartmouth about Santa Muerte without fetishizing the macabre features of the cult, religious practices can also be about "mirroring and working through the struggles of this world." Indeed, as she argued, "To beg for Muerte's power is also to put oneself at the mercy of the power of death . . . because if you fail in your promised devotion she may lead to your harm."[20]

As Enriqueta Romero Romero, founder of one of the most revered altars to Santa Muerte in Tepito never tires of explaining, la Huesuda avenged the death of her son by killing all his murderers, except for the one who has betrayed him, because she had prayed that Santa Muerte leave him incapacitated. To the great delight of Doña Cheta, as she is known locally, this man, once the terror of the neighborhood, now has his diapers changed and takes his sustenance through a popote.[21] As this example of a "therapeutic intervention" to a traumatized population shows, devotees to la Huesuda inhabit a borderline space where they pray to *la Huesuda* to protect *them* from violence and particularly a violent death even as they pray for her to kill or harm those who may seek to harm them.[21] It should come as no surprise, then, that Santa Muerte altars are proliferating across Mexico and increasingly encroaching into Central America and the United States. The sale of the paraphernalia used to create altars to Santa Muerte has skyrocketed and *botánicas*, which once were dedicated to Santería (with a nod to the Virgin of Guadalupe and Mexican folk beliefs in Hispanic neighborhoods of the United States dominated by Mexicans), increasingly carry Santa Muerte paraphernalia. There are also innumerable websites dedicated to the cult expounding on Santa Muerte's symbolism and virtues, as well as academic—and not so academic—studies of the cult.[23]

Once a small, largely invisible cult, the rise in Santa Muerte's importance and visibility has increased in step with Mexico's transformation into a narco and a necro state. As Achille Mbembe notes, necro states have the power to kill and to let live ("el poder de hacer morir y dejar vivir").[24] Indeed, in Mexico today, the state has turned on the civilian population and especially its youth. Think of the 2014 massacre of the forty-three Normalistas at Ayotzinapa (Iguala) that had rocked the nation. But many more victims of state violence come to light on a daily basis as people are forced to live in ever more precarious situations, experiencing heretofore unseen levels of violence amid a generalized state of impunity. Rossana Reguillo, among many others, has repeatedly argued that both the narcos and the state (and the narco state) today have become bulimic monsters that regurgitate the country's youth, vomiting them in the streets tortured and maimed or heaped in clandestine graves. A direct consequence of the imposition of neoliberalism in Mexico, Reguillo sees the emergence of this type of devoring, dismembering, and state-killing machine as the counterpart to the maquiladora industry's literal *incorpo*ration and subjection of workers (mostly young mestizo women) and its spitting them out upon the first sign of resistance. The lowest ranking "soldiers," they are there merely to serve the machine and are readily sacrificed ("en la forma de cuerpos que ingresan a las maquilas como dispositivos al servicio de la máquina . . . como soldados sacrificables en las escalas más bajas de los rangos militares").[25] In sum, thousands upon thousands of Mexican citizens have become completely dispensable and at the mercy of a state deeply implicated with the narcos that sustains itself on the daily administration of death ("la operación cotidiana de un sistema sustentado en la administración de la muerte").[26]

Like the broken doll altar that I stumbled upon, then, the *extremely* grotesque (and quite shocking) forms of representing Santa Muerte—that is, its *necroaesthetics*—have merged in parallel to the (narco) state's necropolitics. When this (to us) grotesque representation is put side by side with the news of beheadings by narcos across Mexico that made the front pages of newspapers worldwide years ago, many might be tempted to talk about a return to barbarism. Reports of gruesome incidents prevail not only in the yellow press but in the media at large. One notorious example rocked the nation when a macabre *Gesamtkunstwerk* of sorts emerged in 1989 after police found that John Schlesinger's 1987 *The Believers* was used as a template for the *narcosatánicos* cult in Tamaulipas, where eleven people were sacrificed in a most gruesome manner, their skeletons used as amulets, and their brains eaten. Another report (*Proceso* March 30, 2012) describes the human sacrifices made by eight followers of a cult to Santa Muerte. The investigation showed that while the three victims had been identified (a woman and two ten-year-olds) the sect, led by a forty-four-year-old woman and including an underage girl, had been doing this since 2009, but the other victims had not been identified. And beheadings such as these abound: "Bodies hung from bridge as 23 more die in Mexico drug war; Human heads dumped at Nuevo Laredo city hall by warring cartel" and would of course only underline this point of view.[27] But these are relatively rare events in contrast to Michoacán's drug cartel La Familia's constant use of violence and beheadings. In 2006, for example, they threw five heads onto a dance floor. The heads were accompanied by a *narcomensaje* that read: "La Familia does not kill for money, does not kill women, does not kill the innocent, those who die are those who must die, let it be known by all, this is: divine justice."[28] That same year, over seventeen decapitations were claimed to have been perpetrated by La Familia. Some narcovideos posted on the Internet have also featured embedded *narcomensajes* in the form of signs featured in the videos or even messages written on the skin of victims. Indeed, "Decapitation, dismemberment, and the deployment of *narcomensajes* have been tightly linked as key elements of what Paula Ovalle (2010) has called the 'visual narrative' of the killings."[29] Alongside the narcomessages "written" on the bodies of victims or which turn the mutilated body into a performance of death (a foot in its mouth, etc.), *narcomantas* are messages written on cloths draped over highways and other very visible public places by means of which the cartels publicize messages to the community or warnings to the government and other cartels. In response to these, the Mexican government has engaged in equally violent actions, equally spectacularly publicized. Carlos Monsiváis denounced the gruesome photos posted of "Jefe de jefes" Arturo Beltrán Leyva, who was killed by the army and depicted with his pants halfway down and covered in the religious amulets and $100 bills he carried with him, as a "semiótica bárbara." In his view, not only were the government and the cartels engaged in a gruesome semiotics, but even worse, the media and the public at large had become addicted to the "teatralización de la muerte" and their media impact. Anthropologist and historian Paul K. Eiss discusses this dynamic as a "narcomedia."[30]

The creations of these scenarios of death, inspired by horror movies, not only drive the actions of the cartels, the government, and the media but also provide narco noir with ample gory material with which to feed the fascination of millions of readers (and the abhorrence of critics). Patrick Bard's *novela de denuncia sobre las muertas de Ciudad Juárez*, for example, was fiercely critiqued by renowned writer Eduardo Antonio Parra for exploiting "the bloody face" of Mexico, for focusing on the country's criminality over its incredible cultural manifestations, and for setting Mexico's "magic aside to privilege [its] barbarism."[31] But the media's sensationalist and grotesque fascination with violent death, particularly that of the so-called "nota roja" or crime-beat press, has to be also seen as part of the underlying folk Baroque sensibility that exists alongside the Day of the Dead altars and Trees of Life. All these strands, unfortunately play out on the bodies of the most vulnerable, and have come together today in the macabre rise in femicides attest.

Indeed, the beheadings in Mexico (as well as those of Daesch in the Middle East) are *not* a sudden return to barbarism, but, as Julia Kristeva reminds us, are part of an age-old practice that stretches as far back in time as 6000 BCE when cultures sometimes depended on beheading enemies, head hunting, and human sacrifices to appease the gods. At other times, Kristeva argues, practices such as "consuming the brain and carving the skull of the other . . . share in the same logic of transition between visible and invisible, life and death, and attest to a religiosity we may find shocking in its savagery, though its complexity demonstrates the presence of authentic psychological anxiety among the first humans."[32] Whether we agree or not with her psychoanalytic explanation of this phenomenon, we are all familiar with key representations such as that of the decapitated head of St. John the Baptist served on a platter or the Baroque's fascination with memento mori. What we might consider, then, as a sudden return to savagery in Mexico, is, in fact, the coming to light of practices hidden from view that underlie *all* cultures and that for Kristeva serve as a bond uniting people or asserting their dominance over others. Artist Pilar de la Fuente famously plays with this Neobaroque in her series "Dándole de comer a los cerdos."[33]

The fast growth of the cult of Santa Muerte has of course worried the Catholic Church, who has issued one condemnation after another, even going so far as to associate the cult with that of Satan. But to no avail. Indeed, the cult is vertiginously spreading beyond Mexico City to Central America and the beyond the northern border into the United States. In Mexico, it is fast filling the vacuum left by the state's absorption and whitening of the Virgin of Guadalupe in the face of which Santa Muerte is providing the only hope of protection against the violence and sheer horror that has become standard fare—that is, a *muerte artera*. According to a *Frontline* report, Calderón's unleashing of the war against the narcos led to over 164,000 homicides between 2007 and 2014—a figure that was much larger than the deaths in Afghanistan and Iraq *combined*.[34] Today, that figure had only grown exponentially. Indeed, researchers such as José Manuel Valenzuela Arce have argued that the death toll is much larger than the official figures released.[35] In fact, Valenzuela Arce traces his genealogy of the violence across Mexico to the femicides that began to be reported along the U.S.-Mexico border, and particularly Ciudad Juárez, in the 1980s. The extreme conditions of "exclusion, vulnerability, precariousness and helplessness" ("exclusión, vulnerabilidad, precarización e indefensión") that began to be seen along the border with the establishment of the maquiladoras and their preference for the cheaper and more "docile" labor of young women upset the dominant patriarchal order. It drew many young women trying to escape that order to the border—a mass migration that not only created conditions of vulnerability in the undoing of family ties, but that also, I suspect, led to an implicit (if unconscious) pact among men to punish those women for their transgression on which feminicidal fury fed. That is, a mass "honor killing" (*sic*) spree that has lasted for decades and that now, "unfortunately" (as Valenzuela Arce unfortunately writes), has spread to vulnerable youth, young children, and the population at large.[36] Indeed, as Eiss notes, "Measures, including the North American Free Trade Agreement (NAFTA), that aimed to facilitate the movement of capital and commodities between Mexico and the United States also facilitated the movement of drugs, money, and arms." Eiss references "a1998 a confidential

U.S. Customs report quot[ing] a onetime Drug Enforcement Administration [DEA] agent"[37] who calls NAFTA "a deal made in narco heaven."[38]

But already in 2007, the documentary *La Santa Muerte/Saint Death*, directed by Eva Aridjis and narrated by Gael García Bernal, tracked the growing importance and visibility of the cult across Mexico and beyond its borders. Even earlier, Homero Aridjis 2003 novella *La Santa Muerte*, according to the author, was the fictionalization of a party he attended at the border in the 1990s hosted by drug traffickers and corrupt government officials. In the narco*wunderkammer* home, there was hall full of African trophies ("Dos tapetes rojos subían al piso de los colmillos y objetos de marfil, cuyo vestíbulo estaba tapizado con pieles de cebra, tigre, oso blanco y leopardo") and a chapel to Santa Muerte, which was the only forbidden space in the house. It had a "necrofridge" (necro-heladera) which held the hands and ears of the family's enemies and the genitals of a policeman it was rumored, as well as the head of a horse and other such niceties.[39] That is, well before the unleashing of Calderón's "war" on the drug trade, the Aridjis's novella and film had signaled how long the violence that now wracks the country had been simmering underneath the surface.

Alongside the growing visibility of Santa Muerte and the Passion Play at Iztapalapa, the narco cemetery, los Jardínes de Humaya, in Culiacán, in the state of Sinaloa (home of many of narco leaders) has become a burial ground so grand as to look like a city at first sight. Rows of compact "villas" displaying the most outrageous architectural details line the peaceful "streets." Some have air conditioning, tinted windows, and their own watchmen. In some, narcos are buried with their "bling" and even their cars. Like the narco lifestyle with all its extremes, los Jardínes de Humaya is excessive in every sense of the word—even in its apparent simplicity. These "gardens" are almost a baroque *trompe l'oeil* since at first sight they seem to be a copy of the more upper class residential areas in Mexico City to which the narcos aspire (and which many are successfully infiltrating)—but it is only after a slight hesitation that you realize this city of gardens is a stage constituted by thousands of grandiose tombs holding some of the worst killers in Mexico.

While those of us who have had the privilege of not being subjected to the shattering violence thousands have experienced across Mexico in the past decades, Santa Muerte's representation is starkly unsettling and even frightening, but to her followers, as I argued above, she is comforting and even beautiful, she is the only source of protection they have in an ever more threatening and chaotic world. Today, then, necropolitics and necroaesthetics go hand in hand. Grotesque levels of violence are inscribed in Santa Muerte's gruesome representations which are then celebrated as "beautiful." Reminding us of the connection of the Baroque to teratology, the new normal is abject and grotesque in every way. In response to this state, the folk Baroque, it would seem, deploys these representations as a normalizing mechanism that makes life bearable for the millions affected by the state of impunity that exists in Mexico today.[40] But if people were ready to resign themselves to this state of affairs, the massive protests Ni Una Más that have shaken Mexico in recent years, and even as we just saw this March 8, 2021, attack the presidential palace as the symbolic bastion of male impunity, things might change. If Saint John the Baptist's head served on a platter is the representation that we associate with the Christian era, Santa Muerte might be the one we will look to as representative of neoliberalism.

NOTES

1. Lomnitz, 27.
2. The most impressive one ever made was a sent as a gift from Mexico to Cuba in 1975 to serve as the centerpiece for the Che Guevara auditorium in Casa de las Américas, Havana. Created by Metepec artist Alfonso Soteno, it is 2.5 meters high and to date the largest in the world.
3. "Mictlantecuhtli." *Ancient History Encyclopedia*, accessed January 20, 2017, http://www.ancient.eu/Mictlantecuhtli/.
4. Zamora, 66.
5. Sandywell, 166.
6. Knechtel, 130.
7. To my knowledge the first to connect the assembling work of the maquiladoras to the disassembling of maquiladora women's bodies was Ursula Biemann in her videoessay, *Performing the Border* (1999).
8. "*Huesos en el desierto* describe la fórmula precisa para cometer crímenes perfectos. Basta pensar en una urbe en la que hubiera libertad para violar, torturar y matar mujeres, los policías encubrieran a los asesinos o fueran sus cómplices, maquinaran la culpabilidad de gente inocente y amenazaran o atentaran contra la vida de quienes se atreviesen a denunciarlos. En consecuencia, los culpables estarían libres y el gobierno cerraría los ojos. Sería una intriga siniestra de la barbarie de género: más de un centenar de victimas de homicidios en serie de cariz sexual. Tal abismo construiría una historia insólita de horror." Back cover.
9. In her review of the translation of González Rodríguez into English (*The Femicide Machine*), Lucía Melgar underlines his conclusions and goes even further arguing that the state of impunity operant in Mexico has normalized the violence against women and girls and is now making all citizens vulnerable to the killing machine. She writes that "La violencia contra las mujeres en México es una violencia estructural, muchas veces institucional e institucionalizada. Forma parte del paisaje. De un paisaje siniestro, sin duda, hoy poblado de fosas clandestinas y agujereado de ausencias: las de los desaparecidos de los que muchos hablan, de las desaparecidas—de las que no se habla lo suficiente—, de las asesinadas con violencia y saña.

Formar parte del paisaje implica en más de un sentido una normalización y naturalización que, lejos de corresponder sólo a una extraña indiferencia social, se deriva de una misoginia persistente y también normalizada y del funcionamiento de lo que podríamos llamar no sólo un "velo" sino una maquinaria de impunidad." Cf. "Alertas de violencia de género: La Sociedad contra la simulación." Sábado 4 de abril 2015. http://nuestraaparenterendicion.com/index.php/blogs-nar/espejos-laterales/item/2762-feminicidio. Accessed September, 25, 2020.

   10. See Hanson and Spilimbergo, 1343.
   11. Eiss, 80.
   12. Roush, 129.
   13. Ibid., 145.
   14. Eliana Gilet, "Los 15 años de la Santa Muerte en Tepito y el fin de la misa de medianoche." *Vice* July 2016. https://www.vice.com/es_latam/article/4w9pan/los-15-anos-de-la-santa-muerte-de-tepito. Accessed August 6, 2020.
   15. Cf. Silvia Spitta, *Misplaced Objects*.
   16. Roush, 130.
   17. "Los cuerpos muertos del narcotráfico son entendidos como mensajeros del terror cubiertos de significaciones" (Ovalle, 106).
   18. Ibid., 111.
   19. Comolli 48.
   20. Hidalgo's "response" presentation at NECLS meeting October 2016.
   21. Cf. Aridjis, *La Santa Muerte/Saint Death* (2007).
   22. Roush, 147.
   23. Cf. Perdigón Castañeda, *La Santa Muerte* and Ovalle.
   24. Qtd. in Reguillo, 62.
   25. Ibid., 65.
   26. Ibid., 68.
   27. *The Guardian*, May 5, 2012.
   28. Eiss, 82.
   29. Qtd. ibid/, 82.
   30. Eiss, 79.
   31. Parra, n.p.
   32. Kristeva, 12.
   33. González Virgen, 27.
   34. Breslow, n.p.
   35. Valenzuela Arce, *Sed de mal: Feminicidio, jóvenes y exclusión social*.
   36. Ibid., 59. These conditions of extreme precariousness and structurally produced conditions of subalternity are also wracking Central America where a genocidal war against women is being unleashed. In Guatemala alone, between 2001 and 2009, 4,867 women have been kidnapped, raped, sexually mutilated, tortured, and killed. Their bodies have been thrown in public places. Guatemala Human Rights Commission/USA (Accessed October 19, 2016).
   37. Eiss, 80.
   38. Ibid., 80; Eaton qtd. in Eiss 80.
   39. Homero Aridjis, 53–54.

40. In the United States, the true nefarious consequences of a neoliberalism run amok so visible in today's un(civil) society in Mexico came to light in the recent election.

WORKS CITED

Aridjis, Eva. *La Santa Muerte/Saint Death*. New Hope, MN: BCI Entertainment, 2007.
Aridjis, Homero. *La Santa Muerte: Sexteto del amor, las mujeres, los perros y la muerte*. Mexico DF: Conaculta Alfaguara, 2003.
Bard, Patrick. *novela de denuncia sobre las muertas de Ciudad Juárez*. Mexico: Grijalvo Intriga, 2004.
Biemann, Ursula. *Performing the Border*. New York, NY: Women Make Movies, 1999.
Blog del Narco Oficial. http://www.elblogdelnarco.com/2014/08/lista-de-v%C3%ADdeos-de-"Bodies hung from bridge as 23 more die in Mexico Drug War." *The Guardian* May 5, 2012. https://www.theguardian.com/world/2012/may/05/bodies-bridge-23-mexico-drug.
Breslow, Jason M. "The Staggering Death Toll of Mexico's Drug War." *Frontline*, July 27, 2015. Accessed October 6, 2016. http://www.pbs.org/wgbh/frontline/article/the- staggering-death-toll-of-mexicos-drug-war/.
Cartwright, Mark. "Mictlantecuhtli." *Ancient History Encyclopedia*. Accessed January 20, 2017. http://www.ancient.eu/Mictlantecuhtli/.
Comolli, Jean-Louis. *Daesch, le cinéma et la mort*. Paris: Editions Verdier, 2016.
Eaton, Tracey. "Report: NAFTA boosts drug trade." *Dallas Morning News*, May 11, 1998.
Eiss, Paul K. "The Narcomedia: A Reader's Guide." *Latin American Perspectives* 41, no. 2 (2014): 78–98. Accessed 10-7-2020. ejecuciones-interrogatorios-y-balaceras. html. Accessed January 20, 2017.
González Rodríguez, Sergio. *Huesos en el desierto*. Mexico: Editorial Anagrama, 2002.
González Virgen, Miguel A. *Pilar de la Fuente*. Monterrey: Universidad Autónoma de Nuevo León, 2008.
Guatemala Human Rights Commission/USA. Accessed October, 19, 2016. http://www.ghrcusa.org/Programs/ForWomensRighttoLive/FAQs.htm.
Hanson, Gordon H. and Antonio Spilimbergo. "Illegal immigration, border enforcement, and relative wages: evidence from apprehensions at the U.S.-Mexico border." *American Economic Review* 89 (1999): 1337–1357.
Hidalgo, Jacqueline. "Response Presentation." *NECLS*, October 2016, Smith College.
Knechtel, John. *Trash*. Cambridge, MA, London, England: MIT Press, 2007.
Kristeva, Julia. *The Severed Head: Capital Visions*. Trans. Jody Gladding. New York: Columbia University Press, 2012.
Lomnitz, Claudio. *Death and the Idea of Mexico*. Brooklyn, NY; Cambridge, MA: Zone Books Distributed by MIT Press, 2005.

Ovalle, Lilian Paola. "Imágenes abyectas e invisibilidad de las víctimas: Narrativas visuales de la violencia en México." *El Cotidiano,* November-December, 2010, 103–15.

Parra, José Antonio. "El privilegio de la barbarie." *Letras Libres.* July 31, 2004. http://www.letraslibres.com/index.php?art=9730. Translation: Silvia Spitta.

Perdigón Castañeda, Katia J. *La Santa Muerte: Protectora de los hombres.* México: Instituto Nacional de Antropología e Historia, 2008.

Reguillo, Rossana, "La turbulencia en el paisaje: De jóvenes, necropolítica y 43 esperanzas." In *Juvenicidio: Ayotzinapa y las vidas precarias en América Latina y España,* edited by José Manuel Valenzuela Arce, 59–77. Barcelona: Ediciones NED, 2015.

Roush, Laura. "Santa Muerte, Protection, and desamparo." *Latin American Research Review* 49 (2014): 129–148.

Spitta, Silvia. *Misplaced Objects: Collections and Recollections in Europe and the Americas* Houston: University of Texas Press, 2009.

Valenzuela Arce, José Manuel. *Sed de mal: Feminicidio, jóvenes y exclusión social.* Tijuana: El Colegio de la Frontera Norte, 2012.

Zamora, Lois. "Baroque Objects and Subjects: *Horror vacui, Naturaleza muerta, Memento mori.*" In *Des/Memorias: Culturas y prácticas mnemónicas en América Latina y el Caribe,* edited by Marta Muñoz, Silvia Spitta y Valeria Wagner, 58–76. Barcelona: Linkgua Ediciones, 2015.

Chapter 6

Carpentier's *Concierto barroco*

Transoceanic Picaresques and Revolution, or All that Glitters Is Not Gold

John Ochoa

Running through the heart of the Baroque-Neobaroque continuum is a geographic axis: Europe-Cuba-Mexico and its reverse, Mexico-Cuba-Europe. Significant journeys go back and forth along this route. It is therefore not surprising that a wandering literary genre—the picaresque—figured prominently in the historical baroque period of the seventeenth and eighteenth centuries and beyond.

A partial list, just on the American side, includes Carlos de Siguenza y Góngora's *Infortunios de Alonso Ramírez* (1690); Fray Servando Teresa de Mier's *Memorias* (1818), reimagined by Reynaldo Arenas in his Neobaroque *La vida alucinante* (1968); and Antonio López Matoso's unexplored gem *Viaje de Perico Ligero al país de los moros* (1816). The picaresque is a genre about empire, if about its margins, but it is also about the need for gold. Empire and gold are also signatures of the Baroque.

A well-worn critical platitude about the picaresque can be found in Benedict Anderson's influential study of the rise of modern national identity, *Imagined Communities* (1982). When Anderson builds his Benjaminian argument that the creation of national consciousness happened because of technology—that is, print journalism, which led to a sense of simultaneity among readers and thus to a modern sense of shared identity—he includes examples from picaresques that chronicle an unmediated and recognizable "reality." His chosen examples are from places that were transitioning from colonialism to post-colonialism: the Philippines and Mexico. Anderson further explains his interest in the genre by noting that the *pícaro*, a marginal wanderer, can offer a unique kind of vantage point, a Foucauldian *tour d'horizon*—a survey of institutions of discipline such as the military, hospitals, debtors' prisons, madhouses, the corrupt lower reaches of the church, and various forms of indentured servitude. The *pícaro* has seen these from the inside, having run afoul of most of them.

Echoing decades of Spanish scholarship, Anderson essentially contends that the picaresque forecasts nineteenth-century realism. Its simplistic and uncomplicated optics, motivated by the protagonist's need to survive and nothing more, provide a morally and aesthetically transparent clarity, and also an existentialism *avant-la-lettre* (as Ortega y Gasset would have it). This clarity—the reason for Anderson's interest in the genre—supposedly captures the essence of "a particular place" in an unmediated way. The collision between the individual subject—the *pícaro*—and the materiality of the real world never weighs down that subject to the point of committing to that particular world. The *pícaro* remains a free-floating signifier if there ever was one, but precisely because of this, he serves as an excellent looking glass.

For all their simplicity, classical picaresques are complicated. They generally lack a clear moral center, given an ontologically and literally hungry main character who must survive above all. The foundational picaresque *Lazarillo de Tormes* (1554) can be read simultaneously as an angry satire, an ideologically motivated critique, or an early example of harsh verisimilitude that initiated novelistic realism. It escapes any attempt to isolate its intentionality. Any corrective message or moral that can be extrapolated from its stoic and minimal narrative is simply that: an extrapolation, a superimposition. Any perceived lesson can be contradicted or explained away as device. Astoundingly, the *Lazarillo* manages to be simultaneously negative and celebratory of the harsh realities it represents. Despite its seething, under-the-surface anger, the main spectacle is not denunciation but rather survival in the face of great odds. The *pícaro's* stoic story of deprivation and harsh living is coupled with an amoral triumph of the will. The real display is simply that the *pícaro* survives to tell the tale. And his ability to survive is what undergirds the genre's huge historical influence and longevity.

The short picaresque novel *Concierto barroco*, published in 1974, came late in the career of Cuban novelist Alejo Carpentier. The action takes place during the eighteenth century, though the novel's timeline gradually folds into an indeterminate present in the twentieth century. The initial setting announces an ethical and stylistic affinity toward the historical Baroque—a very specific period late in the baroque style—thus locating this work within a particular moment in literary history and the rise of the modern novel.

Ian Watt argues forcefully in his *Rise of the Novel* (1957) that the eighteenth century is *the* source of modern sensibility, and that English literature was front and center during that transitional century. According to Watt, the novel did not begin in 1612 with *Don Quixote*—as many critics had argued—but rather with *Don Quixote*'s more "novelistic" British progeny.[1] Whatever the reason for Watt's need to locate the source of realism in the British late eighteenth century, his ideas about the development of the modern, realist novel are compelling. And it is interesting to trace the parallel evolution of the picaresque during this same period. In what is known as the Long Eighteenth Century the character of the *pícaro* evolved from the knowing, cynical, and often amoral opportunist of previous works (such as the *Lazarillo de Tormes* or Mateo Alemán's *Buscón de Alfarache*) to what British Hispanist writer Alexander Blackburn calls an *honnête homme*: an optimistic fellow who is quite often dumb but is tempered by "stoical refusal to give in to adversity."[2]

Alexander Parker, in *Literature and the Delinquent*, likewise comments on the moral shift in the *pícaro*, stating that "roguery exists not in him but in the world around him."[3] This new *pícaro*, "invigorated by Hobbesian optimism and belief in the possibility of salvation for all, [. . .] finds opportunities to show virtue even in the hard-knock realities of the world."[4] There is a noticeable if gradual development in the character of the rake, the archetypal picaresque protagonist. And *pace* Watt, that gradual change does not necessarily point toward "proto-realism." Rather, it points toward the values of a nascent bourgeoisie and how to deal with middle-class comforts, with retail affluence. Both the novel and the picaresque reflected the growing importance of a literature-consuming bourgeoisie.

This newly gentrified eighteenth-century *pícaro* is more morally straightforward than the hungry, cunning, inexperienced (and morally ambiguous) whipping boy of the original picaresque. This new character may be dumb, but he is essentially good. And his mediation with the world provides a different sort of insight into society—a different *tour d'horizon*—than did the story of Lazarillo. Rather than being a tale of a marginal character's stark efforts to survive, this is the story of an optimistic young innocent's collisions with an unforgiving world. In Europe, young protagonists who manage to stay admirably alive despite countless misadventures are featured in Grimmelhausen's *Simplicius Simplicissimus* (1668), Le Sage's *L'Histoire de Gil Blas de Santillane* (1715–1735), Voltaire's *Candide* (1759), Johnson's *Rasselas* (1759), Fielding's *Tom Jones* (1749), and later works such as Kipling's *Kim* (1900). Across the ocean such characters are found in José Joaquín Fernández de Lizardi's *Periquillo Sarniento* (1816–1831) and Mark Twain's *Huckleberry Finn* (1884). The respective attitudes in these works are different from those of the cynical *pícaros* who preceded them. These are fresh young men to whom the world "happens" in spite of themselves, but who nonetheless maintain a certain optimism.

A partial explanation for this development is the influence of what can (and has been) read as yet another offshoot of the picaresque, the second part of *Don Quixote,* published in 1615.[5] Gone is the gratuitous misfortune of the *Lazarillo de Tormes* and its attendant dark and cruel humor, now replaced with clueless optimism. (Other formal similarities to the *Quixote* distinguish the eighteenth-century picaresque from its sources in the *Lazarillo*. The new *pícaro* doesn't travel alone between episodes but tends to travel with a Sancho-like interlocutor—a servant or a sidekick, or sometimes a "wise" teacher.)

Most importantly, there is a turn toward a new, quite lighthearted cosmic joke taken directly from Cervantes: like the Don, the main character simply *doesn't get it*. He certainly "gets" what the world has to offer, because he receives some painful and comical hard knocks to confirm this. But he doesn't *understand* the harshness of that world in a deep epistemological sense. He never truly sees the reasons or meaning behind those knocks. Yet he keeps on going, almost inexplicably, with an almost stupid optimism and resilience, in a way that seems to leave few psychic consequences.

Since he is unaware of the significance of his own story or the impact of his journey, the new *pícaro* is a kind of blind witness. There is a counterintuitive, almost unexplainable sense of unearned value to his view of the world.

It is from this ethos of cluelessness and hollow worth that Carpentier draws to build his protagonists and their journey in *Concierto barroco*. Following the pattern of other bourgeois eighteenth-century *pícaros*, the main character is not a low-life member of the *bajo mundo* or underworld. Instead he is a wealthy Mexican criollo or Mexican of Spanish descent identified only as the "Master," who ventures out with his Indian manservant as his squire.

IN TRANSIT

The novel opens with a scene of preparations for the pair's upcoming, damn-the-expenses trip to Europe. It is an epic device, the Iliadic catalogue, an inventory that here lists, instead of ships, all the luxury items necessary for the pair's invasion of Europe:

> Of silver the slender knives, the delicate forks; of silver the salvers with silver trees chased in the silver of the hollows for collecting the gravy of roasts; of silver the triple-tiered fruit trays of three round dishes crowned by silver pomegranates; of silver the wine flagons hammered by craftsmen in silver; of silver the fish platters, a porgy of silver.[6]

This flashy deployment of "silver" as a modifier, compounded by a fancy use of asyndeton, recalls the baroque language of works such as Luis de Góngora's *Soledades* (1613). Both share a visual ostentation and an obsession with heavily symbolic and overwrought precious metals. More specifically, this is baroque obsession with the *display* of such metals.

Yet in both cases the showy display is so overdone that it is somewhat suspect. Despite the dazzling insistence, there is a kind of obsessive monochromatism that belies a kind of shortage—a silver- and gold-leafed shortage. Spanish writer Dámaso Alonso, in a slightly mischievous essay ("Claridad y belleza de las *Soledades*"), argues that Góngora's palette is actually quite limited, even poor, and full of *metáforas triviales, constantemente repetidas, llegan a construir una manera*—repeated trivial metaphors, a stylized veracity.[7] The sensorial overload ultimately fails to deliver the promised object of grandeur and novelty— *carecen casi siempre de novedad*.[8] Baroque excess can become so stylized and so insistent, declaring its own richness so much, that on some fundamental level it will always be spread thin, superficial. This is a theatrical exuberance that is only gilt-deep. Underneath the gold leaf is, not much.

The story of these *pícaros*, the Mexican Master and his sidekick-servant Filomeno, is an inverse of the European Grand Tour. This was a ritual that served as the capstone of a wealthy young man's education, typically undertaken to admire, and perhaps collect, some of the cultural capital of Europe. Instead, the Master brings his American capital with him and spreads it around, teaching a lesson to the cultured men he encounters. Not only is he traveling with plenty of gold and silver, but he brings with him an American story—the story of Cortés—that he will bestow upon none other than composer Antonio Vivaldi.

The novel's climax on a Carnival night in Venice is at the very center of empire. It echoes an episode of Voltaire's *Candide,* also set in a Venice, when the picaresque travelers discover that their fellow guests at the inn are a collection of deposed monarchs. The Mexican traveler and his sidekick hook up with musical royalty, in this case Vivaldi, George Friedrich Handel, and Domenico Scarlatti. This group sets out into a Joycean night jaunt. They stop at the *Ospedale della Pietà*, an orphanage where girls are trained as musicians, and there Vivaldi leads a baroque/jazz "jam session" (*una mermelada*). During the drunken proceedings, Vivaldi (the "priest") talks to the Mexican about his outlandish costume, a baroque version of Moctezuma's attire:

> "Inca?" he then asks, fingering the Aztec emperor's glass beads. "Mexican," replied the master, launching into a lengthy tale which the priest, already deep in his cups, took to be about a king of giant beetles—the narrator's glossy, green, squamous breastplate did, in fact, resemble a beetle's—who had lived not so long ago, when one considered it, among temples, lakes, and *teocallis*, the ruler of an empire that was wrested from him by a handful of bold Spaniards with the help of an Indian woman who was in love with the chief of the invaders.
>
> "Good story. Good theme for an opera. . ." said the priest, thinking, all at once, of ingenious stage settings, trapdoors, levitations, and *machine* with which

effects of smoking mountains, apparitions of monsters, and earthquakes with collapsing buildings could be most effectively created, since there were master stage technicians so skillful they could reproduce any prodigy of nature and even make a live elephant fly through the air.[9]

Vivaldi becomes quite engrossed by the account and begins to create the concerto of the novel's title, which he completes by the end of the night.

The party then becomes a wine-fueled conga line as Filomeno begins to dominate the music with his Afro-Cuban beat, and it all spills into the street. Baroque figures morph into jazz: "posters announced that Louis Armstrong's incomparable trumpet would be heard in a matter of moments."[10] The parallel between a baroque basso continuo and a jazz ensemble becomes a central motif. It is an astute parallel between two musical modes that improvise upon—"deform"—highly structured forms.

The novel's journey is itself an improvisation on a fixed and recognizable pattern: the Mexico-Cuba-Europe trip. Significant flows have gone back and forth along this axis with regularity for centuries. The first was that of Hernán Cortés, who began in Spain, went to Cuba, and in 1516 led a fleet to Mexico. Once in Aztec territory he went rogue, quickly going from emissary of the crown to outlaw—essentially becoming a picaresque adventurer. He recklessly kidnapped the Aztec emperor, loaded up with gold ransom, and then lost all of it and most of his men in a disastrous retreat.

Cortés's story is the same one underlying the story in *Concierto barroco*: the *concierto* of the title refers to the opera Vivaldi improvised that night, *Motezuma*, an actual work that was still lost at the time Carpentier wrote his novel.[11] His is a speculative novel, proposing that the seed for this work was planted in Vivaldi's imagination by a Mexican grandee traveler who has journeyed all the way to Venice to be at Carnival dressed up as the last Aztec emperor of his homeland. Vivaldi, upon hearing the story of the *conquista*, begins working out loud on the details of an opera based on the tales he hears from the traveler. Time collapses, and the opera is written, rehearsed, and performed that same night. Of course, the storyline of the conquest is drunkenly distorted into a fantastic fugue, prominently incorporating an invented love story between two fictitious characters—Cortés's "younger brother" Ramiro and an Aztec princess, "Teutile" (actually the name of a minor Aztec commander, a frivolity that enrages the Master). Improvisation seems to take over history.

AN EXCESS OF LACK, OR THE PRICE OF REVOLUTION

Additional Europe-Cuba-Mexico patterns of travel figure into the mélange. One is the direct aftereffect of Cortés's initial conquest, a flow that began with the conquest and headed in the other direction: the centuries-long stream of precious metals going from the New World to the Hapsburg Empire. During most of the seventeenth and eighteenth centuries, American silver sustained Spain's empire-building. It supported the wars of religion that were raging in northern Europe and the Mediterranean. American silver and gold also underwrote the aesthetic arm of the Spanish Counter-Reformation, the High Baroque. American wealth provided its gilt. And at the source of the treasure in the Americas, it created a few fabulously wealthy *criollos indianos* like the silver-merchant traveler, the "Master" of the novel.

A third flow along this geographic path also emerges, in subtle *bas relief*, from *Concierto barroco*. This is the story of a flotilla that left Mexico bound for Cuba. In 1956, a repurposed American pleasure yacht named *Granma* left Veracruz carrying eighty-two men, including Fidel Castro, Ernesto "Che" Guevara, and Camilo Cienfuegos. It landed in Oriente Province on December 2, 1956.

Thus began the Cuban Revolution (figure 6.1). This unlikely, poorly armed, ragtag group would ultimately succeed in its mission of ousting dictator Fulgencio Batista. Their journey would arguably conclude with another series of trips, when Ernesto "Che" Guevara, as head diplomat, embarked on a succession of visits to declare the Revolution's victory to the world. He traveled to New York in late 1964 to address the United Nations, then went on to Paris and Algiers to give landmark speeches denouncing both Western capitalism and Soviet autocracy.

Each of these four transoceanic voyages—Cortés's to the Aztec capital, the flow of precious metals in return, the Master's journey to Europe in *Concierto barroco*, and the Cuban Revolution's—is connected to the marshaling and

Figure 6.1 *Granma* landing in Oriente Province, December 2, 1956.

circulation of resources to create incredibly elaborate results—out of not very much. Each of these trips was connected to a display of enormous riches but the "value" of those riches was either a displacement, a repurposing, an ultimate loss, or a fantastic overstatement.

As mentioned previously, the prevailing view about the Spanish Empire is that it was funded by bottomless and ever-expanding New World silver mines, along these lines (see figure 6.2). But the steady increase in numbers did not translate into increased wealth. Despite the growing income, during this period the Spanish Empire was actually in marked economic deterioration, having bankrupted itself several times during the seventeenth century. As recent historians of this global silver trade explain:

> The value of silver began to decline and inflation set in, for as the metal became more abundant, its buying power diminished. This inflationary trend affected the value of all commodities; everything had been valued in silver and silver lost its value. Ramifications of this change touched the lives of almost everyone in the empire. [. . .] As silver lost value, more silver money was required to purchase items that had maintained their value. Price inflation is defined as the surrender of more pieces of money for a given set of items, so

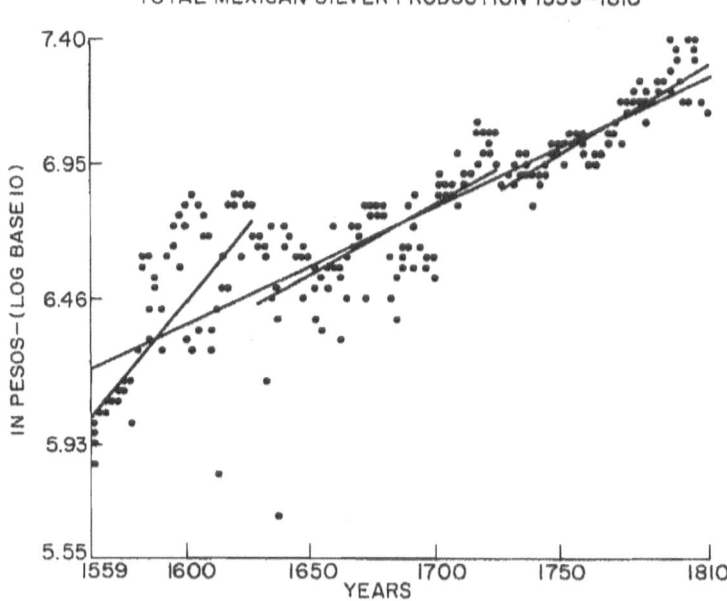

Figure 6.2 Total Mexican Silver Production, 1559–1810.

the descent of silver to its cost of production is what ultimately caused prices to inflate.[12]

There is a parallel dynamic at work in the Baroque. Mexican writer Carlos Fuentes once offered the following insight about the baroque aesthetic, which amounts to an artistic expression of this same economic phenomenon:

> It is the Baroque language of *our* great literary tradition [. . .] defeat, misery, insecurity and historical excess can only be recounted in a language that preserves immediate evidence, an instrument capable of including everything, because in a world where nothing is known for certain everything must be preserved. The Baroque, Alejo Carpentier once told me, is the language of peoples who, not knowing what is true, desperately seek it.[13]

Inventing a rich spectacle to counterpoint a reality of "defeat, misery, insecurity and historical excess" and "not knowing what is true"—both the economic and the literary histories of the seventeenth and eighteenth centuries featured increasingly elaborate displays of a diminishing, or absent, grandeur. The art stands in sharp contrast with the reality behind those rich displays of wealth. And recall that the astounding displays of wealth were underwritten by the sweat and blood of an enormous underclass of slaves, Indians, and mixed races. Extreme poverty and extreme wealth coexist in an open paradox within the dynamics of the Baroque.

The twentieth-century Neobaroque inherited that paradox. The figure and works of José Lezama Lima offer an interesting case in point. Lezama's version of the Neobaroque is known for its ostentation, omnivorous panopticism, and almost blinding artifice. In fact, Chapter 7 of his magnum opus *Paradiso* (1966) gives such an excessively ornate representation of an orgiastic, sumptuous meal that such a feast is now known as the *cena lezamiana*. Lezama's aesthetics are rich, cosmopolitan, constantly alluding to European art and to the material ostentation of a privileged class. But the actual means of production for this novel tell a different story. Lezama himself did not possess that kind of luxury, especially later in life. As biographers have long noted, he led a rather austere life. He did not travel much (except for one short trip to Mexico, which left him deeply impressed with the baroque grandeur he saw). His house, which can still be visited, is a fairly humble affair in a middle-class neighborhood. The opulence in his work is all Neobaroque fantasy: all gold leaf, all imagination, all memory, and all somewhere else.

Alejo Carpentier's choice of the picaresque for *Concierto barroco* figures into this blend of lack and opulence. And by inviting into the Baroque the picaresque—traditionally associated with abject penury—he turns the latter genre on its head with new clothes. This *pícaro* appears as a fabulously wealthy *indiano* who travels in style to the Old World. All of this speaks to a stylized, highly imaginative gold that melts into the air and light of the Neobaroque.

To expand upon this point, it bears looking at the key ideological paradox at the source of the historical Baroque. The Protestant reformation arose in the sixteenth century because of popular disillusion with the exhausted rituals and demands of an out-of-touch and corrupt church. During the first century after Martin Luther, the mission of Protestantism was to simplify spiritual life: by knocking down monasteries, emptying cathedral niches of their distracting saints and virgins, and removing the entitlements of corrupt churchmen. The Bible was translated into vernacular languages to make it accessible to everyone. Protestantism's purpose was to let the faithful speak directly to God, as one does to a neighbor—without mediation, without ornament.

When the Catholic Counter-Reformation vigorously fought back, it did so with a religious revolution of its own. It reinvested in mediation. There was oppression and violence, but there was also sublime art. In the Catholic Mediterranean, Low Germany, Spain, and its Spanish American colonies, the disillusionment and hunger for spiritual connection that had led to Protestantism and simplicity was addressed in a completely opposite way: the startling baroque aesthetic, full of gold leaf and artifice, angels and monsters, fantasy. The hunger was fed through imagination, self-conscious form, and the possibility of opulence. And all this theatricality was paid for with real American gold and silver (and with real blood).

This brings us to a complicated question that arises when considering the relationship between the historical "first" Baroque—that of the Counter-Reformation—and the Neobaroque. How does one reconcile the politics of one with those of the other? The answer comes in true baroque fashion with a sharp juxtaposition of opposites, a chiaroscuro. Remember that the historical Baroque was the aesthetic front of the reactionary Counter-Reformation. It stood for monarchical absolutism and was a tool of cultural and religious oppression. Given its staunch solidity in these matters, it is not surprising that one of its key conceits was *coincidentia oppositorum*, a dynamic way of countering its opposition through incorporation, via destabilizing, inclusionary aesthetics.[14]

Some interpreters of the historical Baroque worked hard to mitigate the pall of absolutism hanging over it by explaining the Baroque as a kind of forward-looking and enlightened despotism—what Spanish historian José Antonio Maravall called "monarchical absolutism," in sharp distinction to "absolute monarchy."[15] According to Maravall, the Hapsburg monarchy, rather than being repressive, offered imagination and whimsy as an emancipatory alternative to the starkness of Protestantism. It would re-energize peoples' faith in the earthly institutions through astonishment, *vislumbre*. This way of addressing spiritual hunger amounts to a prescient egalitarianism, an unprecedented proto-iconoclasm perhaps not seen again until modernism's shock of the new.

Likewise, the Neobaroque thinkers and aesthetic practitioners who were mostly on the political left reinvested the Baroque with their own twentieth-century context to counter the political charge of the original. Like Maravall, they invented an exculpatory parallel: when they saw baroque *trompe l'oeil*, they saw a phenomenon as destabilizing as revolution. While not entirely disregarding the fact that the historical Baroque was fundamentally counter-revolutionary, their discourses either downplay the importance of the absolutist institutions behind it—focusing on the counter-hegemonic presence of the subaltern voices (Lezama Lima's *contraconquista*[16])—or they go even further and try to establish the Baroque as somehow—paradoxically—analogous to the anti-establishment humanists more associated with Protestantism. The Cuban writer Severo Sarduy invokes Copernicus questioning that the earth is the center of the universe, and by extension he questions the centrality of the earthbound church. He connects Copernicus's heretical act of defiance to the Baroque's hallmark: destabilizing, de- and re-centering symmetrical composition. He likens all of this to the epistemological revolutions of the twentieth century, like the "Big Bang" theory for the birth of the universe.[17] This reading attempts to cast the Baroque as transcending its conservative, anti-Reformation shape, moving it into anti-anti-revolution—which more or less amounts to claiming it *as* "revolution."

Much of this argument stems from considering the expression of the Baroque that occurred in the Americas. The *Barroco de Indias* blended indigenous and African elements and was, as Lezama argued, a seamless extension of the baroque aesthetic: the explosions of light, gold and outlandishness, and exoticizing inclusivity were the perfect setting in which the subaltern could really speak. As Lois Parkinson Zamora puts it:

> The Baroque is subversive. Historically, the European Baroque denied the frontal vision of the Renaissance perspective. [. . .] So we arrive at one of the few satisfying ironies of the Spanish colonization of Latin America: the form most associated with the cultural repression of the monological Spanish Counter-Reformation in Latin America—the Baroque—provides the very structure with which to subvert that repression.[18]

The indigenous and African voices, forms, and labor found in the *Barroco de Indias* was further proof of the "subversive"—revolutionary—soul deep within the Baroque. The presence of Black and Indian counter-voices counterpointed and re-energized a tired absolutism at the source of the historical Baroque, if not quite absolving it.

This takes us back to Carpentier's novel: the Master and his musical Black manservant in *Concierto barroco* inject their respective American realities back into the European source, and show them how it's done. As the jam session spills out into the street, Filomeno infects Vivaldi, who is leading his baroque *basso continuo*, with Afro-Caribbean syncopation. "'Black devil!' exclaimed the Neapolitan. 'When I want to carry a certain rhythm, he forces me to follow him. I'll wind up playing cannibal music!'"[19]

Still, despite the best intentions behind this wish for inclusionary, political reimagination, the reality of the seventeenth and eighteenth centuries still grates against the reality of the mid-twentieth century. Any way one looks at it, it is not easy to reconcile the fact that the historical Baroque—the spiritual and ethical source of the Neobaroque—was fundamentally reactionary, counterrevolutionary, repressive, and absolutist. The Baroque has and always will be a tool of an empire looking for a way to revalidate itself and consolidate its hold. And the revolutionary kinship perceived by the modern articulators of the Neobaroque is inescapably a product of their own twentieth-century desires.

The main figures of the twentieth-century Neobaroque were associated with real aesthetic revolution, true iconoclasm—High Modernism, Negritude, *Indigenismo*. They were also tied to actual historical revolution: the Cuban Revolution. So it made sense to find kindred revolution at the source. Neobaroque writers stand fast with the paradox: they keep their contemporary concept of revolution but also their attachment to the historical Baroque by recasting the latter as an unsettling force akin to their own present. This is a wistful and elaborate artifice—gloriously false gilt.

In this way, the paradox also returns us to the picaresque trip along the Mexico-Cuba-Europe axis. In Cuba, Sarduy had been an early and enthusiastic supporter of the revolution, and paroxysmal change became a signature element in his version of the discourse. But Sarduy gradually grew away from the actual revolution. After he left for Europe in 1960, his position evolved little by little the longer he stayed away from Cuba, developing into an internationalist view more in tune with the anti-establishment aesthetic and youth movements of the period. As was the case with his contemporary Reynaldo Arenas, Sarduy's political alignments and awareness—initially hatched in conversation with the intellectuals of the prerevolutionary Cuban bourgeois left such as Lezama Lima and Cintio Vitier—had easily synchronized with the anti-Batista revolution. He joined the charismatic and idealistic *barbudos* who had disembarked from the *Granma* in 1956 and ultimately brought down the dictatorship, and he cut his teeth at the Marxist publications *Diario libre* and *Lunes de revolución*.

But comrade Sarduy necessarily moved on from this early education when he traveled to Europe: he jumped at a chance to study art in Paris.

Subsequently his version of revolution took a different journey. Still left-leaning, he found a new set of resonances in that turbulent decade with the international, pop-inflected culture that soon took to street battles, the May Spring, and free love. Doubtless Sarduy's aesthetics and ideology would have been very different had he not traveled away from Cuba. In Paris, where the style and ethos were driven by winds pungent of tear gas and ironic protest shouts of "underneath the paving stones, the beach," things were in sharp contrast with the way they were developing back in Cuba. Sarduy became more *Tel-Quel* and less *brigadas macheteras* heading into the fields to harvest the sugarcane to the rhythm of work songs laboring to build the socialist future of Cuba.[20]

Finally, via *Concierto barroco*, this returns us to Alejo Carpentier's own journey. Steve Wakefield, in Carpentier's *Baroque Fiction,* presents a compelling interpretation of the difference between Carpentier's earlier, strongly "marvelous real" works and his final novels such as *Concierto barroco* and *El arpa y la sombra* (1978). He sees two elements at work in these later novels. First is the sense that the techniques and aims of magical realism had become exhausted, with "all the appearances of having fossilized into a number of set formulae, that are trotted out from time to time in expectation of the success that accompanied their debut in earlier works."[21] Second was a recommitment to the aims of the Cuban Revolution, although Wakefield characterizes this as "a weakness"—a "Marxist gloss" that Carpentier tried to justify in arguments that edged closer to dogma and ignored the increasingly complex politics of the left in the 1960s, with its youth culture and Western Marxism's turn away from Communist absolutism.[22] Specifically in Cuba, Carpentier failed to take a strong stance on the prosecution of writer Heberto Padilla for criticizing the Revolutionary government, and whose case would create insurmountable rifts in the "Boom" generation of writers.[23] Wakefield suggests something very important at the core of the Neobaroque, an inherent disjunctive always-already within it: the mix of *actual* worth versus the *representation* of worth. Wakefield claims that Carpentier attempted "to keep the spirit of the marvelous real alive by using it in humorous new situations," leavening this short novel through its dip into the picaresque and its anachronistic musical fantasy.[24]

At the conclusion of *Concierto barroco*, the *criollo* Master, upon watching the production of the fanciful opera that deformed history, heatedly argues with Vivaldi about the liberties the musician has taken with the facts:

> "What happened to doña Marina in this whole charade." [asks the Master.]
> "That Malinche was a traitorous bitch, and the public doesn't like traitors. No singer of ours would have accepted such a part." [. . .]
> "Your Mitrena, however, recognizes the superiority of the conquistadors."

"But at the end she's the one who calls for desperate resistance. Such characters are always popular."

The *criollo*, although taken down a peg, continues to insist. "History tells us . . . ."

"Stop giving me that history crap. Poetic illusion is what counts in the theater."[25]

"Poetic illusion," Baroque fantasy, and falsification: the general outlines of the flow are kept, but the content—the actual value of what travels within that flow—is immaterial. The real value is the effect, the poetic illusion itself. False gilt, because of its theatrical excess and astonishing nature, is its own inherent worth.

NOTES

1. It must be noted what Watt meant by "modern" and "novel" was essentially tied to nineteenth-century realism. Interestingly, Gyorgy Lukacz made a parallel claim, if in a vastly different political register. Both Watt's and Lukacz's radings bear connections to empire, optimistically in Watt's unabashedly Anglocentric case, pessimistically in Lukacz's Western Marxist perspective. In *Theory of the Novel*, Lukacz's claim is ultimately agonistic: he argues that the modern novel and the nineteenth-century realism that so impressed Watt amounted to the decay of the Epic, a spiral that had begun with the greatness of Homer and had gone south ever since then.

2. Blackburn, *The Myth of the Pícaro*, 116.

3. Parker, *Literature and the Delinquent*, 121.

4. Blackburn, 116.

5. In comic "rogue's tales" during this period there is a marked conflation between the "true" picaresque featuring the single rake on an existential quest who speaks in first person, and the quixotic traveling pair featuring a master/squire, narrated in third person (see Ochoa, *Fellow Travelers*).

6. Carpentier, *Baroque Concerto*, 23.

7. Alonso, "Claridad, Belleza De Las Soledades," 300.

8. Ibid., 300.

9. *Baroque Concerto*, 60.

10. Ibid., 116.

11. This whimsical libretto (RV 723) existed and was known to Carpentier, but the music was thought to have been lost. The score reappeared in 2002 in the archives of the Sing-Akademie zu Berlin and the opera has since been staged.

12. Flynn and Giráldez, "Born with a 'Silver Spoon,'" 203.

13. Fuentes, "The Novel as Tragedy," 533.

14. As Monika Kaup succinctly explains the internal disjunctive via French philosopher Gilles Deleuze's reading of the Baroque, "Facing the impossibility of settling for one single and universal truth (be it God or Reason), the Baroque solves

the conflict by sorting the inconsistencies into parallel worlds. The Baroque thereby offers an ontological solution to an epistemological impasse. The epistemological questions, 'What is there to be known? How it is known, and with what certainty?' having been exhausted, the Baroque responds ontologically, with the creation of new worlds for each of the conflicting possibilities" (135).

15. Maravall, *La cultura del barroco*, 71.

16. "El 'arte de la Contrarreforma' [. . .] pasó a ser 'arte de la Contraconquista'" ("The 'art of the counter-reformation' [. . .] became the 'art of the counter-conquest.'") ("Curiosidad barroca," 88). Bolívar Echevarría nicely sums up this strong reading of the New World Baroque as a survival strategy of Indians: "In the 17th century, American Indians who had been integrated into the urban life of their Iberian victors and conquerors undertook the task of re-constructing European civilization in practice—a spontaneous, informal endeavor in which they engaged American-born Spaniards. However, already in the 16th century, they had begun to use baroque ethos to restructure roles and functions within what was European: they reinvented Catholic Christianity by translating it into a performance or 'absolute staging'" (42).

17. Sarduy, *Ensayos generales sobre el barroco*, 75.

18. Zamora, *The Inordinate Eye*, 80–81.

19. *Baroque Concerto*, 74.

20. In addition, the open persecution of homosexuals by the Revolution would certainly have affected him. Likewise, the Cuban government eventually imprisoned the openly gay poet Reinaldo Arenas, after which he went into a very difficult period of exile in the United States, where he condemned the Castro regime, contracted AIDS, and ultimately committed suicide.

21. Wakefield, *Carpentier's Baroque Fiction*, 35.

22. Ibid.

23. See Carpentier's late essays "Problemática de la actual novela latinoamericana" (*Ensayos*, 11–44) and "De lo real maravilloso americano" (*Ensayos*, 100–17).

24. Wakefield, 37.

25. *Baroque Concerto*, 103.

WORKS CITED

Alonso, Damaso. "Claridad, Belleza De Las Soledades." In *Estudios y ensayos gongorinos*, 3rd. ed., 316–17. Madrid: Gredos, 1982.

Anderson, Benedict. *Imagined Communities: Reflections on the Origin and Spread of Nationalism*. London: Verso, 1991.

Blackburn, Alexander. *The Myth of the Pícaro: Continuity and Transformation of the Picaresque Novel, 1554–1954*. Chapel Hill: University of North Carolina Press, 1979.

Carpentier, Alejo. *Baroque Concerto*. Translated by Asa Zatz. London: Andre Deutsch, 1991.

———. *Ensayos*. Vol. 13 of *Obras Completas de Alejo* Carpentier. Mexico City: Siglo Veintiuno Editores, 1990.

Echeverría, Bolívar. "Meditations on the Baroque." In *Neo-Baroques: From Latin America to the Hollywood Blockbuster*, edited by Walter Moser, Angela Ndalianis, and Peter Krieger, 30–47. Boston: Brill, 2016.
Flynn, Dennis O. and Arturo Giráldez. "Born with a 'Silver Spoon': The Origin of World Trade in 1571." *Journal of Word History* 6, no. 2 (1995): 201–221.
Fuentes, Carlos. "The Novel as Tragedy: William Faulkner." In Zamora and Kaup, *Baroque New Worlds*, 531–53, 1970.
Kaup, Monika. "Becoming-Baroque: Folding European Forms into the New World Baroque with Alejo Carpentier." *CR: The New Centennial Review* 5, no. 2 (2005): 107–149.
Lezama Lima, José. "La curiosidad barroca." 1957. Chap. 2 in *La expresión americana*, edited by Irlemar Chiampi, 79–106. Mexico: Fondo de Cultura Económica, 1993.
Lukács, Gyorgy. *The Theory of the Novel: A Historico-Philosophical Essay on the Forms of Great Epic Literature*. Cambridge, MA: MIT Press, 1971.
Maravall, José Antonio. *La cultura del barroco: Análisis de una estructura histórica*. Esplugues de Llobregat, Spain: Ariel, 1975.
Ochoa, John. *Fellow Travelers*. Charlottesville: University of Virginia Press, Forthcoming.
Parker, Alexander Augustine. *Literature and the Delinquent: The Picaresque Novel in Spain and Europe, 1599–1753*. Edinburgh: Edinburgh University Press, 1967.
Sarduy, Severo. *Ensayos generales sobre el barroco*. Colección Tierra Firme. Mexico: Fondo de Cultura Económica, 1987.
Vivaldi, Antonio. *Motezuma RV 723*, 1733. MS.
Wakefield, Steve. *Carpentier's Baroque Fiction: Returning Medusa's Gaze*. Woodbridge, UK: Tamesis, 2004.
Watt, Ian. *The Rise of the Novel; Studies in Defoe, Richardson, and Fielding*. Berkeley: University of California Press, 1957.
Zamora, Lois Parkinson. *The Inordinate Eye: New World Baroque and Latin American Fiction*. Chicago: The University of Chicago Press, 2006.
Zamora, Lois Parkinson, and Monika Kaup, eds. *Baroque New Worlds: Representation, Transculturation, Counterconquest*. Durham: Duke University Press, 2010.

Chapter 7

"Breaking the Circle of Perfection"

Baroque Form from Johannes Kepler to Isabelle Stengers

Monika Kaup

The problem of disorder and irregularity is at the heart of the debates on the Baroque. Ever since the neoclassical stigmatization of baroque form as "bizarre," the assumed imperfection of baroque forms has been the lightning rod of censure: the principle of order is stability and regularity. How can something that breaks with these principles be appreciated as beautiful? As is well-known, the debate over baroque form was connected to early modern scientific upheavals that shattered Ptolemaic cosmology, putting in its place the decentered modern universe stretching out to infinity. In effect, what was at stake was the very idea of order as such: a structure that was required to be harmonious, absolute, unchanging, predictable, and perfect. As has been pointed out, even more revolutionary than Copernican heliocentrism was the baroque-era discovery of infinity and of the decentered universe. In Marjorie Nicolson's succinct formulation: "The idea of infinity had demolished the circle of perfection."[1] This essay revisits the parallels between the Baroque and modern science in the reconceptualization of the dominant paradigm of order and structure. It focuses on cross-disciplinary affinities in formulating an alternative model of order that no longer conformed to traditional ideals of absolute stability and perfection. I argue that baroque art pioneered a model of disorderly order that corresponds to a revolutionary new paradigm in science, the systems view. Ultimately, this also involves a redefinition of the real. I propose that the baroque articulates a holistic, context-based, or ecological approach to the real that prioritizes relationships, interdependency, and organized processes and patterns over elemental parts and isolated objects.

In the seventeenth century, links between the Keplerian cosmology of elliptical orbits and the elliptical figures of baroque architecture, art, and literature are familiar and have been the subject of many studies. As Giancarlo Maiorino observes, "When measured against classical standards, infinity spawns excess."[2] The neobaroque, the twentieth- and twenty-first-century recovery of the historical Baroque in literature, art and architecture, and philosophy, investigates the parallels between seventeenth-century science and baroque art. A principal goal of neobaroque theories has been to rehabilitate baroque aesthetics and culture and liberate it from the stigma of the irrational and the retrograde. One way it has done so has been by prying baroque expression loose its historical instrumentalization as a tool of Absolutism and the Counter-Reformation. Cuban writer Severo Sarduy, for example, one of the principal theorists of the Baroque and the Neobaroque, explores Kepler's astronomy of ellipses as the master figure of what he calls the "A Baroque of the Revolution": because the Baroque destabilizes order, it is the "art of dethronement."[3]

Generally, neobaroque theories posit that while functioning as a technology of power in the State Baroque, the Baroque has also been an expression of social and intellectual rebellion and innovation. This is the case not just in the American Baroque most frequently associated with this claim, but also for general theories of the Baroque, the principal focus of this essay. As perhaps the principal spokesperson of the rebellious New World Baroque, Cuban writer José Lezama Lima asserts, in Latin America, the European colonial Baroque was transculturated: the American Baroque became the art of counterconquest. Lezama's claims have recently been historically substantiated by Latin American colonial historian Jorge Cañizares-Esguerra, who shows that Latin America saw developments toward "radical renewal" and "aggressive modernity" coming from *within* baroque epistemologies.[4] Dynamic, extravagant, and capricious, the Baroque is an aesthetics of excess and transgression that sets established forms into variation. As Lois Zamora puts it, baroque forms are "inordinate": "inordinate structures are not normative, not predictable, but eccentric, disparate, uneven" (xxii). Zamora's study *The Inordinate Eye: New World Baroque and Latin American Fiction* (2006) is a landmark of the revitalization of baroque scholarship that began in the early 1990s and that continues to gather steam in the twenty-first century. This new wave of baroque studies has fully developed a key characteristic of the Baroque that had previously been understated or imperfectly understood: thanks to her contribution, and in accordance with its rebellious anti-classical aesthetic, the Baroque is now recognized as an alternative expression of the modern that encompasses multiple nations, continents, and disciplines.[5]

In the seventeenth century, repercussions of Keplerian cosmology in eccentric baroque forms helped contemporaries understand the upheavals of their time. Sarduy's notion of "retombée" (or "epistemological solidarity") conceptualizes these analogies between natural science and baroque art. In the twentieth and twenty-first centuries, the parallels between the Baroque and science continue in surprising ways. As I aim to show, these developments extend significantly beyond what Sarduy envisioned. To this end, I will consider an essay entitled "Breaking the Circle of Sufficient Reason" by philosopher of science Isabelle Stengers, which stages a close encounter between the baroque figure of ellipsis and complexity theory—the "new" twentieth-century science of complexity that replaced classical Newtonian science. Elaborating correspondences between Keplerian cosmology and systems thinking, Stengers recovers the cosmology of Johannes Kepler as the point of departure in a revolutionary scientific paradigm shift from mechanism to systems thinking, thus linking the seventeenth and twentieth centuries. Coupling Kepler's laws of elliptical planetary orbits to Ilya Prigogine's theory of dissipative structures, Stengers contends:

> For me, Prigogine is . . . clearly a descendant of Kepler, who dared to break with the perfection of the circle and to wager on the *relevance* of mathematics to describe the world of phenomena, against the *power* of mathematics to judge this world in the name of a normative ideal.[6]

It is instructive to take a step back to zoom out to a historical overview before proceeding with Stengers's essay. Thinking in wholes and networks emerged during the romantic period and was further developed in the twentieth century as an alternative to the classical modern scientific-analytic method, when, as Fritjof Capra argues, "the holistic perspective became known as systemic."[7] During the first decades of the twentieth century, modern systems thinking was pioneered simultaneously in several disciplines: evolutionary biology, Gestalt psychology, the new science of ecology, and most dramatically, the new physics of quantum theory (ibid.). The basic tension is the relation between parts and wholes. Classical science arose with the analytic-reductive method developed by Descartes, which understands entities as wholes that can be broken down into their smallest parts. It proceeds by determining the properties of the parts and deducing from these the nature of the whole, defined as the sum of elemental parts. But, as Capra explains,

> the great shock of twentieth-century science has been that systems cannot be understood by analysis. The properties of the parts are not intrinsic properties, but can be understood only within the context of the larger whole. Thus, the relationship between the parts and the whole has been reversed. In the systems approach, the properties of the parts can be understood only from the organization of the whole. Accordingly, systems thinking does not concentrate on basic building blocks but rather on basic principles of organization. Systems thinking is "contextual," which is the opposite of analytical thinking. Analysis means

taking something apart in order to understand it; systems thinking means putting it into the context of a larger whole.[8]

This chapter argues that baroque forms are congruent with the contextual or ecological approach of modern systems thinking outlined by Capra. More specifically, I propose that baroque forms were rejected as bizarre and illogical because their characteristic pattern of organization conjoins principles that were thought to be separate and opposed—the idea of order and the principle of instability. From today's vantage point, however, we know that the Baroque came out as the winner in this battle between paradigms of order. The first claim can be illustrated by the conceptual approach taken by the pioneer of the twentieth-century rehabilitation of the Baroque, Swiss art historian Heinrich Wölfflin. The difference between the systems approach and the analytic view corresponds to the opposition between the Baroque and the classic according to Wölfflin. Each of Wölfflin's famous five paired categories opposes a characteristic of classicism to a feature of the Baroque: linear vs. painterly; plane vs. recession; closed vs. open form; multiplicity vs. unity; absolute vs. relative clarity. Underpinning the polarity between classic and Baroque is the antithesis between the systems outlook and the analytic approach: classical compositions prioritize isolated parts over wholes, because wholes can be dissected into parts, which are the primary entities. In contrast, baroque compositions prioritize organized wholes over parts. In the celebrated slogan of Gestalt psychology, "the whole is more than the sum of its parts." This point is most obvious in Wölfflin's fourth pair of antithetical categories, "multiplicity vs. unity." As Wölfflin explains:

> In the system of a classic composition, the single parts, however firmly they may be rooted in the whole, maintain a certain independence.... For the spectator, that presupposes an articulation, a progress from part to part, which is a very different operation from perception as a whole, such as the seventeenth century applies and demands.... [I]n the one case unity is achieved by a harmony of free parts, in the other, by a union of parts in a single theme, or by the subordination, to one unconditioned dominant, of all other elements.[9]

In the classic, the constituent objects are primary. In the Baroque, the system of their interrelationships is primary. The "baroque" effect thus stems from the Gestalt of an irreducible organized pattern.

Wölfflin's categories are commonly considered to be the first neutral and nonevaluative account that pictures the classic and the Baroque as two antithetical, but equally valuable aesthetics. According to Wölfflin, classicism is objective whereas the Baroque is subjective; classicism is rational while the Baroque is emotional. Classicism depicts essences: the world as a collection of solid objects. In contrast, the dynamic Baroque describes appearances and processes: the world as unfolding dynamical change. In Arnold Hauser's view, the "outlook of the Baroque is . . . 'cinematic.'"[10] Wölfflin's achievement required a paradigm shift in conceptual thinking. This new kind of thinking, I argue here, corresponds to the systems and process thinking that was developed concurrently across a variety of disciplines by Wölfflin's contemporaries. According to Capra and Luisi, systems thinking prioritizes "connectedness, relationships, and context" over discernable autonomous objects.[11] In short, Wölfflin is a systems theorist.

In the language of systems theory, baroque artworks are organized systems that take the shape of irreducible wholes. As such, baroque compositions are like ecosystems, collectives of different species that because of their internal interactions can only be understood as units. Like ecological thinking, understanding baroque art requires a figure/ground shift in perspective from seeing isolated objects to seeing patterns of relationships. For instance, in the baroque *Gesamtkunstwerk* such as Bernini's concept of the unification of sculpture, architecture, and painting in the *bel composto* ("beautiful composite"), the interaction between component parts creates a new higher-level unity—Bernini's beautiful composition.[12] Albeit unstable and decentered, this higher-level unity has what systems theory terms "emergent" properties, which do not exist at lower levels. Unlike intrinsic properties, emergent properties arise from the relationships of the parts in the organization of the whole. These properties are destroyed when the system is taken apart. To illustrate this point, one need only consider the interiors of baroque churches such as Bernini's. According to Gauvin Bailey, baroque church interiors

> demonstrate an essentially Baroque concept in which sculpture, painting, and architecture join forces in creating a unifying total effect. Unlike Renaissance churches, in which the different media are separated—sculptures kept within their niches, paintings within their frames and architectural units strictly reflecting their function—Baroque church interiors allow for overlap, so that sculptural stuccos climb up walls and spill into canvases, statues reach out from their frames and the whole interior is covered with similar patterns and motifs.[13]

In the language of systems thinking, the dramatic effect of the baroque ensemble—quintessentially baroque in seizing the spectator's attention and overwhelming her senses— is an emergent property.

These insights into analogies between baroque compositions and systems science allow us to return to Stengers. Stengers is a close collaborator of Nobel laureate and physicist Ilya Prigogine, one of the co-founders of complexity theory and the discoverer of the so-called "dissipative structures." Complexity theory describes self-organization in complex systems.

Prigogine's research showed that in "open" or "dissipative" structures operating far from equilibrium, at critical points of instability, organized structures may spontaneously arise, creating "order out of disorder."[14] Stengers coauthored with Prigogine the best-selling introduction to complexity, whose English translation is entitled *Order Out of Chaos: Man's New Dialogue with Nature* (1979; 1984). The study traces the "conceptual revolution" that replaced the classical paradigm of modern science.[15] The classical Newtonian science of mechanics pictures a world of unchanging mathematical and mechanical laws. Time and change, which govern the phenomenological world where organic and historical beings are born, live, and die, do not exist there. Classical physics denies time: the ideal pendulum without friction and the eternal movements of the planets exist in a universe of eternal beings, where all processes are reversible. Prigogine and Stengers's *Order Out of Chaos* describes the paradigm shift that eroded this view. It traces developments toward a new science that no longer denies change—the arrow of time—and that began in the nineteenth century, with thermodynamics and evolution. Both these new disciplines describe irreversible processes of change. Both the dissipation of heat and the evolution of living beings toward greater diversity are historical processes that required a new concept of science that recognizes time instead of denying it. In the twentieth century, these were joined by relativity theory, quantum mechanics, further advances in astronomy, and the discovery of complex dynamical systems. Writing at the end of the twentieth century, Stengers affirms: "We have now discovered the violence of the universe; we now know that stars explode and that galaxies are born and die."[16] As Prigogine and Stengers declare, "we are discovering the primacy of time and change, from the level of elementary particles to cosmological models."[17]

Obviously, there is a lot more to be said here, but I will focus on the baroque theme of disorderly structures. Prigogine's research on dissipative structures—stable states that arise and maintain themselves in unstable conditions (e.g., hurricanes)—proved that new higher-level order might emerge spontaneously out of lower-level disorder. In thermodynamics, dissipation is associated with waste—entropy. But unlike the closed structures of thermodynamics, dynamical systems are "open": they exchange heat and energy with the outside. Paradoxically, no longer associated with waste, dissipation "becomes a source of new order."[18] As Prigogine and Stengers point out, complexity theory, the new science of open, dynamical systems, advances a "new view of matter" that is "no longer the passive substance described in the mechanistic world view but . . . associated with spontaneous activity."[19] Ultimately, this speaks to the beginning of life by way of the spontaneous self-organization of nonorganic matter. In the field of science, complexity theory thus carries forward the baroque challenge of stable instability:

chaotic structures flaunt classical norms of timeless order. As Prigogine puts it, "order 'floats in disorder.'"[20] It is therefore not surprising that the authors of *Order Out of Chaos* invoke Kepler as their inspiration: they suggest that the so-called "Keplerian revolution" launches the ex-centric new science the authors champion.[21] Prigogine and Stengers's revisionary account elevates Kepler above Copernicus, the established founder of modern cosmology, as the emblematic founding father of the new science that *is rediscovering time*.[22] This is a pointed iconoclastic gesture: dethroning the Copernican Revolution, Prigogine and Stengers's Keplerian Revolution launches the ex-centric new science the authors champion.

Stengers elaborates the Keplerian analogy in her essay, "Breaking the Circle of Sufficient Reason." As she notes, the essay was written with "Kepler as its dominant theme because it was he who transformed the sense of mathematical astronomy by 'breaking' the circles in the name of which the phenomenological evidence of the celestial movements was judged."[23] While overthrowing Ptolemy's heliocentric cosmology for the modern geo-centric system, Copernicus continued to uphold the normative scientific ideal of mathematical perfection. Copernicus transformed the earth into a planet that rotates around the sun, the center of the cosmos. Nonetheless, the cosmos retained its quasi-divine form of a world "untouched by time."[24] Unlike Kepler, Copernican heliocentrism obeyed the classical figure of the circle; "the mathematical figure of perfection" continues to model the motion of the planets.[25] Conversely, by breaking the circle, Kepler's astronomy of elliptical planetary orbits launched the first breach of the timeless mathematical ideal in science. As is known, the hypothesis of elliptical orbits is only the first of Kepler's two laws or conjectures.[26]

An ellipse is best understood not as a finished form, but as a modification of another, the circle. Whereas a circle is produced by tracing a line around a single center at a constant distance, an ellipse is generated by splitting the center into two poles, attaching the ends of a string to both points, and drawing a line at the end of the loop thus formed. By virtue of geometric law, the ellipse is a deformed and decentered circle: the larger the distance between the two centers, the greater the dilation of the elliptical orbit. Kepler's proposition was that "Mars moves in an orbit of elliptical shape with the sun at one focus," while the other focus is invisible, occluded, a mere mathematical point.[27] Kepler's second law states that in his elliptical orbit, Mars "sweeps out equal areas in equal times," which is to say that the planet travels at different speeds in different areas of its course around the sun.[28] Just as Kepler's first conjecture destroyed the ideal of the perfect circle, the second destroyed the ideal of uniform speed, introducing the factor of time into cosmology.[29] Kepler arrived at these conjectures through a torturous path in his protracted "war with Mars." As his biographer Arthur Koestler notes, Kepler reached the crucial breakthrough when he gave up trying to fit cosmology into the norm of formal geometry, and accepted that the "universe was moved by real, physical forces" which would turn out to be gravity.[30] Elliptical orbits could not result from "a single force, as previously assumed," such as a Prime Mover, but could only be produced by "two antagonistic forces" at loggerheads with each other.[31] Like baroque art, Kepler's cosmos is a baroque composition. It stages—to cite Christopher Braider's succinct description of baroque form—a "theatre of ceaseless conflicts."[32] It depicts powerful forces in combat that subject the composition to contrary tensions, disrupting and deforming it.

Stengers extends these observations by contending that, in demolishing the circle of perfection, Kepler's astronomy of elliptical planetary orbits launched the first breach of the timeless mathematical ideal in science. The mathematical analogue to the circle of perfection is German philosopher Gottfried Wilhelm Leibniz's principle of sufficient reason. According to Stengers, what is distinctive about Leibniz's mathematics is the "equals" sign that makes causes and effects fully reversible, and therefore timeless like the pendulum without friction. For Stengers, Kepler is to Copernicus what Prigogine is to Leibniz. Thus, Prigogine completes the decentering of the cosmos begun by Kepler. "As with Freud," Stengers observes, "one could speak here of a wound imposed on human narcissism. Reason had to relinquish the power of judging a priori and submit to empirical observation."[33] For Stengers, the history of science from Newton to complexity theory marks the triumph of the "phenomenological evidence of the arrow of time" over the mathematical ideal of timeless perfection.[34]

What Stengers does not mention—and what this essay aims to recall—is that Kepler's elliptical cosmology is also one of the inaugural moments of the Baroque. As mentioned earlier, the geometry of ellipses links seventeenth-century astronomy with seventeenth-century baroque art and architecture. The substitution of the ellipse for the circle, the classical symbol of perfection exalted by the Renaissance, is a prominent feature in baroque art. This is the case in the European as well as in as the New World Baroque. Elliptical architectural structures appear in the Roman Baroque of Bernini and Borromini as they do in the Brazilian Baroque, from the eighteenth-century churches of New World Baroque artist Aleijadinho (Antônio Francisco Lisboa) to the neobaroque architecture of Brazilian modernist Oscar Niemeyer. The iconoclastic impact of Kepler's conjecture of elliptical planetary orbits on baroque art is elucidated by Severo Sarduy. Keplerian cosmology forms the centerpiece of Sarduy's study *Barroco* (1974), which compares developments in the history of science and baroque art. The chapter on "Baroque Cosmology: Kepler" in particular offers close readings of elliptical compositions in canonical works of European art and literature by Diego Velázquez, Caravaggio, Borromini, El Greco, Peter Paul Rubens, and Luis de Góngora.

He uses Keplerian cosmology as a model to explain parallel phenomena of decentering, dual centers, and anamorphoses of the circle in the visual and verbal arts. As Sarduy explains:

> Something is decentering itself, or rather, duplicating, dividing its center; now, the dominant figure is not the circle, with its single, radiating, luminous, paternal center, but the ellipse, which opposes this visible focal point with another, equally functional, equally real, albeit closed off, dead, nocturnal, the blind center, the other side of the Sun's germinative yang, that which is absent.[35]

Sarduy establishes the explosive political and theological resonances of Kepler's elliptical theory: the Baroque is an "art of dethronement"[36] because of the social connotations of the cosmological "single center" of the sun, symbol of God and King.

In the concluding section of *Barroco*, identical with the conclusion of Sarduy's earlier and influential essay, "The Baroque and the Neobaroque" (1972), Sarduy champions "a Baroque that rejects all instauration, that metaphorizes the disputed order, the judged god, the transgressed law. A Baroque of the Revolution."[37] Sarduy's revolutionary art of dethronement thus mirrors Stengers and Prigogine's Keplerian revolution that overthrows "the idea of an absolute point of view" in science.[38]

As those familiar with his work know, Sarduy also furnishes his own suggestion for a twentieth-century offspring of the Keplerian Revolution, which parallels Prigogine and Stenger's lineage leading from Kepler to the new science of complexity. The fourth chapter on twentieth-century cosmology ("La cosmología después del barroco"; "Cosmology after the Baroque") considers Einstein's special theory of relativity, pointing to its displacement of the idea of absolute space and time via the concept of a four-dimensional continuum of relative space-time ("el Espacio-Tiempo").[39] Sarduy adds that the general theory of relativity subsequently expands the special theory to include gravity. As Sarduy emphasizes, both relativity theories renounce the idea of an absolute point of view ("punta de vista de nadie").[40] Finally, "Big Bang" theory appears as a third descendant of Kepler's decentering cosmology because it posits an ever-expanding universe ("El universo está en expansión").[41] Without doubt, in its central claim to a transhistorical "retombée," that is to say, a correlation between science and art in the seventeenth and twentieth and twenty-first centuries, Sarduy's comments are newly confirmed by Prigogine and Stengers's historical accounts.

In this light, it is instructive to recall Sarduy's 1972 comments in "The Baroque and the Neobaroque." Sarduy characterizes the historical evolution from the seventeenth-century Baroque to the twentieth-century neobaroque as an intensification of decentering and destabilization. He observes that the European Baroque and the early Latin American colonial Baroque present themselves as images of a mobile but decentered but still harmonious universe. . . . On the contrary, the contemporary Baroque, the Neobaroque, reflects structurally the disharmony, the rupture of homogeneity, of the logos as an absolute, the lack that constitutes our epistemic foundation. Neobaroque of disequilibrium, structural reflection of a desire that cannot attain its object.[42]

There is no doubt that Prigogine and Stengers would share Sarduy's assessment. Consider their concluding comments in *Order Out of Chaos*, which also appear in their coauthored essay "The Reenchantment of the World" in a more eloquent version, which I quote here:

At both the macroscopic and the microscopic levels, the sciences of nature are thus liberated from a narrow conception of objective reality, which believes that it must in principle deny novelty and diversity in the name of an unchanging universal law. They are freed from a fascination that represented rationality as closed and knowledge as in the process of completion. They are from now on open to unpredictability, no longer viewed in terms of an imperfect knowledge, or of insufficient control. Thus, they are open to a dialogue with a nature that cannot be dominated by a theoretical gaze.[43]

In conclusion, this essay has illuminated the significant parallels between Sarduy's *Barroco* and Stengers's essay, which extends Prigogine and Stenger's collaborative work. As I have shown, writer and theorist Sarduy supplies the hidden baroque cultural context for Stenger's argument. Conversely, philosopher of science Stengers validates Sarduy's claims about interdisciplinary parallels between art and science.[44] Writing from opposite ends of the "two cultures," their studies form natural twin companion pieces. Developed independently of each other—indeed, unbeknownst to each other—yet profoundly aligned, Stengers's and Sarduy's writings participate in the same celebration of a Keplerian Revolution that unseats absolutes— the scientific "view from nowhere," with its early modern symbolic echoes between the absolute ruler on earth *and* in the heavens. Their agreement on Kepler's demolition of the self-contained "classical" composition bridges the chasm between the "two cultures" of the sciences and the humanities. In the most general terms, my discussion offers fresh insight into the much-discussed transgressiveness of baroque forms. As the example of Stengers's essay shows, the roots of the Baroque's stigmatization go much deeper than previously understood. By opening the door to an undiscovered wing in the baroque labyrinth where the trajectory of the Baroque converges with the history of science, Stengers affords a clearer view of the Baroque's deviance and its revolutionary potential: the Baroque anticipates an alternative paradigm of order that only becomes comprehensible in the twentieth century, as a result of the rise of systems thinking and complexity theory.

This becomes even clearer if we turn to Lezama Lima as an unexpected witness for Prigogine's and Stengers's affirmation of the "arrow of time" in the new science of complexity, which I propose to do in closing. When Lois Zamora and I were at work editing *Baroque New Worlds*, we spent some time puzzling over how to annotate Lezama's cryptic statements about "plutonism" as a unique trait that distinguishes the New World Baroque from the European Baroque. According to Lezama, in the American Baroque, "first, there is tension in the Baroque; second, there is plutonism, an originary fire that breaks the fragments and unifies them."[45] He further adds that "we find in the [American] Baroque a plutonism that burns the fragments, metamorphosing them and impelling them toward their end."[46] Lezama's classical reference to Pluto, god of the underworld, and subterranean fire identify the metamorphic process of rebellious re-creation that produces the American counterconquest Baroque. In light of Prigogine and Stengers's account, it becomes clear that Lezama's plutonist analogy alludes to the irreversible processes that first came to light in the history of science through thermodynamics, the science of heat. As Stengers and Prigogine write, if "fire transforms matter," this transformation is nonreversible.[47] In contrast to mechanical processes, heat "implies material changes of state" that are irreversible.[48] Lezama's Plutonism thus newly appears as yet another distant offspring of Kepler's inaugural deformation of the circle that gave rise to the Baroque. In this respect, it is telling that instead of Kepler's elliptical planetary mechanics, which still adheres to the mechanistic paradigm even if it decenters the classical image of timeless order, Lezama draws on the modern nineteenth-century science of chemistry to characterize the American Baroque. In light of the foregoing discussion, Lezama's deeper meaning becomes clear: the new baroque structures spontaneously emerging in the cultural processes of de-colonizing transformation in the New World are fundamentally irreversible, like matter transformed by fire.

NOTES

1. Nicolson, 165.
2. Maiorino, 184–85.
3. Sarduy, "Baroque and Neobaroque," 290.
4. Cañizares-Esguerra, 320.
5. In addition to Zamora's *The Inordinate Eye*, the extensive research literature on the alternative modernity includes (in alphabetical order): Chiampi, *Barroco y modernidad*; Deleuze, *The Fold*; Echeverría, *La modernidad de lo barroco* and "Meditations on the Baroque"; Egginton, *The Theater of Truth*; González Echevarría, *Celestina's*

Brood: Continuities of the Baroque in Spanish and Latin American Literature; Jay, "Scopic Regimes of Modernity"; Kaup, *Neobaroque in the Americas: Alternative Modernities in Literature, Visual Art, and Film*; Lambert, *On the (New) Baroque*; Ndalianis, *Neobaroque Aesthetics and Contemporary Entertainment*; Young, "How the Baroque Learned to Speak Spanish"; Zamora and Kaup (eds.), *Baroque New Worlds: Representation, Transculturation, Counterconquest* (a list that is necessarily selective).

6. Stengers, "Breaking the Circle," 23–24.
7. Capra and Luisi, 63.
8. Ibid., 66.
9. Wölfflin, 15.
10. Hauser, 176.
11. Capra and Luisi, 79.
12. Bernini's revolutionary concept of the unification of the arts in the *bel composto* is highlighted in Panofsky, "What is Baroque?."
13. Bailey, 275.
14. Capra and Luisi, 160.
15. Prigogine and Stengers, xxviii.
16. Stengers, "Breaking the Circle," 35.
17. Prigogine and Stengers, 306.
18. Capra and Luisi, 159.
19. Prigogine and Stengers, 9.
20. Prigogine qtd. in Capra and Luisi, 160.
21. Prigogine and Stengers, 306.
22. Ibid., xxviii.
23. Stengers, "Breaking the Circle," 28.
24. Stengers (with Prigogine), "Reenchantment," 33.
25. Stengers, "Breaking the Circle," 20.
26. Crowe, 153.
27. Ibid.
28. Ibid., 154.
29. See Kearney, 137.
30. Koestler, 135.
31. Ibid., 151.
32. Braider, 8.
33. Stengers, "Breaking the Circle," 20.
34. Ibid., 23.
35. Sarduy, "Baroque Cosmology: Kepler," 292.
36. Sarduy, "Baroque and Neobaroque," 290.
37. Ibid.
38. Stengers (with Prigogine), "Reenchantment," 39.
39. Sarduy, *Barroco*, 85.
40. Ibid., 90.
41. Ibid., 91.
42. Sarduy, "Baroque and Neobaroque," 289.

43. Stengers (with Prigogine), "Reenchantment of the World," 39.

44. As director of the Hispanic Baroque Research project at the University of Western Ontario, Juán Luis Suárez headed a multiyear investigation entitled "The Hispanic Baroque: Complexity in the First Atlantic Culture." As Suárez explains in "Hispanic Baroque" and as stated in the research plan on the project website, the project utilizes "selected ideas from complexity theory ('emergence,' 'dynamic stability,' or 'efficiency') to analyze three spheres of baroque culture: the baroque constitution; its religious expressions; and its urban aspects." See http://web.archive.org/web/201 31015012111/http://www.hispanicbaroque.ca/

Thus, this essay joins ongoing efforts to explore links between the science of complexity and the baroque, which also includes Kwa (2002).

45. Lezama Lima, "Baroque Curiosity," 213.
46. Ibid., 215.
47. Prigogine and Stengers, 103.
48. Ibid., 106.

WORKS CITED

Bailey, Gauvin Alexander. *Art of Colonial Latin America*. London: Phaidon, 2005.

Braider, Christopher. *Baroque Self-Invention and Historical Truth: Hercules at the Crossroads*. Aldershot, UK: Ashgate: 2004.

Cañizares-Esguerra, Jorge. *How to Write the History of the New World: Histories, Epistemologies, and Identities in the Eighteenth-Century Atlantic World*. Stanford, CA: Stanford UP, 2001.

Capra, Fritjof and Pier Luigi Luisi. *The Systems View of Life: A Unifying Vision*. Cambridge UP, 2014.

Chiampi, Irlemar. *Barroco y modernidad*. Mexico City: Fondo de Cultural Economica, 2000.

Crowe, Michael J. *Theories of the World: From Antiquity to the Copernican Revolution*. 2nd ed. Mineola, NY: Dover, 2001.

Deleuze, Gilles. *The Fold: Leibniz and the Baroque*. 1988. Translated by Tom Conley. Minneapolis: University of Minnesota P, 1993.

Echeverría, Bolívar. "Meditations on the Baroque." In *Neo-Baroques: From Latin America to the Hollywood Blockbuster*, edited by Walter Moser, Angela Ndalianis, and Peter Krieger, 30–47. Leiden and Boston: Brill/Rodopi, 2016.

———. *La modernidad de lo barroco*. Mexico City: Ediciones Era, 1998.

Egginton, William. *The Theater of Truth: The Ideology of (Neo)baroque Aesthetics*. Stanford: Stanford UP, 2010.

González Echevarría, Roberto. *Celestina's Brood: Continuities of the Baroque in Spanish and Latin American Literature*. Durham: Duke UP, 1993.

Hauser, Arnold. *The Social History of Art*. Vol. 2, *Renaissance, Mannerism, Baroque*. New York: Vintage, 1985.

Jay, Martin. "Scopic Regimes of Modernity." In *Modernity and Identity*, edited by Scott Lash and Jonathan Friedman, 178–95. Oxford: Blackwell, 1992.

Kaup, Monika. *Neobaroque in the Americas: Alternative Modernities in Literature, Visual Art, and Film.* Charlottesville: U of Virginia P, 2012.

Kearney, Hugh. *Science and Change, 1500–1700.* New York: McGraw-Hill, 1971.

Koestler, Arthur. *The Watershed: A Biography of Johannes Kepler.* Garden City, NY: Anchor Bks., 1960.

Kwa, Chunglin. "Romantic and Baroque Conceptions of Complex Wholes in the Sciences." In *Complexities: Social Studies of Knowledge Practices*, edited by John Law and Annemarie Mol, 23–52. Durham: Duke UP, 2002.

Lambert, Gregg. *On the (New) Baroque.* Aurora, CO: The Davies Group, 2008.

Lezama Lima, José. "Baroque Curiosity." In Zamora and Kaup, *Baroque New Worlds*, 212–40.

Maiorino, Giancarlo. "The Breaking of the Circle: Giordano Bruno and the Poetics of Immeasurable Abundance." Chap. 2 in *The Cornucopian Mind and the Baroque Unity of the Arts*, 13–46. University Park, PA: Pennsylvania State UP, 1990.

Ndalianis, Angela. *Neobaroque Aesthetics and Contemporary Entertainment.* Cambridge: MIT P, 2004.

Nicolson, Marjorie Hope. *The Breaking of the Circle: Studies in the Effect of the "New Science" upon Seventeenth Century Poetry.* New York: Columbia University Press, 1960.

Panofsky, Erwin. "What Is Baroque?" 1934. In *Three Essays on the Baroque*, edited by Irving Lavin, 19–88. Cambridge: MIT P, 1995.

Prigogine, Ilya and Isabelle Stengers. *Order Out of Chaos: Man's New Dialogue with Nature.* New York: Bantam, 1984.

Sarduy, Severo. "Baroque Cosmology: Kepler." 1974. In Zamora and Kaup, *Baroque New Worlds*, 292–315.

———. *Barroco.* Buenos Aires: Sudamerica, 1974.

———. "The Baroque and the Neobaroque." 1972. In Zamora and Kaup, *Baroque New Worlds*, 270–91.

Stengers, Isabelle (with Ilya Prigogine). "The Reenchantment of the World." Chap. 3 in *Power and Invention: Situating Science*, translated by Paul Bains, 32–58. Minneapolis: U of Minnesota P, 1997.

Stengers, Isabelle. "Breaking the Circle of Sufficient Reason." Chap. 2 in *Power and Invention: Situating Science*, 20–29. Translated by Paul Bains. Minneapolis: U of Minnesota P, 1997.

Suárez, Juan Luis. "Hispanic Baroque: A Model for the Study of Cultural Complexity in the Atlantic World." *South Atlantic Review* 72, no. 1 (2007): 31–47.

Wölfflin, Heinrich. *Principles of Art History: The Problem of the Development of Style in Later Art.* Translated by M.D. Hottinger. New York: Dover, 1950.

Young, Allen. "How the Baroque Learned to Speak Spanish." *Revista Canadiense de Estudios Hispánicos* 38, no. 2 (2014): 351–77.

Zamora, Lois Parkinson and Monika Kaup, eds. *Baroque New Worlds: Representation, Transculturation, Counterconquest.* Durham: Duke UP, 2010.

Zamora, Lois Parkinson. *The Inordinate Eye: New World Baroque and Latin American Fiction.* Chicago: U of Chicago P, 2006.

Part III

LATIN AMERICA IN THE WORLD

Chapter 8

Magical Realism's Synecdoche

Stephen M. Hart

More than fifty years have elapsed since Gabriel García Márquez published *Cien años de soledad* (1967) and launched the new literary genre of magical realism. It may come as a surprise to some that while he is generally acknowledged as the initiator of the genre, García Márquez is not nowadays seen as its most significant writer. The blurb of Maggie Ann Bowers's book, *Magic(al) Realism* (2004) places the Colombian writer in fourth place of significance: "Maggie Ann Bowers [. . .] illustrates her study with fresh readings of the work of eminent writers such as Salman Rushdie, Toni Morrison, Isabel Allende, Gabriel García Márquez and Angela Carter."[1] In this essay I wish to re-evaluate magical realism, starting with the ingredients as they came together in *One Hundred Years of Solitude* in 1967, and conclude with a brief discussion of the magical-realist formula as it has been exported to the rest of the world in the fifty-year period since that date. I will be building on some of the ideas sketched in an essay I wrote in 2010 on García Márquez's short fiction where I proposed that, while he was busy writing his short stories throughout the 1950s, the great Colombian novelist was actually experimenting with and, in effect, polishing the five literary techniques that—once they were gathered together—would be the ingredients of the new style of magical realism that would make him the most famous Latin American writer in the world.[2] In this essay I also want to focus on five literary techniques—which I will be calling "essences" in this essay—and particularly on the fifth, which I suggest was the quintessence exported to the rest of the world. The five essences are: (i) old wives' tales, (ii) popular Catholicism, (iii) phenomenological morphing after Kafka, (iv) irony, and (v) the political allegorization of the divide between the West and the non-West.

I. OLD WIVES' TALES

It is García Márquez himself who points the way to the first characterization of the essence of magical realism in terms of the old wives' tale. I should add that the individual playing the role of the "old wife" in this drama is none other than García Márquez's grandmother, Tranquilina Iguarán Cotes. Here's how the Colombian writer told the story. On July 9, 1965, he decided to take his family to Acapulco on vacation and, while driving away from Mexico City, suddenly the novel on which he had been working for years was "solved": "One day, as Mercedes and I were driving to Acapulco with the children, it came to me in a flash. I had to tell the story the way my grandmother used to tell me hers."[3] The first sentence of the novel came into his head: "Muchos años después, frente al pelotón de fusilamiento, el coronel Aureliano Buendía había de recordar aquella tarde remota en que su padre lo llevó a conocer el hielo."[4] García Márquez's description of the experience of how the novel came to mind is similar to Muhammad's account of the birth of the Qu'ran—it is as if he were simply the scribe of a story already written. It's a great story, and Apuleyo Mendoza, who was interviewing García Márquez at the time, needed to get all the details:

> *Q. Is it true that you turned the car around on the motorway and started writing it?*
> *A. It's true, I never got to Acapulco.*[5]

García Márquez turned around the car, headed back to Mexico City and began to write the novel that would change his life.

But a question inevitably asserts itself: What was it about the way that Tranquilina used to tell her stories that García Márquez was referring to? We need to go no further than the excellent work of García Márquez' official biographer, Gerald Martin, who offers a vivid picture of Tranquilina Iguarán Cotes:

> Dressed always in mourning or semi-mourning, and always on the verge of hysteria, Tranquilina floated through the house from dawn to dusk, singing, always trying to exude a calm and unflustered air, yet always mindful of the need to protect her charges from the ever-present dangers: souls in torment ("hurry, put the children to bed!"), black butterflies ("hide the children, someone is going to die"), funerals ("get the children up, or they'll die too").[6]

When I visited García Márquez' house in Aracataca on February 26, 2009, Rubiela Reyes—who gave me an excellent tour of the house—gave a slightly different version of what butterflies meant for Tranquilina; if a butterfly came in through the window, Tranquilina would say "Someone is going to arrive."[7] And, indeed, there is an excellent example of the use of Tranquilina's omen-laden oral style of speech in the third chapter of *Cien años de soledad*:

> Y mientras [Úrsula] se lamentaba de su mala suerte, convencida de que las extravagancias de sus hijos eran algo tan espantoso como una cola de cerdo, Aureliano fijó en ella una mirada que la envolvió en un ámbito de incertidumbre.
> —Alguien va a venir—le dijo.[8]

Aureliano, following in the footsteps of Gabo's grandmother, uses his sixth sense to "perceive" the future—he therefore "knows" that someone is going to come into the house. Aureliano has no need to explain his truth; like Tranquilina, he simply knows it, and says what he "feels" will happen. I will return to this episode later on in this essay, but for the time being let us note that García Márquez—perhaps a bit like the Spanish poet, Federico García Lorca—used the poetry of everyman, the old wives' tales and the superstitions, in order to stitch together his vision of the world. I say "stitch" deliberately because, as we shall see, the Colombian writer combined the discursivity of the old wives' tale with four other techniques.

II: POPULAR CATHOLICISM

Given García Márquez's interest in popular culture—including the stories that he used to hear told by everyday people when he went to carnivals—it is perhaps not surprising that he should have taken an interest in popular Catholicism.[9] Catholicism is a vein that runs through the Colombian's work—one of the most illustrative examples is *Del amor y otros demonios* (2004) though, even here, the canonic theme of exorcism is mediated by a backdrop pulsating with *santería*—and perhaps the most Catholic text García Márquez wrote was the short story "La Santa," the second of the stories collected in *Doce cuentos peregrinos* (1992). It is a rather curious story about the attempts made by an individual called Margarito Duarte to have his daughter, who died of fever at the age of seven, canonized as a result of the discovery, when her body was exhumed, that it was incorruptible:

> Como todos los habitantes de la región, Margarito desenterró los huesos de sus muertos para llevarlos al cementerio nuevo. La esposa era polvo. En la tumba contigua, por el contrario, la niña seguía intacta después de ocho años. Tanto, que cuando destaparon la caja se sintió el vaho de las rosas frescas con que la habían enterrado. Lo más asombroso, sin embargo, era que el cuerpo carecía de peso.[10]

This short story was clearly inspired by Gabo's experience of studying in Rome during the 1950s at the Centro Sperimentale di Cinematografia—Cesare Zavattini even makes a cameo entrance in the story—but what is also clear from the above quote is that the depiction of the saint in the story is based on the recorded life of the Peruvian saint, Santa Rosa de Lima (1586–1617). When the body of the saint in "La santa" was exhumed, like Santa Rosa, it smelled of roses;[11] and a number of the miracles attributed to Rosa revolved around weight and, particularly, weightlessness,[12] and weightlessness is precisely the quality that Margarito Duarte is using in order to prove his daughter's sanctity. An interest in Santa Rosa may have been inspired by the fact that Gabo and Mercedes's first son, Rodrigo, was born on August 24,[13] that is, the date on which, in 1617, Santa Rosa died.[14]

Santa Rosa's "ghost," as it were, also hovers behind some of the scenes depicting Catholic culture in *Cien años de soledad*. In the novel's fifth chapter, for example, Father Nicanor Reyna arrives in Macondo in order to officiate in Aureliano Buendía's marriage and, after Mass, he takes it upon himself to prove that God really does exist to the inhabitants of Macondo:

> Al final, cuando los asistentes empezaron a desbandarse, levantó los brazos en señal de atención.
> —Un momento—dijo. Ahora vamos a presenciar una prueba irrefutable del infinito poder de Dios.
> El muchacho que había ayudado a misa le llevó una tasa de chocolate espeso y humeante que él tomó sin respirar. Luego se limpió los labios con un pañuelo que sacó de la manga, extendió los brazos y cerró los ojos. Entonces el padre Nicanor se elevó doce centímetros sobre el nivel del suelo. Fue un recurso convincente. Anduvo varios días por entre las casas, repitiendo la prueba de la levitación mediante el estímulo del chocolate, mientras el monaguillo recogía tanto dinero en un talgo, que en menos de un mes emprendió la construcción del templo.[15]

The portrayal of Nicanor Reyna's levitation as well as the apparently insignificant detail of the cup of chocolate that is intimately associated with that miracle can both be traced back to Santa Rosa de Lima: Santa Rosa is famous for her ability to remain awake all night, hanging by her hair from a nail drilled into the wall of her bedroom, and she is also famous for her love of drinking chocolate, which she associated with Christ.[16] The parishioners accept and are impressed by Father Reyna's "Catholic" miracle, dig into their pockets and help fund the building of the first church in Macondo. I should add that I am not suggesting that the positive presentation of Father Reyna's miracle means that *Cien años de soledad* is a Catholic novel. It clearly is not, and this is evident if we compare the reaction on the part of the inhabitants of Macondo to Father Reyna's miracle with their reaction to Melquíades's magic and circus tricks described in the first chapter of the novel. In fact the reaction of the "pueblo" is similar in each case—one of awe when confronted with an uncanny or supernatural event. In each case García Márquez has wrapped the event in a sheen of empirical details—for example, as part of the detailed description of Father Reyna's actions prior to levitation the text provides a precise figure for the distance between Father Reyna's feet and the ground (12 centimeters). One last point: it is important to underline that the logic operating within this scene (namely, Father Reyna's levitation) derives not from theological dogma but from popular Catholicism. (It is, after all, unlikely that the objective description of an event of this kind would be accepted by the Holy See as evidence of a miracle.)[17] Although García Márquez was once called the "Third Pope" by Fidel Castro,[18] his interest was not in matters of canonization; rather he saw the texts of popular Catholicism, like the narratives embedded within old wives' tales and superstition, as a fertile soil which he would plunder—mercilessly—in order to create his own finely nuanced magical-real narratives.

III: PHENOMENOLOGICAL MORPHING AFTER KAFKA

García Márquez referred several times to the importance of the work of the great Czech writer, Franz Kafka, for the elaboration of his literary style. As he once stated in an interview:

> ya cuando entré a la facultad de derecho, en Bogotá, una noche entré a la casa, al cuarto de la pensión de estudiantes donde vivía . . . tenía un amigo que leía mucho y me pasó un librito amarillo y me dijo: "léete eso," como era el único que le quedaba disponible en ese momento, entonces yo me acosté. Leía mucho, leía todo lo que me caía en las manos y abrí esto y decía: "una mañana Gregor Samsa se encontró convertido en un gigantesco insecto." Yo tengo . . . lo recuerdo como si me hubiera caído de la cama en ese momento y fue una revelación, es decir, si esto se puede hacer, esto sí me interesa.[19]

The first sentence of *The Metamorphosis*, Kafka's master novel, is, indeed, justly famous: "When Gregor Samsa awoke one morning out of restless dreams, he found himself in his bed transformed into a monstrous bug." As Roy Pascal suggests: "From this moment the narrator identifies himself almost completely with Gregor, sees and hears through his eyes and ears, and accepts the truth of his metamorphosis as the victim himself must."[20] The opening sentence of Kafka's novel no doubt inspired the Colombian writer to hone his own skills at writing the killer opening sentence in a novel. (The first sentence of *Crónica de una muerte anunciada* is, after all, at least as good if not better than the first sentence of *Cien años de soledad*.)[21] The narrator's eyes in *The Metamorphosis* then alight on Gregor's legs: "His many—in relationship to his pitifully thin bulk—legs waved helplessly before his eyes. 'What has happened to me?' he thought. It was no dream." He has become an "Ungeziefer," a disgusting creature, an "uncreature" as Martin Greenberg suggests.[22] But there is one other feature of Kafka's novel that needs to be drawn out for it was destined to become an even more important tool in García Márquez' garden shed.[23] Thus far—that is, in the opening paragraphs of *The Metamorphosis*—the text is not that different from any number of nineteenth-century Gothic texts in which the monstrous within the human mind emerges to devastating effect. What is different about Kafka's novel is what happens next. Amazingly, rather than screaming out that he is now a monster, or going mad, or something of the kind, Gregor simply observes that he has not yet packed his briefcase, and he starts thinking about various ways in which he can catch the 7:00 a.m. train so he can get to work early enough to avoid a telling-off from his boss. He even tries to change the tone of his voice when he speaks to his mother—who is outside his bedroom door, worried about the fact that her son is late for work—so that she will not realize that he has changed into an insect! Gregor in effect is trying to rationalize his transformation into a "monstrous insect" and accepts that transformation as if it were something normal. And Kafka's novel is a tour de force in its creation of a completely absurd situation that the protagonist, at every turn, attempts to rationalize.

In fact, there are a good number of examples of the use of this technique in García Márquez's work. When José Arcadio Buendía, for example, in the first chapter of the novel, is looking for Melquíades, and finds some gypsies, the following magical event occurs:

> Por último llegó hasta el lugar donde Melquíades solía plantar su tienda, y encontró a un armenio taciturno que anunciaba en castellano un jarabe para hacerse invisible. Se había tomado de un golpe una copa de la sustancia ambarina, cuando José Arcadio Buendía se abrió paso a empujones por entre el grupo absorto que presenciaba el espectáculo, y alcanzó a hacer la pregunta. El gitano lo envolvió en el clima atónito de su mirada, antes de convertirse en un charco de alquitrán pestilente y humeante sobre el cual quedó flotando la resonancia de su respuesta: "Melquíades murió." Aturdido por la noticia, José Arcadio Buendía permaneció inmóvil, tratando de sobreponerse a la aflicción, hasta que el grupo se dispersó reclamado por otros artificios y el charco del armenio taciturno se evaporó por completo.[24]

Here we have an example of a phenomenological and visible transformation of one substance into another. In this case it is a gypsy, a taciturn Armenian, who is transformed with the help of some syrup first into a puddle and then into thin air (when he disappears completely). The puddle is the intermediate substance between the taciturn Armenian's body and nothingness, and their interrelationship allows it to be both a puddle and a (speaking) man. Thus the answer that the man/puddle provides, revealing that Melquíades has died, "floated" for a while on the puddle ("quedó flotando"). This sequence of actions and description of a magical action is presented as if it were plausible and real, and its "objective" existence is ratified, as it were, by the public's reaction. The most important spectator of all, however, is José Arcadio Buendía who "remained motionless," and his reaction is not typical for someone who has just seen something as incredible as a man who has turned before his very eyes into a pool of tar. Instead José Arcadio is overwhelmed by the sad news that Melquíades has died. The event is made even more plausible by the blasé reaction of the spectators who soon disperse once the gypsy has disappeared, and go off in search of other more interesting things to spectate. This episode in Gabo's fiction shares the phenomenological morphing technique we saw in Kafka's *Metamorphosis*. In both cases, whether a man turns into an insect or into a puddle of tar, the same reaction is elicited—acceptance of an absurd event followed by an attempt to rationalize the event. García Márquez was clearly inspired by Kafka's technique—as he was happy to acknowledge in the interview quoted above—and he used it to excellent effect in his own fiction, using it as a palimpsest to underpin the oral speech patterns of Tranquilina Iguarán.

IV: IRONY

Irony appears in *Cien años de soledad* in many different forms, but the common denominator is the contrast that is articulated in a phrase or an event that means the opposite of what was originally expected. A good example is the reaction of José Arcadio Buendía's son when he is presented by his father with the discovery of the philosopher's stone:

> De tanto mostrarlo, terminó frente a su hijo mayor, que en los últimos tiempos apenas se asomaba por el laboratorio. Puso frente a sus ojos el mazacote seco y amarillento, y le preguntó: ¿Qué te parece?
> José Arcadio, sinceramente, contestó:
> —Mierda de perro.[25]

With these ironic three words the entire and life-absorbing quest for alchemy is thrown into disarray, and the shock to José Arcadio Buendía's system is devastating. Another good example of irony occurs when the Corregidor, Don Apolinar Moscote, arrives in Macondo; he rents a room in the center of town, and orders all the houses to be painted blue in order to celebrate the anniversary of national independence, only to find that José Arcadio Buendía rejects his authority: "En este pueblo no mandamos con papeles—dijo sin perder la calma —. Y para que lo sepa de una vez, no necesitamos ningún Corregidor porque aquí no hay nada que corregir."[26] José Arcadio's comment is witty as well as ironic and draws its force from its skilled play on the root meaning of "Corregidor," which derives from the verb "corregir" (to correct). Gabo's irony is, indeed, rarely unaccompanied by humor. As we read in chapter 6:

> [A José Arcadio Buendía] lo fatigó tanto la fiebre del insomnio, que una madrugada no pudo reconocer al anciano de cabeza blanca y ademanes inciertos que entró en su dormitorio. Era Prudencio Aguilar. Cuando por fin lo identificó, asombrado de que también envejecieran los muertos, José Arcadio Buendía se sintió sacudido por la nostalgia. "Prudencio—exclamó—. ¡cómo has venido a parar tan lejos!"[27]

José Arcadio's comment is supremely ironic, for how can the dead get old? All of these uses of verbal irony in *Cien años de soledad* are based on a subversion of the reader's expectation, and are in each case examples of dialogue based on witty one-liners, a technique that García Márquez perfected while writing his short stories in the 1950s.[28]

V: THE POLITICAL ALLEGORIZATION OF THE DIVIDE BETWEEN THE WEST AND THE NON-WEST

This fifth essence, which is most common in the first chapter of *Cien años de soledad* —the political allegorization of the divide between the West and the non-West—resembles some degree to Kafka's phenomenological morphing technique, but with the crucial difference that the fifth component uses the technique of transforming reality to underline the difference between understanding reality in the First World compared with in the Third World. The inhabitants of Macondo, for example, do not understand how magnets work and accept Melquíades's explanation at face value that they have spirits ("todo es cuestión de despertarles el ánima," as he tells them).[29] Nor do they understand that ice is frozen water produced by a refrigerator, preferring instead to see it as "el diamante más grande del mundo."[30] The inhabitants of Macondo also "discover" that the earth is "redonda como una naranja" (José Arcadio Buendía is the voice of Macondo, in this sense).[31] The parallelism is worked out consistently in García Márquez's novel in that the technological inventions of the First World, such as dentures, the telegraph, and the cinema, are presented as if they were magical things in Macondo (the Third World). Rather than being a phenomenological transformation like the taciturn Armenian who becomes a puddle of tar, the conversion is something that takes place in the mind of the perceiver (the ice "becomes" a diamond). This transformation—or, rather, misprision—has, of course, a political dimension. According to José Arcadio: "En el mundo están ocurriendo cosas increíbles—le decía a Úrsula —. Ahí mismo, al otro lado del río, hay toda clase de aparatos mágicos, mientras nosotros seguimos viviendo como los burros."[32] The gap between the two interpretations of the same object—is it ice or is it a diamond—produces a space where the allegory of the struggle between the First World and the Third World is born.

VI: THE FIVE ESSENCES OF MAGICAL REALISM

Having extracted what I have referred to as the five essences of García Márquez's magic-realist universe—(i) the old wives' tale, (ii) popular Catholicism, (iii) phenomenological morphing after Kafka, (iv) irony, and (v) the political allegorization of the divide between the West and the non-West—I want to turn to the way in which these components are blended together in some passages drawn from *Cien años de soledad*. The first example draws on four of these ingredients and the second uses the five essences.

Let's begin with the famous episode in the second chapter of the novel in which Prudencio Aguilar insults José Arcadio Buendía for his lack of virility ("A ver si por fin ese gallo le hace el favor a tu mujer"),[33] at which point José Arcadio Buendía spears him to death:

> Prudencio Aguilar lo esperaba. No tuvo tiempo de defenderse. La lanza de José Arcadio Buendía, arrojada con la fuerza de un toro y con la misma dirección certera con que el primer Aureliano Buendía exterminó a los tigres de la región, le atravesó la garganta. [. . .] El asunto fue clasificado como un duelo de honor pero a ambos les quedó un malestar en la conciencia. Una noche en que no podía dormir, Úrsula salió a tomar agua en el patio y vio a Prudencio Aguilar junto a la tinaja. Estaba lívido, con una expresión muy triste, tratando de cegar con un tapón de esparto el hueco de su garganta. No le produjo miedo, sino lástima. Volvió al cuarto a contarle a su esposo lo que había visto pero él no le hizo caso. "Los muertos no salen—dijo—. Lo que pasa es que no podemos con el peso de la conciencia." Dos noches después, Úrsula volvió a ver a Prudencio Aguilar en el baño, lavándose con el tapón de esparto la sangre cristalizada del cuelo. Otra noche lo vio paseándose bajo la lluvia.[34]

The episode is based on a story that told Gabo in his grandparents' house—how his grandfather killed Medardo Pacheco Romero in 1908—and which Gabo found very moving.[35] It also expresses—in the description of the ghost of Prudencio Aguilar who enters the courtyard and then comes directly into the Buendía house and there tries to staunch the flow of the blood that comes from his wound in his neck caused by José Arcadio—a leitmotif derived from popular Catholicism, that is to say, the soul in purgatory forever doomed to walk on earth for all eternity. It is interesting to note how the Colombian novelist gradually builds up a picture of Prudencio's ghost—Prudencio Aguilar is first of all seen in the courtyard, then in the bathroom in the Buendía household, and then walking in the rain—which pulls the wool over the reader's eyes, making him feel gradually more accustomed to the supernatural life of a dead man. And then García Márquez gives the final twist to the technique of rationalization of absurdity that we saw in Kafka's work:

> José Arcadio Buendía, fastidiado por las alucinaciones de su mujer, salió al patio armado con la lanza. Allí estaba el muerto con su expresión triste.
> —Vete al carajo—le gritó José Arcadio Buendía—Cuantas veces regreses volveré a matarte.[36]

Arcadio Buendía's assertion is, of course, supremely ironic for how can one kill a man who is already dead? It is also a case of the rationalization of the absurd explored in *The Metamorphosis*. This episode, as we see, manages to combine various essences of magic realism, such as the old wives' tale (although in this case it might be called an old granddads' tale), popular Catholicism, the technique of rationalization of the absurd derived from Kafka, and the exploitation of irony.

Our second example is the episode that begins with Aureliano's premonition—which I have already quoted above—that someone (unknown) is about to arrive. As we have already noted the scene is drawn specifically from Tranquilina's omen-laden speech, and particularly her "ability" to predict the future based on seemingly fortuitous events. In order to see how this episode draws on a number of levels, we need to place the original quote in a broader context:

> Y mientras [Úrsula] se lamentaba de su mala suerte, convencida de que las extravagancias de sus hijos eran algo tan espantoso como una cola de cerdo, Aureliano fijó en ella una mirada que la envolvió en un ámbito de incertidumbre.
> —Alguien va a venir—le dijo.
> Úrsula, como siempre que él expresaba un pronóstico, trató de desalentarlo con su lógica casera. Era normal que alguien llegara. Decenas de forasteros pasaban

a diario por Macondo sin suscitar inquietudes ni anticipar anuncios secretos. Sin embargo, por encima de toda lógica, Aureliano estaba seguro de su presagio.
—No sé quién será—insistió—pero el que sea ya viene en camino.

El domingo, en efecto, llegó Rebeca. No tenía más de once años. Había hecho el penoso viaje desde Manaure con unos traficantes de pieles que recibieron el encargo de entregarla junto con una carta en la casa de José Arcadio Buendía, pero que no pudieron explicar con precisión quién era la persona que les había pedido el favor. Todo su equipaje estaba compuesto por el baulito de la ropa, un pequeño mecedor de madera con florecitas de colores pintadas a mano y un talego de lona que hacía un permanente ruido de cloc cloc cloc, donde llevaba los huesos de sus padres. La carta dirigida a José Arcadio Buendía estaba escrita en términos muy cariñosos por alguien que lo seguía queriendo mucho a pesar del tiempo y la distancia y que se sentía obligado por un elemental sentido humanitario a hacer la caridad de mandarle esa pobre huerfanita desamparada, que era prima de Ursula en segundo grado y por consiguiente pariente también de José Arcadio Buendía, aunque en grado más lejano, porque era hija de ese inolvidable amigo que fue Nicanor Ulloa y su muy digna esposa Rebeca Montiel, a quienes Dios tuviera en su santo reino, cuyos restos adjuntaba la presente para que les dieran cristiana sepultura. Tanto los nombres mencionados como la firma de la carta eran perfectamente legibles, pero ni José Arcadio Buendía ni Úrsula recordaban haber tenido parientes con esos nombres ni conocían a nadie que se llamara como el remitente y mucho menos en la remota población de Manaure.[37]

As we can see, both of Aureliano's predictions turn out to be true—the first that someone would arrive and the second that the person involved is already on their way to the Buendía house, since she arrives within a few days of Aureliano's prediction—and so, at first glance, this would seem to indicate the beginning of an episode based on one of Tranquilina's old wives' tales. But then the narrative changes tack and, at first, appears to be leading us into a mysterious dead end—although the letter says that Rebecca, the young girl who has just arrived, is a relative of theirs, neither Ursula nor José Arcadio has any recollection of her. Even more unsettling, the orphan has arrived with a canvas sack containing her parents' bones, and not only that, the bones are heard making "a permanent cloc cloc cloc sound." As the text clarifies, the souls of Rebecca's parents will never find peace until they receive a "Christian burial," and thus García Márquez's text is alluding to the notion of the soul wandering in purgatory, a stock notion of popular Catholicism. What is interesting about this portrayal of the supernatural—encapsulated by the clicking, living bones—is that García Márquez uses a technique that has clear similarities with Gregorius Samsa's modus operandi when he discovered that he had turned into a "monstrous bug"—namely, the rationalization of the absurd: "Since there was no cemetery in Macondo at that time, for no one had died up till then, they kept the bag of bones to wait for a worthy place of burial, and for a long time it got in the way everywhere and would be found where least expected, always with the clucking of a broody hen."[38] And the bones even turn later on in the novel when Ursula decides to build an extension on the house, and the workmen were "exasperados por el talego de huesos humanos que los perseguía por todas partes con su sordo cascabeleo."[39]

The scourge of oblivion that the town experiences soon after Rebecca's arrival also has to do with the fifth ingredient of magic realism in the sense that it expresses the allegorization of the divide between the West and the non-West. When Rebecca arrives she is described as only able to understand an indigenous language ("los indios le preguntaron en su lengua si quería un poco de agua y ella movió los ojos como si los hubiera reconocido y dijo que sí con la cabeza").[40] The arrival of Rebecca is thus to be understood as an allegory of the destruction of the Indies and the Americas carried out by the Spanish conquistadors—the conquest in effect resulted in virtually total amnesia of indigenous culture in the New World, both its language and its culture. That is why Rebecca's arrival operates in an allegorical way in the text, and coincides with the scourge of oblivion:

> el alba del lunes sorprendió despierto a todo el pueblo. Al principio nadie se alarmó. Al contrario, se alegraron de no dormir, porque entonces había tanto que hacer en Macondo que el tiempo apenas alcanzaba. Trabajaron tanto, que pronto no tuvieron nada más que hacer, y se encontraron a las tres de la madrugada con los brazos cruzados, contando el número de notas que tenía el valse de los relojes.[41]

The antics that Arcadio Buendía subsequently gets up to in order to try to deal with the absurdity of the new situation also brings to mind Gregor Samsa's strategies in *The Metamorphosis*:

> El letrero que [José Arcadio Buendía] colgó en la cerviz de la vaca era una muestra ejemplar de la forma en que los habitantes de Macondo estaban dispuestos a luchar contra el olvido: *Esta es la vaca, hay que ordeñarla todas las mañanas para que produzca leche y a la leche hay que hervirla para mezclarla con el café y hacer café con leche.* Así continuaron viviendo en una realidad escurridiza, momentáneamente capturada por las palabras, pero que había que fugarse sin remedio cuando olvidaran los valores de la letra escrita.[42]

As we see, the episode of Rebecca's arrival in the Buendía household begins like one of Tranquilina's old wives' tales, then becomes a discourse inspired by popular Catholicism (namely, the clicking bones of purgatory), before being transformed into an ironic allegory of the struggle between the West and indigenous culture, and ends up resorting to the Kafkaesque technique of rationalization of the absurd (the villagers hang a sign around the cow's neck to help them remember that she must be milked each day to produce a substance they can put in their coffee to make it more tasty). In this episode the various essences of magical realism merge into one another to such an extent that it is difficult to discern where one ends and the other begins.

By merging old wives' tales, popular Catholicism, phenomenological morphing, irony, and the allegorization of the divide between the West and the non-West, García Márquez had in effect created a new self-coherent formula with which to portray Latin American culture. As touched on in the following section, this formula—especially its quintessence—attracted the attention of many novelists around the world, and inspired them to use this recipe to describe the cultural complexities they found in their own countries.

VII: EXPORTING MAGICAL REALISM TO THE REST OF THE WORLD

Fifty years after the publication of *Cien años de soledad*, the world has changed so much that it is almost unrecognizable. The paradigms that sustained that universe—including the notions of the First, Second, and Third Worlds—no longer exist. Today books tout magical realism as a highly successful modern literary genre—there are, for example, European, African, American, Asian, Middle Eastern, and Antipodean writers who have employed the formula of magical realism to express their respective visions of the world in which they live.[43] The migration of magical realism from Colombia to other countries led, of course, to its globalization, but it also had the unexpected result of obscuring its originary roots, as noted above.

One of the reasons magical realism seems to have attracted the attention of a wide range of writers was its force as a "decolonizing agent" able to express what Naipaul has called "half-made societies" in which "the impossibly old struggles against the appallingly new."[44] As Jean-Pierre Durix has pointed out in a memorable way, the "imperialist powers deprived colonized people not only of their territories and wealth, but also of their imagination,"[45] and, indeed, a novel like Salman Rushdie's *Midnight's Children*, was an example, of the non-West using García Márquez's formula to wrest power back from the West. Especially for the writers of countries that had recently escaped the tentacles of colonialism, magical realism appeared to become, in Homi

Bhabha's much-quoted words, "the literary language of an emerging postcolonial world."

To conclude: it is worth asking if magical realism has the same valency in the work of, for example, Salman Rushdie and Ben Okri as in García Márquez's work. In spite of some superficial resemblances, I do not think so. With hindsight it is now clear that the magical realism exported to the rest of the world was the quintessence of magical realism with its vision of the divide, articulated ironically, between the West and its non-West, and it was a version from which the old wives' tales, the popular Catholicism, and the phenomenological morphing *à la Kafka* had been alchemically drained out. Magical realism's articulation of the struggle between two worldviews—the magical vision of the diamond compared to the empirical and scientific perspective ("it is ice")—was a formula that captured the imagination of many writers across the world who wanted to express the cracked, distorted, and "incredible" world they lived in. It was, in effect, a synecdoche of the magical-realist brand—namely, the first chapter of *Cien años de soledad*— which was exported from Colombia and re-purposed by writers across the whole world. At least, though, they had the good sense to keep the irony.

NOTES

1. Blurb on back cover: *Magic(al) Realism* (London: Routledge, 2004).
2. The five features were (i) the deadpan description of uncanny events; (ii) the portrayal of time as a dislocated reality; (iii) punchy dialogue, including lapidary one-liners; (iv) a humor that is often absurd and sometimes black; and (v) the use of political allegory; see Hart, "The Short Stories." I also draw on Lois Parkinson Zamora's wonderful essay on Borges and the prehistory of magical realism which she kindly offered for inclusion in my edited volume, *A Companion to Magical Realism*.
3. See Mendoza, *The Fragrance of Guava*, 74.
4. García Márquez, *Cien años de soledad*, 7.
5. Apuleyo Mendoza, 74.
6. Martin, *Gabriel García Márquez*, 35.
7. See my eight-minute documentary on García Márquez, *Sin título*, which includes an interview with Rubiela Reyes.
8. *Cien años de soledad*, 38.
9. In a number of conversations I had with Russell Porter, when he was Head of Documentary at the Escuela Internacional de Cine y Televisión, he would tell me that García Márquez often said that while critics looked for the secret of magical realism in literary texts, they missed the obvious—the stories came from the weird and wonderful people he met at carnivals all over Latin America.
10. "La Santa," 60–61.

11. "Y de la caja en que estaba salió un suave olor semejante al de las rosas secas, muy diferente del que suelen tener los cuerpos muertos en semejante estado" (Hart, ed., *Edición crítica del Proceso Apostólico de Santa Rosa de Lima*, fols. 1026r-v, 757).

12. For an example of Santa Rosa's ability to make very heavy objects seem weightless, see Hart, ed., *Edición crítica del Proceso Apostólico de Santa Rosa de Lima*, fols. 209v-210r, 221.

13. Rodrigo was born on August 24, 1959; see Hart, *Gabriel García Márquez*, 64.

14. Santa Rosa's saint day, however, is August 30, since August 24 was already taken by St Bartholomew.

15. *Cien años de soledad*, 72.

16. Hart, *Santa Rosa de Lima*, 207 and 364.

17. For discussion of the Holy See's interpretation of a miracle, and Santa Rosa's case is as good as any other, see Stephen M. Hart, *Santa Rosa de Lima*, 75-140.

18. Hart, *Gabriel García Márquez*, 159.

19. Bilon and Martínez-Cavard, "La escritura embrujada: Entrevista con Gabriel García Márquez," n. p.

20. Pascal, "The Impersonal Narrator of *The Metamorphosis*," 95.

21. "El día que lo iban a matar, Santiago Nasar se levantó a las 5.30 de la mañana para esperar el buque en que llegaba el Obispo" (García Márquez, *Crónica de una muerte anunciada*, 9).

22. Greenberg, "Gregor Samsa and Modern Spirituality," 20.

23. For a helpful discussion of the influence that Kafka's work had on Gabo's fiction, see Hahn, *The Influence of Kafka on Three Novels by Gabriel García Márquez*.

24. *Cien años de soledad*, 19.

25. Ibid., 29.

26. Ibid., 51.

27. Ibid., 68.

28. See Hart, "The Short Stories," 132–34.

29. *Cien años de soledad*, 7. For an excellent discussion of the ways in which magical-realist writers depicted magic as inhering in objects, see Zamora, "Swords and Silver Rings."

30. Ibid., 20.

31. Ibid., 10.

32. Ibid., 13.

33. Ibid., 23.

34. Ibid.

35. Hart, *Gabriel García Márquez*, 20.

36. *Cien años de soledad*, 23-–4.

37. Ibid., 38–39.

38. García Márquez, *One Hundred Years of Solitude*, 41.

39. *Cien años de soledad*, 50.

40. Ibid., 39.

41. Ibid., 42.

42. Ibid., 44.
43. For a discussion of the expansion of the genre of magical realism around the world, see Hart and Ouyang, eds., *A Companion to Magical Realism*, esp. the introduction.
44. See Faris, *Ordinary Enchantments*, 38.
45. Durix, *Mimesis, Genres, and Post-Colonial Discourse*, 187.

WORKS CITED

Apuleyo Mendoza, Plinio. *The Fragrance of Guava: Conversations with Gabriel García Márquez*. London: Faber & Faber, 1983.

Bilon, Yves, and Mauricio Martínez-Cavard. "La escritura embrujada: Entrevista con Gabriel García Márquez"; https://calledelorco.com/2015/05/27/la-metamorfosis-de-kafka-fue-una-revelacion-gabriel-garcia-marquez/. Accessed July 1, 2016.

Bloom, Harold, ed. *Franz Kafka's "The Metamorphosis."* Philadelphia: Chelsea House Publishing, 1988.

Bowers, Maggie Ann. *Magic(al) Realism*. London: Routledge, 2004.

Durix, Jean-Pierre. *Mimesis, Genres, and Post-Colonial Discourse: Deconstructing Magical Realism*. London: Macmillan, 1998.

Faris, Wendy B. *Ordinary Enchantments: Magical Realism and the Remystification of Narrative*. Nashville: Vanderbilt University Press, 2004.

García Márquez, Gabriel. *One Hundred Years of Solitude*. Translated by Gregory Rabassa. London: Picador, 1978.

———. *Cien años de soledad*, 3rd edition. Barcelona: Editorial Argos Vergara, 1980.

———. *Crónica de una muerte anunciada*. Barcelona: Bruguera, 1985.

———, "La Santa." In *Doce cuentos peregrinos*, 57–77. Buenos Aires: Editorial Sudamericana, 1992.

Greenberg, Martin. "Gregor Samsa and Modern Spirituality." In *Franz Kafka's "The Metamorphosis,"* edited by Harold Bloom, 19–35. Philadelphia: Chelsea House Publishing, 1988.

Hahn, Hannelor. *The Influence of Kafka on Three Novels by Gabriel García Márquez*. New York, 1993.

Hart, Stephen M. *Gabriel García Márquez*. London: Reaktion Books, 2010.

———. "The Short Stories." In *The Cambridge Companion to Gabriel García Márquez*, edited by Philip Swanson, 129–43. Cambridge: Cambridge University Press, 2010.

———. *Sin título*, Documentary, 8 mins. (2010).

———. *Gabriel García Márquez*. Translated by Nadia Stagnaro. Lima: Cátedra Vallejo, 2016.

———. *Santa Rosa de Lima: La evolución de una santa*. Translated by Nadia Stagnaro. Lima: Cátedra Vallejo, 2017.

———, ed. *Edición crítica del Proceso Apostólico de Santa Rosa de Lima (1630–1632): Congr. Riti Processus 1573, Archivum Secretum Vaticanum*. Lima: Cátedra Vallejo, 2017.

Hart, Stephen M., and Wen-chin Ouyang, eds. *A Companion to Magical Realism*. Woodbridge: Tamesis, 2004.
Martin, Gerald. *Gabriel García Márquez: A Life*. London: Bloomsbury, 2008.
Parkinson Zamora, Lois. "Swords and Silver Rings: Magical Objects in the Work of Jorge Luis Borges and Gabriel García Márquez." In *A Companion to Magical Realism*, edited by Stephen M. Hart and Wen-chin Ouyang, 28–45. Woodbridge: Tamesis, 2004.
Pascal, Roy. "The Impersonal Narrator of *The Metamorphosis*." In *Franz Kafka's "The Metamorphosis*," edited by Harold Bloom, 95–104. Philadelphia: Chelsea House Publishing, 1988.

Chapter 9

Epistemology of the Ineffable
Octavio Paz and India
Wendy B. Faris

This discussion focuses on Octavio Paz's encounter with India in his 1995 essay *Vislumbres de la India* (translated as *In Light of India*), together with brief discussions of poems written during his appointment as ambassador to India (1962–1968) originally published in *Ladera Este* (1962–1968; East Slope), *Hacia el comienzo* (1964–1968; Toward the Beginning) and *Blanco* (1966; White).[1] I will also consider his 1974 narrative *El mono gramático* (translated as *The Monkey Grammarian*), in order to further understand his particular sensibility as well as the international scope of his work.[2] In addition, given the intercultural nature of this artistic encounter with a foreign culture, we also gain a sense of Paz as a sensitive cultural comparatist.

PAZ'S ART OF THE GLANCE

To excavate *Vislumbres de la India* reveals what we might call an epistemology of the ineffable, which characterizes Paz's encounter with India. And, taking a cue from his title, we can see that he employs a strategy of the glance to discern and register that ineffable. Beginning with a brief interlude on Paz's initial stay in India (in 1958) as secretary in the newly established Mexican embassy, the essay is a free-ranging excursion encompassing brief anecdotes from his travels throughout India during his ambassadorship and lengthy reflections on various historical, political, and cultural issues. Paz himself lingers a moment on the title: "creo que su título define su carácter: *Vislumbres de la India*. Vislumbrar: atisbar, columbrar, distinguir apenas, entrever. Vislumbres: indicios, realidades percibidas entre la luz y la sombra" ("I think its title defines its character: *Glimpses* of India. To glimpse: discern, make out, barely distinguish, begin to see").[3] As if to suggest the difficulty of defining the word, he parses both verb and noun. Similarly, he leads up to this discussion of the title by referring to the gaps ("lagunas") in his essay, which correspond to the impossibility of adequately encompassing his subject: "el tema . . . es rebelde a la síntesis" ("the subject . . . rebels against synthesis").[4] In the end, the essay "no es hijo del saber sino del amor" ("is the child not of knowledge but of love").[5]

Like the dichotomies in Indian culture that he explores, calling them "violentos contrastes: modernidad y arcaísmo, lujo y pobreza, sensualidad y ascetismo, incuria y eficacia, mansedumbre y violencia" ("extreme contrast: modernity and antiquity, luxury and poverty, sensuality and asceticism, carelessness and efficiency, gentleness and violence"), Paz's art of the glance is something of a double mode.[6] We perceive, but just barely. We see and we almost don't see; we only glimpse. Adopting an often visionary mode, Paz relies on intuitive knowledge gleaned from visual glimpses and fleeting moments rather than on rational knowledge obtained by methodically gathered information; that kind of knowledge is also included, although, I would argue, it is less significant. The title thus implies an epistemology of cultural encounter appropriate to its subject, a way of knowing India that is oblique rather than direct. Therefore, as Paz explains the rationale underpinning *Vislumbres de la India*, "este libro no es sino una larga nota al pie de página de los poemas de *Ladera Este*, . . . no vital sino intelectual" ("this book is no more than a long footnote to the poems of *Ladera Este* . . . not vital but intellectual").[7]

This strategy of the glance and suggestions of implicit affinity pervade the essay, appropriately, it seems to me, inasmuch as the actual content presenting India is not especially revealing, often recapitulating well-known cultural facts gleaned from clearly acknowledged secondary sources. Following Paz, I focus on his sensibility as he encounters the culture of India rather than on his later cultural and political analyses. Near the end, after excusing his disquisitions on historical and political topics as necessary to the hour, he claims that he would have preferred to write about "lo que amo y siento: la India no entró en mí por la cabeza sino por los ojos, los oídos, y los otros sentidos" ("what I love and feel: India did not enter me through my mind but through my senses").[8] The sociopolitical analysis filling about fifty pages at the center of the book thus constitutes something of a hiatus between evocations of his—and of India's—underlying and more profound sensibility. He focuses on that very concept for a moment, as he introduces his Spanish-language versions of several Indian epigrams or "kavyas," which close *Vislumbres*. In so doing—while also introducing his practice of intermingling his own voice with that of Indian poetry in translation—he confirms this idea of transient yet epiphanic perception as an important if not a constant focus in the essay:

en los tratados de poética aparece una categoría estética difícil de definir en una lengua occidental: *rasa*. La palabra quiere decir *sabor* pero Ingalls [translator of Sanskrit poems], con buen juicio, prefiere traducirla por *mood*. ¿Y en español? ¿Talante, humor, estado de ánimo? Rasa es todo eso y más: *gusto*. No nada más sabor ni sensación sino "sensibilidad para apreciar las cosas bellas y criterio para distinguirlas" (María Moliner, *Diccionario de uso del español*).

(in treatises on poetics an aesthetic category that is difficult to define in a Western language appears: *rasa*. The word means *flavor* but Ingalls, with good reason, prefers to translate it by *mood*. And in Spanish? Mood, humor, state of mind? "Rasa" is all this and more: *taste*. Not nothing but flavor nor sensation but "the sensitivity for appreciating beautiful things and the judgment for perceiving them." [María Moliner, *Diccionario de uso del español*].)[9]

Given its delicate nature, such a sensibility is best apprehended in "vislumbres," glances, intuitions.[10]

As I am suggesting here, Paz's discursive coming to terms with India years after his stays there in *Vislumbres* reveals a particular epistemology of the ineffable as perceived in the glance and embodied in the titular word "vislumbres." Beside and beyond the book's cultural explorations, the translations of Indian epigrammatic verse that conclude the volume themselves provide perhaps the most dense concentration of *vislumbres*. That Paz chose this particular short poetic form to close the volume suggests that the glance indeed characterizes his encounter with Indian sensibility. An epigram, a *kavya*, is like a glance: He calls the titles he gives them "flechas de indicación" ("directional arrows")—suggesting the tentative and delicate nature of the epigrams as a way of knowing for the reader.[11] Besides being brief, they are varied, a scattering of topics; he has chosen oblique glances, not sustained investigations. And he includes a *kavya* entitled "Retórica" to serve as a manifesto of such an epistemology:

La belleza no está
en lo que dicen las palabras
sino en lo que, sin decirlo, dicen:
no desnudos sino a través del velo
son deseables los senos.

(Beauty is not
in what words say
but in what, without saying, they say:
not nude but through the veil
are breasts desirable.)[12]

Similarly, Paz's initial encounter with India as he first explores the "realidad insólita" ("unimagined reality") of Bombay, abandons a logically structured account in favor of listing glimpses of miscellaneous sights: "oleadas de calor," "torrentes de autos," "la aparición de una muchacha como una flor que se entreabre," "luna llena sobre la terraza del sultán" ("waves of heat," "torrents of cars," "the apparition of a girl like a half-opened flower," "full moon over the sultan's terrace").[13]

Such fleeting insights in the incorporated epigrams and the initial list of sights recall the perennial concern with linear and circular time, profane and sacred realities that pervade Paz's poetry. Moving beyond the terminal epigrams included in *Vislumbres* to focus briefly on the poems written in India and collected in *Ladera Este* (East Slope) confirms what I have been calling Paz's epistemology of the ineffable in small ways. At the same time, this epistemology of the inexpressible does not deviate from his characteristic preoccupations with time and eternity, the solid and the fluid, unity and diversity, silence and words, the self and the beloved.

When, writing to a fellow poet ("Carta a León Felipe"; "Letter to León Felipe"), Paz says that "lo instantáneo / Es nuestro oficio" ("the instantaneous / is our trade") and that "La poesía / es la ruptura instantánea / instantáneamente cicatrizada" ("Poetry / is a sudden rupture / suddenly healed"), he suggests such an epistemology by proposing that as poets they work not to write commentaries.[14] He recommends that they should instead "Aprender a leer / el hueco de la escritura / en la escritura" ("learn to read / the written gap / in writing").[15]

Thus, as we are seeing, immersed in this epistemology of the ineffable, the reader begins to know India through glimpses of places, people, and the poet. A few more examples will further elucidate the point. Appearing "Cerca del cabo Comorín" ("Near Cape Comorin")—the title phrase of a poem from *Ladera Este*—"El martín pescador es un topacio / instantáneo" ("The kingfisher [is] a topaz flash").[16] Or consider the six-line poem "La exclamación" ("Exclamation"), which provides a glimpse of a hummingbird:

Quieto
          no en la rama
en el aire
No en el aire
en el instante
          el colibrí

(Stillness
          not on the branch

in the air
>	Not in the air
in the moment
>	hummingbird)[17]

Equally illuminating, the three line poem "Prójimo lejano" ("Distant Neighbor") presents a momentary encounter with a world attempting to speak:

Anoche un fresno
a punto de decirme
algo—callóse

(Last night an ash tree
was about to tell
me something—and didn't)[18]

Both the surrounding city and the self-partake of this momentary sensibility. In a poem named for the speaker's perch on a balcony in Delhi, Paz introduces the Indian capital through an associative reference to its typography: "Dos sílabas altas / Rodeadas de arena e insomnio" ("Two tall syllables / surrounded by insomnia and sand").[19] In the closing lines, a tentative pulse of the self awaits its own arrival in this unfamiliar place: "La hora me levanta / hambre de encarnación padece el tiempo / mas allá de mí mismo / en algún lado aguardo mí llegada" ("The hour lifts me / time hungers for incarnation / Beyond myself / somewhere / I wait for my arrival").[20]

PILGRIMAGE, WITH (HARDLY ANY) MONKEYS

After this initial investigation of Paz's art of the glance, and before pursuing other related aspects of *Vislumbres*, I propose a brief hiatus to consider Paz's other most substantial narrative based in India, *El mono gramático* (*The Monkey Grammarian*). This is because the kind of visionary moments that I argue are essential to Paz's encounter with India appear at significant points in this other literary homage to India. The book is a lyrical, impressionistic narrative chronicling a trip to a remote and somewhat disheveled temple, resonant with numinous moments of scenic perception. Its journey is a double journey—to and through a temple and within language itself. And its voice seems to exist at the heart of the glance in the knowledge that flickers on and off:

> vamos y venimos entre la palabra que se extingue al pronunciarse y la sensación que se disipa en la percepción—aunque no sepamos quién es el que pronuncia la

palabra ni quién es el que percibe, aunque sepamos que aquél que percibe algo
que se disipa también se disipa en esa percepción: sólo es la percepción de su
propia extinción.

(we come and go between the word that dies away as it is uttered and the sensation that vanishes in perception—although we do not know who it is that utters
the word nor who it is that perceives, although we do know that the self that
perceives something that is vanishing also vanishes in this perception: it is only
the perception of that self's own extinction.)[21]

Perhaps the essay is a kind of Mallarméan deconstructive discourse mas-
querading as and coexisting with an atmanic/brahmanic merging of self and
universe, interior and exterior.[22]

As Paz begins this textual and mental pilgrimage of sorts, he evokes what I
am calling his epistemology of the ineffable obtained by the glance: "visiones
y semipensamientos que aparecen y desaparecen en el espacio de un par-
padeo, mientras se camina al encuentro de.... El camino también desaparece mientras lo pienso, mientras lo digo" ("images, memories, fragmentary
shapes and forms—all those sensations, visions, half-thoughts that appear and
disappear in the wink of an eye, as one sets forth to meet.... The path also
disappears as I think of it, as I say it").[23] These glances approximate but can't
capture the ineffable reality encountered. An early example describes a brief
moment in which Paz "me quedo quieto" ("remain[s] completely at rest"):
"La fijeza es siempre momentánea. Es un equilibrio, a un tiempo precario y
perfecto, que dura lo que dura un instante" ("Fixity is always momentary. It
is an equilibrium, at once precarious and perfect, that lasts the space of an
instant").[24] And soon, as if to stress that mode of perception as the virtually
impossible attempt to capture ineffable reality, he lingers on the phrase "la
fijeza es siempre momentánea" ("fixity is always momentary"), repeating it
several times.[25]

Later on in his journey, Paz accepts the incomplete glimpses of a *sadhu*—
one of the many wandering ascetics and beggars frequenting Indian tem-
ples—that he is given:

Busca la ecuanimidad, el punto donde cesa la oposición entre la visión interior
y la exterior, entre lo que vemos y lo que imaginamos. A mí me gustaría hablar
con el sadhu pero ni él entiende mí lengua ni yo hablo la suya. Así de vez en
cuando me limito a compartir su té, su bhang y su quietud.

(He is searching for equanimity, the point where the opposition between inner
and outer vision, between what we see and what we imagine, ceases. I should
like to speak with the sadhu, but he does not understand my language and I do

not speak his. Hence I limit myself to sharing his tea, his bhang, and his tranquility from time to time.)[26]

That "de vez en cuando" ("from time to time") embodies the acceptance of what comes in disparate and unpredictable moments, rather than the attempt to control one's experience, and affirms the momentary and ineffable. Immediately thereafter, looking down at the temple compound, Paz experiences a luminous moment in which implicit holiness is composed of disparate elements that magically coalesce (in what is hard not to see as also a Baudelairian embodiment of "correspondences"):

Todo resplandece: las bestias, las gentes, los árboles, las piedras, las inmundicias. Un resplandor sin violencia y que paca con las sombras y sus repliegues. Alianza de las claridades, templanza pensativa: los objetos se animan secretamente, emitan llamadas, responden a las llamadas, no se mueven y vibran, están vivos con una vida distinta de la vida. Pausa universal.

(Everything is radiant: the animals, the people, the trees, the stones, the filth. A soft radiance that has reached an accord with the shadows and their folds. An alliance of brightness, a thoughtful restraint: objects take on a secret life, call out to each other, answer each other, they do not move and yet they vibrate, alive with a life that is different from life. A universal pause.)[27]

Similarly, at another point, he reflects on his momentary glimpse of the ineffable as a combination of material and spiritual (note his willingness to correct himself, to try and get this glimpse of this unfamiliar culture right):

El bote de basura desborda de inmundicias y es un altar que se consume en una exaltación callada: los detritus son una gavilla de llamas bajo el resplandor cobrizo de la cubierta oxidada. Transfiguración de los desperdicios—no, no transfiguración: revelación de la basura como lo que es realmente: basura. No puedo decir "gloriosa basura" porque el adjetivo la mancharía. La mesita de madera negra, el bote de basura: presencias. Sin nombre, sin historia, sin sentido, sin utilidad. Porque sí.

(The garbage can with the lid half open burns with a quiet, almost solid glow. The light runs down the brick wall as though it were water. A burned water, a water-that-is-fire. The garbage can is overflowing with rubbish and it is an altar that is consuming itself in silent exaltation; the refuse is a sheaf of flames beneath the coppery gleam of the rusty cover. The transfiguration of refuse—no, not a transfiguration: a revelation of garbage as what it really is: garbage. I cannot say "glorious garbage" because the adjective would defile it. The little dark wooden table, the garbage can: presences. Without a name, without a history, without a meaning, without a practical use: just because.)[28]

At the heart of this journey is a meditation on language as both destructive and creative of itself and the universe, a series of valiant attempts to catch glimpses of the ineffable reality of the world, as he is seeing it now in India. As he contemplates pools of stagnant water, banyan trees, and other items on the way to the sanctuary of Galta, Paz reflects that

> cada una de estas realidades es única y para decirla realmente necesitaríamos un lenguaje compuesto exclusivamente de nombres propios e irrepetibles, un lenguaje que no fuese lenguaje . . . . Pues bien, el camino de la escritura poética se resuelve en la abolición de la escritura: al final nos enfrenta a una realidad indecible . . . . La realidad que revela la poesía y que aparece detrás del lenguaje—esa realidad visible sólo por la anulación del lenguaje en que consiste la operación poética—es literalmente insoportable y enloquecedora. La poesía nos alimenta y nos aniquila, nos da la palabra y nos condena al silencio. Es la percepción necesariamente momentánea (no resistiríamos más) del mundo sin medida.

> (each one of these realities is unique and to truly express it we would require a language composed solely of proper and unrepeatable names, a language that would never be a language. . . . Hence the path of poetic writing leads to the abolition of writing: at the end of it we are confronted with an inexpressible reality. . . . The reality that poetry reveals and that appears behind language—the reality visible only though the destruction of language that the poetic act represents—is literally intolerable and maddening. Poetry gives us sustenance and destroys us, it gives us speech and dooms us to silence. It is the necessarily momentary perception (which is all that we can bear) of the incommensurable world.)[29]

Thus, like the doubleness of the glance that flickers on and off, language is double: both sign of the world with which we are denied innate contact and an attempted way back into intimate relation to the world via words, especially evocative poetic words that recreate the world: "el lenguaje es la consecuencia (o la causa) de nuestro destierro del universo, significa la distancia entre las cosas y nosotros. También es nuestro recurso contra esa distancia" ("language is the consequence (or the cause) of our exile from the universe, signifying the distance between things and ourselves. At the same time it is our recourse against this distance").[30] As he writes his journey to Galta, Paz produces a "decir que apenas dicho se evapora, decir que nunca dice lo que quiero decir. Al escribir, camino hacia el sentido; al leer lo que escribo lo borro, disuelvo el camino" ("a saying of something that the moment it is said evaporates, a saying that never says what I want it to say. As I write, I journey toward meaning: as I read what I write, I blot it out, I dissolve the path").[31]

This leads Paz to a reflection on the difference between propositional and poetic language. The fate of discursive writing seems to be continual dissolution, a linear journey in time, which incorporates momentary acts of fleeting perception but constantly attempts—unsuccessfully—to reach an end point of meaning. After this reflection on non-transcendence, presenting the impossibility of finding and evoking a world of meaning in language, Paz explains how poetry—"el reverso del . . . lenguaje" ("the reverse of . . . language")—is empty of such linear vicissitudes:[32] "no quiere saber qué hay al fin del camino" (it "does not attempt to discover what there is at the end of the road"), but rather satisfies itself by producing "momentáneas configuraciones" ("momentary configurations").[33] Paradoxically, however, as if by not searching, it finds: "La visión de la poesía es la convergencia de todos los puntos. Fin del camino" ("the vision of poetry is that of the convergence of every point. The end of the road").[34] As if himself momentarily inhabiting that space of poetry, which he says is empty, offering a place of appearance and disappearance, the poet takes a breath:

> Respiro: estoy en el centro de un tiempo redondo, pleno como una gota de sol . . . . El baniano es una araña que teje desde hace mil años su inacabable telaraña. Saberlo me produce una alegría inhumana: estoy plantado en esta hora como el baniano en los siglos.
>
> (I breathe deeply: I am in the center of a time that is fully rounded, as full of itself as a drop of sunlight. . . . The banyan tree is a spider that has been spinning its interminable web for a thousand years. Discovering this causes me to feel an inhuman joy: I am rooted in this hour as the banyan tree is rooted in time immemorial.)[35]

Experiencing a sense of a dissolving individual self, "siento que me desprendo de mí mismo: estoy y no estoy en donde estoy" ("I feel that I am coming loose from myself: I am where I am and at the same time I am not where I am").[36] The section ends with a cosmic equivalent of that self-perception: "Cada tiempo es diferente; cada lugar es distinto y todos son el mismo, son lo mismo. Todo es ahora" ("each time is different; each place is different and all of them are the same place, they are all the same. Everything is now").[37] These moments of spatial and temporal reconciliation are visions of profound unity, of, we might say, Paz's version of *brahman*, the Hindu concept of all-pervading Godhead, the oneness of self and universe. Echoing the *brahmanic* sense of each place being different and yet all being the same place, there are four versions of the same photo of Galta in *El mono gramático*, three positive images, which differ slightly from each other in the way that they are printed, and one photographic negative. Like the Hindu all-pervading Godhead, they differ and yet are also the same.

SPIRIT REALMS: SACRED AND SENSORY

As we return to *Vislumbres*, the foregoing account of Paz's self-conscious pilgrimage in *El mono gramático* prompts us to ask precisely how Paz experiences the spiritual realm within Indian culture. On the surface of it, relatively minimally. However, given his sensibility, which might be characterized as the ineffability of the sensory—reflected in his description of the god Shiva and his consort Parvati's happiness as "al mismo tiempo terrestre e inalcanzable" ("both terrestrial and unreachable")—Indian spirituality intrigues Paz.[38] However, it does not dominate the essay, and the text suggests that he approaches this strong spiritual tradition cautiously, obliquely, with a delicate kind of perception—through *vislumbres*, as I've been suggesting. The root of the word *vislumbre* is light, behind which we might discern a concern with enlightenment, an undefinable realm we can only glimpse. From this angle, the light touch of the *vislumbre* contrasts with the "cháchara clerical" ("clerical chatter") of the mullahs, with "el ruido de sus discusiones y debates" ("the racket of their discussions and debates") that Paz contrasts to the mode of the seventeenth-century writer and prince Dara Shiko, whom he paints in a positive light as a mystic and free thinker.[39]

While Paz never really makes his interest in the spirit explicit, we do catch glimpses of it—largely couched in his own sensorial mode. Paz's embedding of the spiritual in the worldly is exemplified by his meeting with a spiritual teacher to whom he goes for advice as to whether he should accept a prize for his poetry. Paz is disinclined to accept this prize since at that point poetry was for him a private not a public affair and accepting the prize would change that. Before speaking to him, as she is occupied with another visitor, she unexpectedly tosses him an orange, which he manages to catch. In a moment, she counsels him to accept the prize, but in a spirit of humility and fortuity, just as he had caught the orange:

> Sea humilde y acepte ese premio. Pero acéptelo sabiendo que vale poco o nada, como todos los premios. No aceptarlo es sobrevalorarlo. . . . Falsa pureza, disfraz del orgullo . . . . El verdadero desinterés es aceptarlo con una sonrisa, como recibió la naranja que le lancé.

(Be humble and accept this prize. But accept it knowing that is [sic] worth little or nothing, like all prizes. To not accept it is to overvalue it. . . . A false purity, a mask of pride . . . . True disinterest is accepting it with a smile, as you received the orange I threw you.)[40]

He remembers the meeting and follows the advice. Just as he accepts pragmatic advice from a spiritual teacher, so a number of Paz's Indian poems are imbued with a combination of sacred and sensory impulses. Citing the final lines from his poem "Felicidad en Herat" ("Happiness in Herat") in *Vislumbres*, he expresses a similar combination of spiritual and terrestrial. He evokes the infinite normally supposed to pervade a sacred place but affirms that the meaningful experience is of this finite world:

No tuve la visión sin imágenes,
No vi girar las formas hasta desvanecerse
En claridad inmóvil,
El ser ya sin substancia del sufí.
No bebí plenitude en el vacío,
[. . .]
Vi un cielo azul y todos los azules,
del blanco al verde
todo el abanico [sic] de los álamos,
y sobre el pino, más aire que pájaro,
el mirlo blanquinegro.
Vi al mundo reposar en sí mismo.
Vi las apariencias.
Y llamé a esa media hora:
Perfección de lo Finito.

(I did not have the imageless vision,
I did not see forms whirl until they vanished
in unmoving clarity,
the being without substance of the Sufis.
I did not drink the plenitude of the void
[. . .]
I saw a blue sky and all the blues,
from white to green,
the spread fan of the poplars,
and on a pine, more air than bird,
a black and white mynah.
I saw the world resting on itself.
I saw the appearances.

And I named that half-hour
The Perfection of the Finite.)[41]

José Antonio de Ory cites the poem as exemplifying Paz's immunity to India's mysticism: "he doesn't allow himself be trapped by the attraction to mysticism, as do many who are drawn to India."[42] However, I think this is not so simple; one might interrogate Paz's poetic statement regarding his experience a bit differently. Is Paz claiming not to have experienced any mystical feelings at all or not to have experienced them in the traditional Indian forms? Both his introduction of the fragment describing the inspiring experience and the poem itself reveal a glancing, implicit sense of the sacred. The aura of ineffability—embodied in that saying without saying—pervades his experience. The resulting poem—"Felicidad en Herat"—distinguishes his own version of the sacred from those he has seen in the texts of India, such as "la visión sin imágenes," "claridad inmóvil," "el ser ya sin substancia del sufi," "las treinta y dos señales del Bodisatva cuerpo de diamante" ("the imageless vision," "unmoving clarity," "the being without substance of the Sufis," "the thirty two signs of the diamond-bodied Bodisatva").[43] In seeming contrast, Paz sees the varied blues of the sky, trees, a white and black bird, and the actual world resting in itself and its appearances, calling them "Perfección de lo Finito" ("the Perfection of the Finite")—rather than of the infinite. And yet, when, in *Vislumbres*, he says—just preceding the reproduction of "Felicidad en Herat" in that volume—that "el mausoleo puede compararse a un poema compuesto no de palabras sino de árboles, esangues, avenidas de arena y flores" ("the mausoleum is like a poem made not of words but of trees, pools, avenues of sand and flowers"),[44] he recalls the cosmic interconnectivity evoked in one of his most-cited poems, "Himno entre ruinas" ("Hymn among Ruins"). Here, Paz writes: "palabras que son flores que son frutos que son actos" ("words that are flowers that are fruits that are acts").[45] In both cases, the cosmic connectivity often associated with the sacred is expressed by the merging of words and things, so that an implicit sense of the sacred is intertwined with the very essence of poetic expression. In other words, the spiritual pervades not only the realm of the worldly and corporeal but also the sphere of poetry.

As we observed in *The Monkey Grammarian*, in which the pilgrimage to a sacred site is also a self-conscious reflection on language itself, Paz's sacral/sensory poems occasionally turn metapoetical. The eight line poem "El mausoleo de Humayún" ("The Mausoleum of Humayun") provides a fleeting image of a holy place that silences language:

> Al debate de las avispas
> la dialéctica de los monos
> gorjeos de las estadísticas

opone
>	(alta llama rosa
>	hecha de piedra y aire y pájaros
>	tiempo en reposo sobre el agua)
>	la arquitectura del silencio

(To the debate of wasps
the dialectic of monkeys
twittering of statistics
it opposes
>	(high flame of rose
formed out of stone and air and birds
time in repose above the water)
silence's architecture)[46]

In a similar spirit of imagining the fate of language in the world, the poem "Lectura de John Cage" ("Reading John Cage") offers a glimpse of the mental conundrum that results from attempting to put the sacred into words or music, thus creating verbal puzzles that are virtually impossible to parse:

> Música:
> >	oigo adentro lo que veo afuera
> >	veo dentro lo que oigo fuera.
>
> [. . .]
> >	Soy
> una arquitectura de sonidos
> instantáneos
> >	sobre
> un espacio que se desintegra
> [. . .]
> Silencio es música
> >	música no es silencio.
> Nirvana es Samsara
> >	Samsara no es Nirvana.
>
> (Music:
> >	I hear within what I see outside,
> I see within what I hear outside.
> [. . .]
> >	I am
> an architecture
> >	of instantaneous sounds
> on a space that disintegrates.

[. . .]
Silence is music,
                Music is not silence.
Nirvana is Samsara,
                Samsara is not Nirvana.)[47]

Perhaps the last lines mean (although the rather inscrutable mode of the discourse seems to challenge any attempt to extract a clear meaning) that the eternal is the transitory but not the reverse because the transitory is the way we intuit the eternal; you see the eternal in the now (Nirvana is Samsara) but you don't see the now in the eternal because the latter is too abstract to perceive. Similarly, "un allá no sé donde" ("a beyond I cannot tell where") is the eponymous "Tumba del poeta" ("Tomb of the Poet") of another poem, but it also suggests the sense of a nonspecific sacredness—brahman (the all-pervasive world spirit).[48] As does the ending of "Cuento de dos jardines" ("A Tale of Two Gardens") which evokes a pure sense of being without specific content: "El jardín se abisma, / Ya es un nombre sin substancia. / Los signos se borran: / yo miro la claridad" ("The garden sinks. / Now it is a name with no substance. / The signs are erased: / I watch clarity").[49] Similarly, such a sense of the ever puzzling world that encompasses both implicitly sacred and profane also characterizes "Cerca del cabo Comorín" ("Near Cape Comorin"), a poem envisioning an overarching unity of opposites: "universal indiferencia / donde la forma vil y adorable / prosperan y se anulan: vacíos hervideros" ("the universal indifference / where base form and the sacred / thrive and are negated: boiling voids").[50] Amid these more generalized glimpses of the sacred, unusually, in "La higuera religiosa" ("The Religious Fig") God is specifically evoked, and Paz cites (in the footnotes) religious poems from the Punjab for this poem on a pipal tree.[51]

Finally (and much too briefly, I admit), in the long poem *Blanco* (1966), we frequently experience a sense of fruitful emptiness that resembles the preceding glimpses of the implicit sacredness of the sensual world:

Aerofanía,
   boca de verdades,
claridad que se anula en una sílaba
diáfana como el silencio:
no pienso, veo
                —no lo que pienso,
la cara en blanco del olvido,
el resplandor de lo vacío.
Pierdo mi sombra,
                avanzo

entre los bosques impalpables,
las esculturas rápidas del viento,
los sinfines,
                        desfiladeros afilados
avanzo,
        mis pasos
                    se disuelven
en un espacio que se desvanece
en pensamientos que no pienso.

(Translucence,
                    mouth of truths,
clarity effaced by a syllable
diaphanous as silence:
I don't think, I see:
                    —not what I think,
blank face of forgetting,
radiant void.
I lose my shadow,
                I walk
through innumerable forests,
sudden sculptures of the wind,
endless things,
                sharpened paths,
I walk,
        my steps
              dissolving
in a space that evaporates
into thoughts I don't think.)[52]

This implicit sacredness of the corporeal, perhaps best encapsulated in the phrase "resplandor de lo vacío" ("radiant void") is achieved by evoking clarity, emptiness, silence, voids, disappearances, non-thoughts, and in repeated paradoxes in which words and the world, the lover and the beloved, the body and the spirit are constantly intermingled. In this way, changes are rung on different entities—words, elements, the lover's body—each becoming emblems of each other, to form a kind of ineffable vibration of being; difficult, virtually impossible to describe, but just possible to experience. What's more, from a Hindu perspective, inasmuch as its title embodies the poem's many comings and goings of body and spirit, might *Blanco* refer to the erasure of content from consciousness, thereby suggesting union with a world soul?[53]

Returning to *Vislumbres* in this context of all-pervading spirit present in a kind of holy nothingness, we hear Paz recall an afternoon in a tiny mosque he came upon by chance in which "pasé un largo rato sin hacer ni pensar en nada. Momento de beatitud, roto al fin por el pesado vuelo circular de los murciélagos. Sin decirlo, me decían que era hora de volver al mundo" ("I stayed for hours, thinking of nothing. A moment of beatitude, broken finally by the heavy circular flight of the bats who had appeared in the fading light. Without saying it, they told me it was time to return to the world").[54] Such implicit and non-doctrinal sacrality, the abstract and cosmic questioning is something that Paz also admires in the oldest sacred texts of Hinduism, the *Rigveda*.[55] In the cultural system of India's ancient epics and tales, "Vedic hymns are in verse, and some of them are poetry of the highest order."[56] But "the texts themselves are not classified as *kavya* (poetry)" because they are "of divine origin and hence sacred, whereas human poetry . . . is made by human authors and hence always mundane."[57] Yet in Paz's view, the Vedic Creation Hymn—"uno de los himnos más hermosos del *Rig Veda*" ("one of the most beautiful hymns of the *Rig Veda*")—is poetry incarnate, thus resembling Paz's own cosmically reverent and often quite abstract verses, many of which—like the abovementioned "Himno entre ruinas"—are also entitled hymns. Paz's quotes the Creation Hymn in his own Spanish translation:[58]

No había nada, ni siquiera la nada
no había aire, ni, más allá, cielo.
¿Que cubría al cosmos, donde estaba?
¿Quién lo regía? ¿Había sólo agua y abismo?

No había muerte ni inmortalidad,
no se encendía ni apagaba la antorcha del día y la noche.
El Uno respiraba sin aire, se sostenía sin apoyo.
Sólo había el Uno y no había nadie.

(Then even nothingness was not, nor existence.
  There was no air then, nor the heavens beyond it.
What covered it? Where was it? In whose keeping?
  Was there then cosmic water, in depths unfathomed?

Then there was neither death nor immortality
  Nor was there then the torch of night and day.
The One breathed windlessly and self-sustaining.
  There was that One then, and there was no other.)[59]

Following that passage, he recites another Vedic verse: "los sabios, que han buscado en sus almas a la sabiduría, saben que son hermanos lo que es y lo que no es" ("The sages who have searched their hearts with wisdom / know that which is, is kin to that which is not").[60] He comments that "todo lo que puede decirse sobre el ser y el no-ser está en esa línea enigmática y sublime" ("all that can be said about being and nonbeing are in those enigmatic and sublime lines"), a description that could be applied to many of his own verses.[61] In dealing with such general questions of origins and immortality, the abstractions reveal an inherent but nonspecific spiritual dimension. As I have suggested above, this is a sensibility akin to the generalized sense of the sacred in the non-dualist Hindu concept of brahman, the all-pervasive sacred consciousness of the universe, in which we all participate. [62]

THE QUESTION OF THE EROTIC

Related to these moments of all-pervading and omnipresent sacrality are Paz's thoughts on an aspect of Indian sensibility close to his own: the combination of the sensual, sometimes embodied in the erotic, and the spiritual.[63] He affirms that sensibility as he ends these reflections: "la hermosura física también posee una irradiación que, a su manera, es magnetismo espiritual" ("physical beauty also possesses a force that is, in its way, a spiritual magnetism").[64] The final Indian cultural duality he cites is an "encarnación de una totalidad que es plenitude y vacuidad, transfiguración del cuerpo en una forma que, sin dejar de ser corporal y sensible, es espiritual" ("incarnation of a totality that is plenitude and emptiness, the transfiguration of the body into form that, without abandoning sensation and the flesh, is spiritual").[65] Such a delicate and ineffable combination, again, is best apprehended glancingly—in a *vislumbre*. Paz implies that idea in his discussion of the late twelfth-century philosopher-poet Dharmakirti, who, according to Paz, embodies "esta desconcertante unión entre pensamiento y sensualidad, abstracción y deleite de los sentidos" ("this disconcerting union of thinking and sensuality, abstraction and delight in the senses").[66] This is a sensibility clearly close to Paz's own. For Paz, Dharmakirti's thought about the world embodies what we might term an epistemology of the ineffable: "Dharmakirti sostuvo que el hombre percibe a la realidad pero que esa percepción es *instantánea e inefable*" (my emphasis; "argues that we indeed perceive reality, but our perception is *momentary and ineffable*").[67]

These reflections on Indian sensuality, as we shall see shortly, constitute something of an opposing dyptich in the realm of sexual love to Paz's essay of two years previous, *La llama doble* (*The Double Flame*), where he analyzes the Western tradition of courtly love with its encoding of high chastity, and of the sequence of transgression, punishment, and redemption, as well as his own departure from that tradition in the realm of love. Paz largely follows Denis de Rougement there, although he disagrees with de Rougemont's view of love as necessarily heretical in valuing the beloved above God. As Paz wonders, "¿el amor también es una heresía del budismo, el taoísmo, el visnuismo y el Islam?" ("Is love also a heresy for Buddhism, Taoism, Vishnuism, Islam?")[68] The implication is that it is not. Paz claims that because it allows us a glimpse of eternity but only momentarily, inevitably returning us to the contradictory time of now and never, "todo amor, incluso el más feliz, es trágico" ("all love, even the most blissful, is tragic").[69] Nevertheless, when he states that "nuestra poesía mística está impregnada de erotismo y nuestra poesía amorosa de religiosiad" ("our mystic poetry is suffused with eroticism and our amorous poetry with religiosity"), he claims that "en esto nos apartamos de la tradición grecorromana y nos parecemos a los musulmanes y a los hindúes" ("in this respect we depart from the Greco-Roman tradition and resemble the Muslims and Hindus").[70] In Paz's view, those Eastern traditions unite the erotic and the spiritual more closely.

Paz speculates that the mystical and the erotic are connected in poetry, because both orgasm and mystical experience embody the instantaneous union of opposites, a mysterious process that is therefore "indecible" ("unspeakable").[71] But characteristically, his introduction seems to touch the subject lightly, performing once again an epistemology of the ineffable expressed in a glance: "Añado, de paso, una observación que podría quizá ayudar un poco a esclarecer el fenómeno" ("I add, in passing, an observation that might help shed a little more light on the phenomenon").[72] Note all the tentative and non-assertive terms in addition to the modesty of "observación": "añado" ("I add"), "de paso" ("in passing"), the subjunctive, "quizá" ("might"), "un poco" ("a little"). Paz compares platonic and yogic coupling, and, different as he says they are, he makes them into mirror images of each other.

> Tanto el cuerpo que contempla el amante platónico como la mujer que acaricia el yogui, son objetos, escalas en una ascensón hacia el cielo puro de las esencias o hacia esa región fuera de los mapas que es lo incondicionado. El fin que ambos persiguen está mas allá del otro.

> (Both the body that the Platonic lover contemplates and the woman who embraces the yogin are objects, steps in an ascent toward the pure heaven of essences, or toward that region shown on no map, the unconditional. The end that both pursue lies beyond the other).[73]

Inasmuch as they abolish otherness, Platonic and yogic coupling are the opposite of love as he has described it for the most part in *La llama doble*: "el amor no es la búsqueda de la idea o la esencia; . . . no busca nada mas allá de sí mismo, ningún bien, ningún premio; tampoco persigue una finalidad que lo trascienda" ("love is not the search for the idea or the essence . . . . love seeks nothing beyond itself—no good, no reward. . . . It is indifferent to any sort of transcendence").[74] This latter type of love reveals glimpses of a totality beyond the finite individual but it does not abolish her: "es una atracción por un alma y un cuerpo; no una idea: una persona. Esa persona es única y está dotada de libertad . . . . Posesión y entrega son actos recíprocos" ("it is an attraction exerted by a soul and a body, not by an idea. By a person. That person is unique and endowed with freedom. . . . Possession and surrender are reciprocal acts").[75] To repeat: this love unites with while recognizing a unique and free individual, whereas the platonic and yogic embraces transcend that worldly state in favor of a "visión de la esencia" ("vision of essence") in which "*el otro* desaparece" ("the Other disappears").[76] In any case, whether or not love affirms individual bodies and souls or searches beyond them for a transcendental realm, the ecstatic experiences are *vislumbres*; they happen fast in "un instante" ("an instant").[77]

Returning to *Vislumbres*, we should mention that Paz maintains—via an evocative image of a fan ("abánico")—that the greatest difference between Western and Oriental love poetry is the idea of an ensemble of transgressions and violations (Western) versus one characterized by a host of possibilities (oriental): "Bataille afirmaba que el erotismo esencialmente es transgresión. El arte erótico hindú lo desmiente; el erotismo no es un código sino un abánico. Al desplegarse, replegarse y volver a desplegarse, el abánico muestra todas las gamas del placer" ("Bataille emphasizes that eroticism is essentially transgression: Hindu erotic art proves him wrong. It is not a legal code but a fan: unfolding, refolding, unfolding again, displaying the whole range of pleasures").[78] The Christian tradition as Paz sees it growing out of Platonism's distancing of the divine from the body contrasts with the Hindu, in which "la actividad del universo es vista a veces como una inmensa cópula divina" ("the activity of the universe is sometimes seen as an enormous divine copulation").[79] Therefore "condenar al cuerpo y a la sexualidad humana en una tradición como la hindú habría sido condenar a los dioses y a las diosas, agentes de la poderosa sexualidad cósmica. Así pues, la castidad y el ascetismo hindú tienen otro orígen" ("to condemn the body and human sexuality in a tradition like Hinduism would be to condemn the gods and goddesses, the manifestations of a powerful cosmic sexuality. Hindu chastity and asceticism must have another source").[80] Desire is sacred energy, "sexualidad como energía cósmica" ("sexuality as cosmic energy").[81] And so chastity serves to conserve that valuable force, so that it may be turned to a vital end: "la castidad nos da poder para la gran batalla: romper la cadena de las transmigraciones" ("chastity gives strength for the great battle: breaking the chain of rebirths").[82] (That Paz takes up this subject in both *Vislumbres* and *La llama doble* in very similar terms suggests its importance for him.) Chastity gives the sage the force to free himself from reincarnations; you don't condemn sexual energy because it is a cosmic force, but you do contain it to use it for enlightenment:

> El yogui debe evitar la eyaculación y esta práctica obedece a dos propósitos: negar la función reproductivo de la sexualidad y transformar el semen en pensamiento de iluminación. Alquímica erótica: la fusión del yo y del mundo, del pensamiento y la realidad, produce un relámpago: la iluminación, llamareda súbita que literalmente consume al sujeto y al objeto. No queda nada: el yogui se ha disuelto en lo incondicionado . . . alcanza la indiferencia del diamante: impenetrante, luminoso y transparente.

> (The yogin avoids ejaculation, with two objectives: denying the reproductive function of sexuality, and transforming his semen into illuminated thought. An erotic alchemy: the fusion of ego and world, thought and reality produces a blinding flash of illumination, a burst of flame that literally consumes subject and object. Nothing is left; the yogin has dissolved into the unconditional . . . he achieves the indifference of the diamond: impenetrable, luminous, transparent).[83]

Again, note the words—"relámpago" ("flash"), "llamareda súbita" ("a burst of flame"), indicating that it happens fast—in the time of a *vislumbre*. In this way, "aquél que busca la liberación no ve en su cuerpo un obstáculo sino un instrumento" ("he who seeks liberation does not see his body as an obstacle, but rather as an instrument").[84] This is an idea also suggested by an epigraph to *Blanco* from *The Hevajra Tantra*: "By passion the world is bound, by passion too it is released."[85] Further focusing on the body as an instrument of freedom, he explains that "el liberado vive en un eterno presente y habita un sitio que es todas partes y ninguna" ("the liberated lives in an eternal present and inhabits a place that is all places and nowhere").[86] Further, "no es ni un yo ni un tú ni un él" ("it is neither an I nor a you nor a he nor a she"), stressing the abstract and paradoxical nature of this state: "es un estado paradójico a un tiempo negativo y positivo" ("it is a paradoxical state that is both negative and positive").[87]

THE CAUTIOUS CULTURAL COMPARATIST

To conclude: Broadening our perspective to consider Paz's cultural comparative mode in *Vislumbres*, we can note that he undertakes this study of sensibilities under the (now unfashionable) modernist banner of universal humanity. In the introduction to the final set of incorporated Indian poems (*kavyas*) that ends the volume, he declares: "las pasiones y los sentimientos apenas si se transforman . . . . La naturaleza humana es universal y perdurable, es de todos los climas y de todas las épocas. Este es el secreto de la perennidad de ciertos poemas y de algunos libros" ("passions and feelings hardly change. . . . Human nature is universal and enduring, it belongs to all climates and all eras. This is the secret of the durability of certain poems and some books").[88] Within this generalized humanistic approach, however, he most often notes India's unique qualities, shifting back and forth between similarities and differences from Mexico, his most frequent site of comparison. But he approaches these comparisons cautiously, as if wishing to make sure not to subsume one culture under another. In a section of *Vislumbres* entitled "La singularidad de la historia India" ("The Singularity of Indian History"), he says that "uno de los temas recurrentes de la historia de la India es el choque de civilizaciones. De ahí que no me haya parecido impertinente comparer a veces esos choques con los que ha sufrido México" ("a recurrent theme of Indian history is the clash of civilizations. Here it seems to me not irrelevant to compare those conflicts with the ones that Mexico has suffered").[89] Notice the apologetic introduction of the comparison: "no me haya perecido impertinente" ("it seems to me not irrelevant"). And he follows an initial comparison by emphasizing difference: "el imperio británico, como el español en América, fue el agente de la unificación. Pero ahí termina el parecido. El legado inglés no fue religioso ni artístico sino jurídico y político" ("the British Empire, like the Spanish in America, was the agent of unification. But there the similarity ends. The British legacy was neither religious nor artistic, it was judicial and political").[90] Therefore I think that Paz cannot be accused of "taking India for the Indies," so to speak, in the sense of attributing Latin American characteristics to India.[91] More generally, he notes of India's history "el rasgo que la distingue de las otras civilizaciones: más que sucesión de épocas: su historia ha sido superposición de pueblos, religiones, instituciones y lenguas" ("more than a succession of epochs, its history has been a superimposition of peoples, religions, institutions, and languages").[92] Finally, with regard to cultural comparisons, one can also see the strategy of *vislumbres*, or incomplete glimpses, as performing cultural humility, inasmuch as they acknowledge incomplete knowability.

In terms of cultural sympathies, writing in 1995, Paz critiques Nehru's politics of "non-alignment" as allying India with non-democratic leaders such as Tito, Nasser, and Sukarno, and ultimately serving Soviet interests.[93] However, in his actual encounter with India during the late 1950s and 1960s, he as a Mexican seems to have felt an affinity with India in its generally non-aligned status. They are two nations with cultural identities of difference. He prefaces his discussion of similarities between the two countries by apologizing for writing briefly as a Mexican, justifying that stance on personal grounds, and once again, apologizing for the comparison, eager not to subsume Indian under Mexican culture: "Pido perdón al lector por ese circunloquio: después de todo, soy mexicano" ("I beg the indulgence of the reader for this digression, but I am, after all, a Mexican").[94] He then states that "entre los indios era muy viva la consciencia de sus diferencias con otros pueblos. Es una actitud que comparten los mexicanos. . . . el hecho de ser mexicano me ayudó a ver las diferencias de la India . . . desde mis diferencias de mexicano" ("Indians are very conscious of their difference from other people. It is an attitude shared by Mexicans . . . the fact of being Mexican helped me to see the difference of being Indian—from the difference of being Mexican").[95]

In the end, then, taking account of Paz's view of love in *La llama doble* in conjunction with his thoughts on India in *Vislumbres*, in both cases, Paz bases himself in the acknowledgment of difference, in individualism, a philosophy of not abolishing the other.[96] Just as in his individual-centric notion of love, in which the lover unites with but does not abolish the identity of the beloved, so too in his cultural comparisons Paz does not, as I have said, subsume India under the Indies, attributing characteristics of Latin America to India. In the end, then, he feels a profound affinity with India, but clearly differentiates himself from it. In love, two individual people; in cultural comparisons, two individual civilizations, sharing a sensibility not an identity.

That attitude of appreciating genuine affinities while acknowledging cultural differences embodies the best comparative work, as Lois has exemplified it in her many texts that have provided us with such illuminating comparisons between cultures, principally within the Americas, but also beyond them. Her most recent book, *The Inordinate Eye: New World Baroque and Latin American Fiction* is of course an outstanding example, but I might recall that I first met Lois as the result of a panel on "Transatlantic Intertextuality" that I was organizing and in which Lois presented a brilliant paper on "European Intertextuality in Vargas Llosa and Cortázar." Finally, and further illustrating her broad cultural reach (and, appropriately enough, given my topic here), Lois ended her distinguished administrative career by heading up a new program in "Comparative Cultural Studies" at the University of Houston, which includes India.

NOTES

1. These poems were reproduced in the 1987 bilingual edition *The Collected Poems of Octavio Paz, 1957–87*, edited by Eliot Weinberger, where they appear next to (mostly) new translations by the editor. All quotations of Paz's poetry after 1957 and their English translations are from the *Collected Poems*.

2. The ideas I discuss here are clearly relevant to all of Paz's poetry, and especially that written in India. But while I treat the latter briefly, to do justice to it as such would be a whole other project.

3. Paz, *Vislumbres*, 43; *In Light*, 33. English doesn't seem to have such a variety of words for glimpsing. Dictionaries usually give "glimpse" for all of the words Paz uses, though sometimes adds the ones I have used here to give a sense of the variety in Paz's text, which is omitted from the English translation.

4. Paz, *Vislumbres*, 43; Paz, *In Light*, 33.

5. Ibid.; ibid.

6. Paz, *Vislumbres*, 44; Paz, *In Light*, 37.

7. Ibid., 42; ibid., 32.

8. Ibid., 159; ibid., 137.

9. *Vislumbres*, 223. All *kavyas* and Paz's introductions to them are omitted from the English translation, *In Light*. Thus, here and below, their translations are mine.

10. Shyama Ganguly describes a sensibility that seems very close to what I have been terming Paz's epistemology of the ineffable, expressed in the word "vislumbre," and connected to the cosmos, as a constant in Paz's work. The difficulty of perceiving and then capturing "that 'unnameable' something, . . . buried in the most hidden part of ourselves,' which, for lack of a precise name, he calls 'Hope' ("Al Polvo"), causes him to try, via words, to reconcile the duality of material and idea, life and death" (Ganguly, "La recepción India," 224). She also implicitly validates the idea of the *vislumbre* as capable of capturing the ineffable in life as encapsulating Paz's poetics: "already in *Las peras del olmo* Paz had said that 'poetic knowledge—the imagination that produces images in which contraries are reconciled—lets us glimpse ['vislumbrar'] the cosmic analogy" (Ibid., 225).

11. *Vislumbres*, 230.

12. Ibid., 237; my translation.

13. *Vislumbres*, 13–15; *In Light*, 10–11.

14. "Carta a León Felipe" ("Letter to León Felipe"), in *Collected Poems*, 244–53; 245, 246; 248, 249. In *Collected Poems*, Spanish original and English translation are printed on opposite pages, running parallel on even- and odd-numbered respectively. Therefore, page totals for multipage poems cannot be given separately for original and translation.

15. Ibid., 248, 249.

16. "Cerca del cabo Comorín" ("Near Cape Comorin"), in *Collected Poems*, 198–201; 200, 201.

17. "La exclamación" ("Exclamation"), in *Collected Poems*, 234, 235.

18. "Prójimo lejano" ("Distant Neighbor"), in *Collected Poems*, 234, 235.

19. "El Balcón" ("The Balcony"), in *Collected Poems*, 164–71; 164, 165.

20. Ibid., 170; 171.

21. *El mono gramático*, 54; *The Monkey Grammarian*, 55–56.

22. In his discussion of how *mono* partially coincides with the ideas of the eleventh-century Indian literary critic and philosopher Abhinavagupta, Oscar Pujol confirms that Paz's textual journey investigates poetry's philosophical engagement with ultimate reality beyond appearances, and also that the perception of such reality

is momentary. However, in contrast to my idea that Paz does seem to realize the ineffable beyond in certain visionary moments, for Pujol, the cultural difference between Paz and Abhinavagupta means that while the latter considers the reality poetry reveals behind ordinary language as "radiant with the light of pure consciousness," for Paz it remains only "insufferable and crazy-making" (Pujol, "El mono gramático," 17).

23. *El mono gramático*, 12; *The Monkey Grammarian*, 4.
24. Ibid., 15–16; ibid., 8–9.
25. Ibid., 27–30; ibid., 20–23.
26. Ibid., 69; ibid., 74.
27. Ibid., 70; ibid., 75–76.
28. Ibid., 99; ibid., 113.
29. Ibid., 113–14; ibid., 132–33.
30. Ibid., 114; ibid., 133.
31. Ibid., 115; ibid., 134.
32. Ibid., 114; ibid., 133.
33. Ibid., 134; ibid., 155.
34. Ibid.
35. Ibid., 117; ibid., 135.
36. Ibid., 119; ibid., 139. According to Ganguly, Paz's sensibility resonates with India's because he already sought such an annihilation of the self in the universe, a "state (of emptiness) of absolute truth (the *paramartha*) where all contradictions are reconciled until the difference between being and non-being disappears" (Ganguly, "La recepción India," 223).

37. *El mono gramático*, 121; *The Monkey Grammarian*, 141. As with the echo of the notion of Baudelairian correspondences noted above, these lines seem to evoke T. S. Eliot's vision of eternal presentness here and elsewhere in *The Four Quartets*: "And the end and the beginning were always there / Before the beginning and after the end. / And all is always now" (Eliot, *Collected Poems*, 180). Such resonances confirm that India is a powerful presence for Paz but always in conjunction with his other literary influences.

38. *Vislumbres*, 18; *In Light*, 14.
39. Ibid., 57; ibid., 48.
40. Ibid., 36; ibid., 26.
41. I am citing the poem as it appears in *Collected Poems*. "Felicidad en Herat" ("Happiness in Herat") in *Collected Poems*, 204–09, 208, 209.
42. Ory, 34.
43. "Felicidad en Herat" ("Happiness in Herat"), 208, 209.
44. *Vislumbres*, 23; *In Light*, 18.
45. Himno entre ruinas," in *La centena*, 83–85, 83; "Hymn among Ruins," in *Selected Poems*, 20–24, 24.
46. "El Mausoleo de Humayún" ("The Mausoleum of Humayun"), in *Collected Poems*, 176–77; 176, 177.
47. "Lectura de John Cage" ("Reading John Cage"), in *Collected Poems*, 234–41; 236, 237.

48. "Tumba del poeta," ("Tomb of the Poet"), in *Collected Poems,* 228–33; 228, 229.

49. "Cuento de dos jardines" ("A Tale of Two Gardens"), in *Collected Poems,* 290–307; 306, 307.

50. "Cerca del cabo Comorín" ("Near Cape Comorin"), in *Collected Poems,* 198–201; 200, 201.

51. "La higuera religiosa" ("The Religious Fig"), in *Collected Poems,* 172–77.

52. "Blanco" ("Blanco"), in *Collected Poems,* 309–31; 322–24; 323–25.

53. C.N. Srinath concurs, saying of *Blanco*: "The meaning of the title 'Blanco' comes alive to us in line after line leading us through labyrinths of being to the glow of nothingness. The poetry of translucence is achieved only after an intense struggle in the vortex of the self shedding all its trappings. It is the transition from the dynamic to the meditative that is the strength of Octavio Paz's poetry" (Srinath, "Octavio Paz," 27). In her analysis of "Cuento de dos jardines," Teresa Costa-Gramunt also recognizes Paz's implicit affinity with the notions of atman and brahman: "The poet's intuition precisely describes the image of one's own center merging with nature, incorporating itself into it. *Atman* fusing with *Brahman*" (Costa-Gramunt, "El jardín del poeta," 22). Amid his analysis of its Simultaneism, Roberto Cantú provides a similar (and much more complete) interpretation of *Blanco,* as embodying verbal nothingness, as well as combining the sensual and the sacred. After having cited a scholar describing the union of Shiva and Shakti in the Tantric tradition, Cantú proposes that "the poem's *telos* or 'target' (*blanco*) is thus *samadhi* ("the One-without-a-second"), the sacred union that leads to the cosmic androgyny, a yogin's condition in which 'the experience and bliss of *this* degree of *samadhi* is silence'" (Cantú, "Octavio Paz and India," 67).

54. *Vislumbres*, 24; *In Light*, 18–19.

55. The "Rigveda" (Sanskrit: "The Knowledge of Verses") is "the oldest of the sacred books of Hinduism, composed in an ancient form of Sanskrit about 1500 BCE, in what is now the Punjab region of India and Pakistan. It consists of a collection of 1,028 poems grouped into 10 'circles' (*mandalas*)." *Encyclopaedia Britannica Online,* s.v. "Rigveda," https://www.britannica.com/topic/Rigveda.

56. "India's Ancient Epics and Tales," 1115.

57. Ibid.

58. He draws on an English-language source, which Paz's notes identify A. L. Basham's 1954 *The Wonder that Was India* (*Vislumbres,* 162).

59. *Vislumbres*, 162; *In Light,* 139.

60. Ibid., 162; ibid., 140.

61. Ibid.; ibid. Similarly, concluding her essay on *Vislumbres,* Elsa Cross defines the generalized elements that unite Paz and India's spiritual traditions: "silence, pauses, vision . . . that we find in ecstatic contemplation that some tantras propose as ways into the center of reality, appear also in Paz's poetry and thought" (Cross, "Sobre *Vislumbres,*" 44).

As Ory has noted, "in Mahayana Buddhism he is attracted fundamentally to the notion of *Sûnyata,* non-being, emptiness, zero" (Ory, "Octavio Paz y la India," 36). As he explains, Paz recognizes the self-negating properties of such nothingness: "the concept of emptiness denies even itself: everything is relative and even so, opposites, life and death, permanence and flow, are reconcilable ('Muerte y vida se confundían,' ['Death and life were jumbled'] 'El presente es perpétuo' ['The present is motionless'] he says in *Ladera Este*; 'El movimiento sólo es una illusión de la inmovilidad' ['Fixity is always momentary'] in *El mono gramático*)" (Ibid.).

62. Non-dualism consists in the belief that there is no division between the self and the universe, in contrast to a "dualist" view in which the self contemplates the divinity of the universe as a separate entity.

63. As Eunice Hernández perspicaciously notes, the two epigraphs to *Blanco*, from Mallarmé and *The Hevajra tantra,* encompass the double impulse behind the poem: emptiness and eroticism—sacred and profane (Hernández, "Octavio Paz: La India," 87). Similarly, Anil Dhingra gives an example of Paz's unification of the erotic and the spiritual. Quoting Paz's poem "Cuento de dos jardines" ("A tale of two gardens") Dhingra writes, "it is through his passion for his wife that he experiences the truth of *Sunyata*, the nothingness of the entire universe: 'Olvidé a Nagarjuna y a Dharmakirti / En tus pechos, / En tu grito los encontré: / Maithuna, / Dos en uno, / Uno en todo, / Todo en nada, / ¡*Sunyata!*'" (Dhingra, "La India en la obra," 163).

64. *Vislumbres*, 199; *In Light*, 185.
65. Ibid., 200; ibid, 185.
66. Ibid., 165; ibid, 142.
67. Ibid; ibid.
68. *Llama doble*, 95; *Double Flame*, 114.
69. Ibid., 111; ibid, 135.
70. Ibid., 110; ibid, 133.
71. Ibid.; ibid.
72. Ibid.; ibid.
73. Ibid., 209; ibid, 260.
74. Ibid., 210; ibid, 260.
75. Ibid., 210; ibid, 260–61.
76. Ibid., 208–09; ibid, 260–61.
77. Ibid., 204; ibid, 253.
78. *Vislumbres*, 171; *In Light*, 154.
79. Ibid., 182; ibid., 170.
80. Ibid., 182; ibid., 171.
81. Ibid., 183; ibid., 170–71.
82. Ibid., 184; ibid., 171.
83. *Llama doble*, 208–09; *Double Flame*, 258–60.
84. *Vislumbres*, 184; *In Light*, 172.
85. "Blanco" ("Blanco"), in *Collected Poems*, 309–31, 309. My translation. The epigraph does not appear in version of the poem reproduced in *Collected Poems*.
86. *Vislumbres*, 188–89; *In Light*, 174–76.
87. Ibid.; ibid.
88. *Vislumbres*, 228–9; my translation. R.H. Khare accepts Paz's standpoint of individualistic global humanism, complimenting Paz for "meaningfully triangulat[ing] India, Mexico, and Europe across a wide swath of historical and cultural difference" and maintaining that "his poetic aestheticism and philosophical erudition effortlessly

stood alongside a politically prudent globalism because he did not see himself just as a distant diplomat or a poetphilosopher but as a co-traveler with humanity, whether these were the learned, the rich, or the poor in India, Mexico, Europe, or anywhere else. . . . Erudite, he had no Orientalist historical-cultural ghosts to fight while addressing India, and he richly gave to and received from India" (Khare, "Changing India," 45). For a contrasting opinion, see Vasant G. Gadre's article "Vislumbres de la India: Viciadas por el prisma del pensamiento occidental de Octavio Paz," who argues that Paz imposes a Western view of Indian history and culture that ignores the country's ancient and continuing cultural and linguistic unity predating the British. Such disagreements regarding Paz's historical and cultural comments in *Vislumbres* confirm my idea that we should look in his sensibility rather than his cultural criticism for the most meaningful aspects of his encounter with India.

89. *Vislumbres*, 106; *In Light*, 90.
90. Ibid., 154; ibid, 130.
91. I owe this intriguing formulation of a possible attitude to Monika Kaup. And the initial suggestion that Paz goes in an opposing direction to Dave Faris.
92. *Vislumbres*, 100; *In Light*, 86.
93. *In Light*, 143.
94. *Vislumbres*, 94; *In Light*, 81.
95. Ibid., 94–95; ibid, 81.
96. Ganguly agrees that Paz's general openness to others—"his universal artistic vision and his sensitivity toward others that pushes him toward a planetary cosmovision"—guides his approach to Indian culture, but that this is not specific to his Indian sojourn (Ganguly, "La recepción India," 221). Likewise, Gladys Ilarregui considers Paz's poetic encounter with India to travel a non-orientalist and yet universal poetic "road outside of his window in Delhi (outside the Western window, as Said wanted) on the other side from the 'soft drink,' in full contact with his 'desgarramientos' as a Mexican and a poet" (Ilarregui,*El mono gramático*, 198). *El mono gramático* is such a journey that in its genuine encounter of another culture encodes the lingusitic and philosophic uncertainty such a journey necessarily entails: "the linguistic route can only be uncertain when it's a question of trying to relate to another culture, leaving behind Western practices of time and language" (Ibid., 190).

WORKS CITED

Cantú, Roberto. "Octavio Paz and India: *Blanco,* Modernity, and the Poetics of Simultaneism." In *One World Periphery Reads the Other: Knowing the 'Oriental' in the Americas and the Iberian Peninsula*, 56–81. Newcastle: Cambridge Scholars, 2010.

Costa-Gramunt, Teresa. "El jardín del poeta." In Dhingra, *Octavio Paz and India*, 21–24. New Delhi: Centre of Spanish Studies, Jawaharlal Nehru University and Embassy of Mexico, 1999.

Cross, Elsa. "Sobre *Vislumbres de la India* de Octavio Paz." In Dhingra, *Octavio Paz and India*, 39–44.

Dhingra, Anil, ed. *Octavio Paz and India: Some Reflections.* New Delhi: Centre of Spanish Studies, Jawaharlal Nehru University and Embassy of Mexico, New Delhi, 1999.

———. "La India en la obra de Octavio Paz: Algunas reflexiones." In Lerner, Nival, and Alonso, *Actas del XIV Congreso*, 161–168.

Eliot, T. S. *Collected Poems: 1909–1962.* New York: Harcourt Brace and World, 1970.

Gadre, Vasant G. "Vislumbres de la India: Viciadas por el prisma del pensamiento occidental de Octavio Paz." In Lerner, Nival, and Alonso, *Actas del XIV Congreso*, 205–212. Newark, DE: Juan de la Cuesta, 2004.

Ganguly, Shyama. "La recepción India y la otredad en la poesía de Octavio Paz." In Lerner, Nival, and Alonso, *Actas del XIV Congreso*, 221–225. Newark, DE: Juan de la Cuesta, 2004.

Hernández, Eunice. "Octavio Paz: La India como un palimpsesto." *Revista de la Universidad Nacional Autónoma de* México, no. 90 (August 1, 2011): 83–88.

Ilarregui, Gladys. "*El mono gramático*: Orientalismo y poética de Octavio Paz." In *Moros en la costa: Orientalismo en Latinoamérica*, edited by Silvia Nagy-Zekmi, 187–99. Madrid and Frankfurt: Iberoamericana/Vervuert, 2008.

"India's Ancient Epics and Tales." In *The Norton Anthology of World Literature*, edited by Martin Puchner et al., vol. A, 1113–21. 4th ed. New York: Norton, 2018.

Khare, R. S. "Changing India-West Cultural Dialectics." *New Literary History* 40, no. 2 (Spring 2009): 223–245.

Lerner, Isaías, Robert Nival, and Alejandro Alonso, eds. *Actas del XIV Congreso de la Asociación Internacional de Hispanistas: New York, 16–21 de Julio de 2001.* Newark, DE: Juan de la Cuesta, 2004.

Moliner, María. *Diccionario de uso del español.* Madrid: Gredos. 1966.

Ory, José Antonio. "Octavio Paz y la India." *Cuadernos Hispanoamericanos* 581 (November 1998): 33–38.

Paz, Octavio. *La centena (Poemas: 1935–1968).* Barcelona: Seix Barral, 1969.

———. *El mono gramático.* Barcelona: Seix Barral, 1974.

———. *La llama doble: Amor y erotismo.* 1993. Mexico City: Seix Barral, 2014.

———. *Selected Poems.* Edited by Eliot Weinberger. New York: New Directions, 1984.

———. *The Monkey Grammarian.* Translated by Helen Lane. New York: Arcade Publishing, Little, Brown, 1990.

———. *In Light of India.* Translated by Eliot Weinberger. New York: Harcourt, Brace & Company, 1997.

———. *Ladera este seguido de Hacia el comienzo y Blanco.* 1969. Barcelona: Círculo de Lectores, 1996.

———. *The Collected Poems of Octavio Paz: 1957–1987.* Edited by Eliot Weinberger. New York: New Directions, 1987.

———. *The Double Flame: Love and Eroticism.* Translated by Helen Lane. New York: Harcourt Brace & Company, 1996.

———. *Vislumbres de la India*. 1995. Mexico City: Seix Barral, 1996.
Pujol, Oscar. "El mono gramático y el sabio alquimista: Algunas reflexiones en torno a la poética de Octavio Paz en *El mono gramático*." In Dhingra, *Octavio Paz and India*, 10–20.
Srinath, C. N. "Octavio Paz: A Note." *The Literary Criterion* 41, nos. 3–4 (Jan 2006): 20–27.

Chapter 10

Alchemist of the Tropics

Alexander von Humboldt and Gabriel García Márquez's Cien años de soledad

Ralph Bauer

In his final days the enigmatic character Melchíades in the late Gabriel García Márquez's *Cien años de soledad* withdraws into the seclusion of one of the bedrooms in the Buendía home, spending "horas y horas garabateando su literatura enigmática en los pergaminos que llevó consigo" (hours on end scribbling his enigmatic literature on the parchments that he had brought with him) and talking to himself in inscrutable monologues. The only thing that could be made out was an "insistente martilleo de la palabra equinoccio equinoccio equinoccio, y el nombre de Alexander von Humboldt" (insistent hammering on the word *equinox, equinox, equinox*, and the name of Alexander von Humboldt).[1] Although this is the only time that Humboldt is mentioned by name, the famous Prussian traveler and naturalist seems to have a pervasive if occult presence in the novel through his association with the ancient (and ageless) Melchíades. Indeed, as John Ochoa has observed, the reader has a sense that "Humboldt was there when memory began" in Macondo.[2] Yet, few literary critics seem to have attempted a sustained inquiry into the relationship between Humboldt and Melchíades in *Cien años de soledad*.[3] This is somewhat surprising, given not only the noted meta-historical interests of García Márquez's epochal novel but also Humboldt's importance for Latin America's modern cultural identity and literary history.[4] Indeed, there is a long tradition of writers who have hailed Humboldt as the "second discoverer" of America, a veritable "second Columbus." Simón Bolívar even allegedly once declared that Humboldt was "The *real* discoverer of South America . . . for captivating the world with his depictions of the region's aesthetic and scientific wonders."[5] In García Márquez novel, however, his association with the character of Melchíades seems to suggest a more critical view of

Humboldt's legacy in Latin America; for, as the reader learns on the last page of the novel, it was Melchíades—Mephistophelan alchemist, chronicler, and prophet of scientific progress—who had condemned Macondo to 100 years of solitude and its apocalyptic end in his enigmatic manuscript, which, written in the ancient Indo-European language of Sanskrit, is finally translated by the last of the Buendías in the moments before his own demise.[6] Thus, in the manuscript, it was foretold

> que la ciudad de los espejos (o los espejismos) sería arrasada por el viento y desterrada de la memoria de los hombres en el instante en que Aureliano Babilonia acabara de descifrar los pergaminos, y que todo lo escrito en ellos era irrepetible desde siempre y para siempre porque las estirpes condenadas a cien años de soledad no tenían una segunda oportunidad sobre la tierra. (172)

> (that the city of mirrors (or mirages) would be wiped out by the wind and exiled from the memory of men at the precise moment when Aureliano Babilonia would finally finish deciphering the parchments, and that everything written on them was unrepeatable since time immemorial and forever more, because races condemned to a hundred years of solitude did not have a second opportunity on earth, 422).

If, in his Nobel Prize address, "The Solitude of Latin America," García Márquez later reiterated this dramatic ending with a twist—calling for a "utopia of life" in Latin American writing, "where the races condemned to one hundred years of solitude will have, at last and forever, a second opportunity on earth"—he underscores the novel's metafictional indictment of a Melchíadean utopia of death, which had entrapped Latin Americans within a "city of mirrors" for a 100 years. Moreover, García Márquez suggests that Melchíades's manuscript was but one version of a much older European master script written about Latin America, a master script that is at least as old as Antonio Pigafetta's account of Magellan's first circumnavigation during the sixteenth century. In presenting "a strictly accurate account that nonetheless resembles a venture into fantasy," says García Márquez, Pigafetta's narrative "already contained the seeds of our present-day novels." In his narrative, Pigafetta had related how, during their stayover in Patagonia, Magellan's men encountered a "giant" who, when confronted with a mirror given to him by the Europeans, "lost his senses to the terror of his own image."[7] The metafiction of *Cien años de soledad* can thus be seen as a reflection on Latin America's traumatic experience with a culture of modernity that has continuously forced Latin Americans to look at themselves through the eyes of European technologies of representation. The novel's "magic realism" that has sometimes been hailed by modern literary critics as an autochthonous literary expression of a distinctly Latin American "magical" ontology turns out to be a tragicomic parody of an age-old European discourse that has been "inventing" Latin America since the fifteenth century.[8] And by being singled out in their association with Melchíades's manuscript—" equinoccio equinoccio equinoccio"—Humboldt's scientific travel writings about the "equinoctial regions of the New World" (as his *Personal Narrative* was subtitled) seem to play a special role in the long literary history of this linguistic city of mirrors in which the modern Latin American novelist writing in a European language must inevitably participate.

In this essay, I take García Márquez's metafictional critique of Melchíades's master script as a starting point for exploring the novel's intertextual dialogue with Alexander von Humboldt's travel writings about the South American tropics.[9] I will argue that, although Humboldt's presence is largely hidden from the surface of the novel's plot, this intertextual dialogue is a central feature of *Cien años de soledad* and Humboldt's scientific rhetoric of (re-)discovery a major subject of its meta-historical critique. Thus, Humboldt's travel writings about the American tropics are an important source of inspiration not only for the novel's central motif of Latin America's "solitude" but also for several of its ancillary themes, such as the tropical entanglement of nature and culture in Macondo as well as its historical amnesia. But a re-reading of Humboldt as a Melchíaden "alchemist of the tropics" has an important bearing not only for our understanding of the historical sources of García Márquez's meta-historical novel but also for the recent critical debate about the role that Humboldt's legacy played in the history of Neocolonialism in Latin America.[10] Specifically, García Márquez's metafictional engagement with Humboldt through the character of Melchíades the alchemist forces us to see the significance of Humboldt's nineteenth-century writings in the context of the longue durée of a European discourse of discovery that reaches back to the sixteenth century—and even beyond to the late Middle Ages, when alchemy first entered the Latin West through transmission from the Arabic. In other words, by his association with the character of Melchíades the alchemist, Humboldt is placed in a long line of European conquerors, travelers, and natural philosophers who participated in the ideological project that the Mexican philosopher of history Edmundo O'Gorman once called "the history of the idea that America was discovered" by Europeans.[11] Moreover, by interrogating how (Latin) America was invented as an object (rather than a subject) of European science, the novel sheds light on how the European conquest of America *legitimated* the modern scientific idea of discovery itself. In the terms of Bruno Latour, we might say that *Cien años de soledad* engages with Humboldt's voluminous travel writings about South America as a central text in the construction of science's "Modern Constitution,"[12] which casts the European naturalist at the "center of calculation" where he separates nature from culture as well as American objects from European subjects of scientific discovery. South America, by contrast, emerges from Humboldt's travel writings as a sort of "crucible of the tropics"—a geographic analogue to the medieval alchemist's alembic, Robert Boyle's early modern air pump, or the modern scientific laboratory—where the secrets of (South American) nature are revealed to the (northern European) "philosophical traveler'" equipped with instrumentation but never to the South American Native him- or herself.[13] In a permanent state of arrested development (or "solitude"), Humboldt's tropical America becomes the foil against which the modern Western narrative of scientific progress unfolds. If this progressivist narrative had been underwritten by the language of Christian alchemical apocalypticism since the fifteenth century, Humboldt's crucial intervention lies in the secularization of its millenarian telos as the transcendent aesthetic experience captured by the German Romantic concept of *Ruhe* (solitude, rest, peace, calm).

ALEXANDER VON HUMBOLDT AND THE CRUCIBLE OF THE TROPICS

Alexander von Humboldt (1769–1859) arrived in the Americas during the final years of the Spanish Empire, not long before Spain's own invasion by Napoleon's forces in 1808. He had originally hoped to join Napoleon's expedition to Egypt, but after those plans were thwarted, traveled instead to Madrid, where he received a warm welcome at the Bourbon court—and, remarkably, a passport to travel to South America in order to conduct scientific observations and measurements. Having served the Prussian state as an inspector of mines in the 1790s, the polymath from Berlin had witnessed, at the Second Congress of Rastatt in 1797, the beginning of the end of another empire that once included Spain—the 1,000-year-old Holy Roman Empire of the German Nation, whose territories were now being carved up by France, Prussia, and Austria. Thus, when Humboldt embarked for America on the *Pizarro* together with his scientific partner, the French botanist Aimé Bonpland, they left an Old World in tremendous political turmoil and transformation. They disembarked at Cumaná, Venezuela, on July 16, 1799, with hundreds of boxes containing scientific instruments and tools to commence their epic five-year-long journey crisscrossing Spanish America—through the Orinoco delta to Caracas; through the Caribbean to Colombia, Ecuador, and Peru; and finally to New Spain (Mexico).[14]

Upon his return to Paris five years later, in 1804, Humboldt launched what would become one of the most spectacularly prolific careers in the history of scientific authorship with the publication of his *Essai sur la géographie des plantes* (1807). The first fruit of his American travels, the *Essai* would be joined by his monumental *Le voyage aux régions equinoxiales du Nouveau Continent, fait en 1799–1804, par Alexandre de Humboldt et Aimé Bonpland,* which eventually came to comprise thirty volumes published in the course of forty years or so and which collectively presented an unparalleled study of American flora, fauna, and geology, lavishly illustrated and supplemented by learned treatises on pre-Columbian Mexica history, detailed statistical information about the political economy of Cuba and New Spain, as well as an intellectual history of the geographic discoveries of European explorers during the fifteenth and sixteenth centuries.

As a travel writer about the tropical regions of the world, Humboldt had been inspired by a number of eighteenth-century predecessors—Louis Antoine de Bourgainville, James Cook, Georg Foster, and Charles Marie La Condamine.[15] As a natural philosopher, he had prominent eighteenth-century models among the Enlightenment *philosophes*—Raynal, Diderot, Montesquieu, Buffon, de Pauw. But unlike most of these Enlightenment philosophes writing about the overseas world before him, Humboldt gave due credit also to the great sixteenth-century Spanish collectors and natural historians, who had gathered naturalist information from indigenous informants. Thus, he wrote that "when we indulge in the study of the earliest historians of the conquest of America—such as Acosta, Oviedo, and García—and we compare them with the examinations with more recent travelers, we are amazed that often the seed of the most important physical truths can already be found in the Spanish writers of the sixteenth century . . . questions that still occupy us today—about the unity of mankind and the diversification from a common origin."[16] Unlike his Spanish Renaissance predecessors, however, Humboldt was primarily interested not in information that could be garnered from Native knowledge about American nature, but rather in information that could be produced through scientific measurement with instruments built in Europe—information that would reveal the occult forces of nature and make manifest the underlying laws and principles connecting all surface phenomena. Before embarking from Spain for America, he explained the purpose of his journey in a letter to a friend in Berlin:

> I will collect flora and fauna; I will investigate the heat, elasticity, and magnetic and electrical charge of the atmosphere, and chemically analyze it; I will determine latitudes and longitudes, and measure mountains. But all this is not the aim of my voyage. My sole true object is to investigate the confluence and interweaving of all physical forces, and the influence of dead nature on the animate animal and plant creation. To this end, I have had to instruct myself in every empirical discipline. Thence the complaints of those who have no idea what I'm doing, that I'm pursuing too many things at once. We

have botanists, we have mineralogists, but no physicists, as [Bacon] called for in the *Sylva Sylvarum*.[17]

Perhaps the most well-known contribution that Humboldt's project in "physical geography" made to modern science lay in his invention of the isobar and the isotherm—lines on the map connecting points of the same atmospheric pressure or median surface temperature. It was this method of making manifest the occult principles of physical geography that came to represent Humboldtian science per se.[18] But the description of his empirical eclecticism as "chemical" analysis and his reference to Francis Bacon (1561–1626) are significant, for it was Bacon who had systematized a general methodology of the "empirical discipline[s]" embraced by Humboldt. In his *Sylva Sylvarum* (1626), in particular, Bacon had proposed a new method of natural history based on the general principles of scientific discovery that he had elaborated in his earlier *Novum Organum*, the second book of the *Instauratio Magna* (1620). There Bacon had distinguished three modes of scientific discovery: by observing the regular operations of nature; by observing its "errors" (such as deformed creatures); and by placing nature into "bonds," that is by transforming it through human art. Thus, Bacon's discoverer must "hound nature" and force it to reveal its secrets by subjecting it to the violence of human artifice, experiment, and instrumentation. For, "like as a man's disposition is never well known or proved til he be crossed, nor Proteus ever changed shapes till he was straitened and held fast; so nature exhibits herself more clearly under the *trials and vexations of art* than when left to herself."[19]

Like Bacon's, Humboldt's ideas about scientific curiosity and discovery had first been inspired by chemical experimentalism, especially by what Humboldt called the "vital chemistry" of such French chemists such as Antoine Lavoisier, Pierre Simon Laplace, and Claude Berthollet, whose forays into calormetry and eudiometry by way of elaborate scientific instruments such as the eudiometer, barometer, thermometer, and electrometer he had studied as a student of mining at the University of Freiburg and that he had himself applied in his program to reform the mining industry while serving the Prussian state as an inspector of mines in Ansbach-Bayreuth, Franconia.[20] Humboldt's patent curiosity about the power of artificial experiment in the discovery of the secrets of nature found its first literary expression with one of his earliest scientific tracts, the *Versuche über die Gereitzte Muskel- und Nervenfaser* (Experiments on Stimulated Muscle and Nerve Fibers). "For several years now," he wrote there,

> I have been engaged in the comparison of the phenomena of organic matter with the laws of inanimate nature. In the course of this work, I conducted successful experiments that led to the discovery of the chemical process of life. A severed animate organ, with irritable and sensible fibers, can be stimulated in

the course of a few seconds from a state of profound numbness to the highest level of sensitivity toward external stimuli, and vice versa be reduced to a state of numbness.[21]

In the course of his experiments in organic chemistry, he discovered that the stimulation of organic matter does not, as previously believed, depend merely on the amount of oxygen but also (and mainly) on mercury and hydrogen, or rather on "a combination of effects and the antagonism between multiple substances."[22] It was in the course of these experiments in organic chemistry, which he performed in various cities throughout Germany and Austria, that Humboldt also cultivated his characteristic habit of traveling with scientific instruments.

Humboldt's chemical experimentalism became the foundation of his later pursuits in natural history as a "terrestrial physics." As he wrote to a friend in 1797,

> in the three years of chemical experiments I discuss in this work, I have sought to demonstrate that the vital action is analogous to the processes of chemical composition and decomposition. I have discovered that irritability [Reizung] can be eliminated and restored in sensitive and irritable fibers 7 to 20 times in succession.... I now plan to devote myself entirely to chemistry, meteorology, and anatomy. I am trying to penetrate the secrets of organization and to bring the sciences together.[23]

Humboldt's notion of *Reizung* (irritation) facilitating the penetration of the secret operations that connect the whole of nature that are hidden from our natural eyes sheds light on his fascination with the American tropics. There, he believed, the secrets of nature are revealed to the philosophical traveler unlike in any other region on earth, due to the extraordinary power of the sun. "If [tropical] America does not occupy an important place in the history of mankind," he wrote in his *Personal Narrative*, "it does offer a wide field for the naturalist. Nowhere else does nature so vividly suggest general ideas on the cause of events, and their mutual interrelationships."[24] And in his later *Cosmos* he wrote that

> the regions of the torrid zone not only give rise to the most powerful impressions by their organic richness and their abundant fertility, but they likewise afford the inestimable advantage of revealing to man, by the uniformity of the variations of the atmosphere and the development of vital forces and by the contrasts of climate and vegetation exhibited at different elevations, the invariability of the laws that regulate the course of heavenly bodies, reflected as it were in terrestrial phenomena.[25]

Due to the exceptional power of the sun, the tropics, like the alchemical crucible, reveal the secrets of nature through *Reizung*—Humboldt's translation of Bacon's "vexation."

In broadest terms, we might say that Humboldt's Baconian curiosity about the New World's volcanoes, caves, isothermal patterns, and magnetic fields is the nineteenth-century manifestation of what Hans Blumenberg has called a "theoretical curiosity" about the occult, a curiosity that had been condemned by Christian theologians as "vain" (*vana curiositas*) throughout the Middle Ages and the history of which links Humboldtian science to Leonardo da Vinci's fifteenth-century *Virgin of the Rocks* on one end and, on the other, to the rise of nuclear physics a 100 years later.[26] But while this curiosity about the occult has often been seen as a distinctly "modern" phenomenon by Blumenberg and others, its history in fact extends beyond the Renaissance and the so-called Age of Discovery to the late Middle Ages, which saw the influx of Arabic-Aristotelian alchemy into the Latin West.[27] Although Bacon had condemned the alchemists for their obscurantist mysticism and their tendency to mix science with religion, his project in scientific reform was, as William Newman has shown, profoundly influenced by the alchemical tradition, especially regarding the alchemical belief in the power of human art to emulate, imitate, and manipulate nature.[28] Western alchemy had developed during the early centuries CE in Hellenistic Egypt and entered the Latin West via translations from the Arabic since the twelfth century. Based on the general principles of Aristotelian natural philosophy, alchemy was, in Christian medieval Europe, regarded not as an academic branch of its own within natural philosophy but rather as a sort of applied science and technical art that explored the practical uses of fire in a number of artisanal fields. Although the attempt to find an artificial way to effect "transmutation" of base metals into gold (chrysopoeia) was always a central aspect of alchemy, its practitioners were engaged in a broad range of experimental activities, including metallurgical essaying, the refining of salts, the manufacture of dye, pigment, glass, and ceramics, artificial gemstones, incendiary weapons, as well as the brewing and distilling of drugs. An artisanal practice whose trade secrets were strictly guarded, alchemy had, over the course of centuries, developed a distinctly esoteric textual tradition that was steeped in the figurative language of emblems, symbols, and allegories. Already in many of the Arabic source texts that were being translated into Latin from the twelfth century onward, this esoteric language of alchemy had also teemed with spiritual, prophetic, and apocalyptic mysticism, some of which had already originated in Islam (especially Ismailism); some in Hellenism (especially Hermeticism); and some in Christianity (especially Joachimism). Promising the recovery of esoteric and arcane knowledge, writers of alchemical literature such as the Catalonian physician and prophet Arnald of Villanova and the French Franciscan monk

John of Rupescissa synthesized science with religion, hereby offering a theological justification— a sort of "state of exception"[29]—for the scientific inquiry into the occult, prohibited by Christian (especially Augustinian) theology. While alchemy was long seen as distinctly premodern and prescientific, historians of science now generally appreciate the important continuities between alchemy and modern chemistry, hereby gradually retiring the notion of a radical rupture between the premodern and the modern. Indeed, one of the constants of alchemical literature was the implicit notion that human art was not weaker than nature but that it was, in fact, more powerful. It hereby played an important role during the late Middle Ages and the early modern period in what has been called the "Two Scientific Revolutions"—that of the thirteenth and that of the seventeenth century— which saw a gradual transformation of science from the Scholastic Aristotelian paradigm of syllogistic demonstration to the modern (Baconian) notion of the empirical finding of new facts and the "uncovering" of the occult forces of nature.[30] As we will see in the next section, the alchemical hermeneutics of discovery is an important theme still in *Cien años de soledad*.

ALCHEMY IN MACONDO

As literary criticism has shown, Gabriel García Márquez's engagement with the language and ideas derived from alchemy is pervasive in *Cien años de soledad*. And, beginning on the first page, it is associated with the enigmatic character of Melchíades.

> Un gitano corpulento, de barba montaraz y manos de gorrión, que se presentó con el nombre de Melquiades, hizo una truculenta demostración pública de lo que él mismo llamaba la octava maravilla de los sabios alquimistas de Macedonia. Fue de casa en casa arrastrando dos lingotes metálicos, y todo el mundo se espantó al ver que los calderos, las pailas, las tenazas y los anafes se caían de su sitio, y las maderas crujían por la desesperación de los clavos y los tornillos tratando de desenclavarse, y aun los objetos perdidos desde hacía mucho tiempo aparecían por donde más se les había buscado, y se arrastraban en desbandada turbulenta detrás de los fierros mágicos de Melquíades. (1)

> (A heavy gypsy with an untamed beard and sparrow hands, who introduced himself as Melchíades, put on a bold public demonstration of what he himself called the eighth wonder of the learned alchemists of Macedonia. He went from house to house dragging two metal ingots and everybody was amazed to see pots, pans, tongs, and braziers tumble down from their places and beams creak from the desperation of nails and screws trying to emerge, and even objects

that had been lost for a long time appeared from where they had been searched for most and went dragging along in turbulent confusion behind Melquíades' magical irons, 1–2).

Melchíades himself is described in language that is replete with alchemical motifs. Thus, his hands are birdlike ("manos de gorrión," [1]) and his hat, a "sombrero grande y negro, como las alas extendidas de un cuervo" (4) (large black hat that looked like a raven with widespread wings, 6), not only reminds the reader of the winged Hermes (god of alchemy and commerce) but also invokes the alchemical motif of the purification of the alchemist's soul and the first stage of the alchemical process, called the *negrido*, or *capus corvi*, and *separatio*.[31] Apparently in possession of the miraculous Philosopher's Stone, he has "alcanzado inmortalidad" (32) and the ability to cure diseases (such as the insomnia plague that strikes Macondo).

After his arrival in Macondo, Melchíades befriends José Arcadio Buendía, the village patriarch, and presents him with the gift of an alchemical laboratory.

> El rudimentario laboratorio—sin contar una profusión de cazuelas, embudos, retortas, filtros y coladores—estaba compuesto por un atanor primitivo; una probeta de cristal de cuello largo y angosto, imitación del huevo filosófico, y un destilador construido por los propios gitanos según las descripciones modernas del alambique de tres brazos de María la judía. Además de estas cosas, Melquíades dejó muestras de los siete metales correspondientes a los siete planetas, las fórmulas de Moisés y Zósimo para el doblado del oro, y una serie de apuntes y dibujos sobre los procesos del Gran Magisterio, que permitían a quien supiera interpretarlos intentar la fabricación de la piedra filosofal. Seducido por la simplicidad de las fórmulas para doblar el oro, José Arcadio Buendía cortejó a Úrsula durante varias semanas, para que le permitiera desenterrar sus monedas coloniales y aumentarlas tantas veces como era posible subdividir el azogile. (5)

> (The rudimentary laboratory—in addition to a profusion of pots, funnels, retorts, filters, and sieves—was made up of a primitive water pipe, a glass beaker with a long thin neck, a reproduction of a the philosopher's egg, and a still the gypsies themselves had built in accordance with modern descriptions of the three-armed alembic of Mary the Jew. Along with those items, Melquíades left samples of the seven metals that corresponded to the seven planets, the formulas of Moses and Zosimus for doubling the quantity of gold, and a set of notes and sketches concerning the processes of the Great Teaching that would permit those who could interpret them to undertake the manufacture of the philosopher's stone. Seduced by the simplicity of the formulas to double the quantity of gold, José Arcadio Buendía paid court to Úrsula for several weeks so that she would let

him dig up her colonial coins and increase them by as many times as it was possible to subdivide mercury; 7).

It is foretold that Melchíades's gift of the alchemical laboratory "había de ejercer una influencia terminante en el futuro de la aldea" (3) (was to have a profound influence on the future of the village; 5). And, indeed, the apocalyptic end of the town will come to pass in the laboratory when Aureliano Buendía-Babilonia deciphers Melchíades's manuscript there a 100 years later.[32] Along the way, there are many more references to alchemical prophecy that lead up to this apocalyptic climax. Thus, shortly before Macondo's end, a mysterious Catalonian book seller appears who scribbles in notebooks that are reminiscent of Melchíades's manuscript and who is intimately familiar with the personal secrets of the "nigromante" (necromancer) Arnald of Villanova, but who soon returns to his native Mediterranean village, "derrotado por la nostalgia de una primavera tenaz" (165) (overcome by a yearning for a lasting springtime; 405). More immediately, José Arcadio Buendía eagerly buys from Melchíades and his gypsies all the scientific gadgets and secrets they offer for sale, including a magnet and a magnifying glass. With the magnet, José Arcadio Buendía hopes to become rich by extracting gold from the ground, promising his wife Úrusla that "Muy pronto ha de sobrarnos oro para empedrar la casa" (3) ("Very soon we'll have gold enough and more to pave the floors of the house"; 2). And with the secret formulas of Zosimo he hopes to double the family's wealth in gold. Apparently, José Arcadio Buendía had already harbored a fascination with gold even before Melchíades's arrival in Macondo. Thus, he had named one of his sons "Aureliano" (from Latin *aureo*, "gold"), who is said to have been born with open eyes, hereby resembling a fish. A common symbol for Christ, the fish represents in alchemical symbolism the Philosopher's Stone,[33] and it also signifies the alertness and concentration needed to complete the alchemical opus.[34] Indeed, Aureliano "había revelado desde el primer momento una rara intuición alquímica" (12) (from the first had revealed a strange intuition for alchemy; 25). After his return from fighting in the civil war, "Colonel" Aureliano Buendía continues his metallurgical pursuits by crafting little golden fish.

In a foundational study of the language of alchemy in *Cien años de soledad*, Chester Halka has argued (informed by Jungian psychoanalytic interpretation of alchemy) that there are two alchemical traditions in Macondo—the material quests of the "Arcadio" line (José Acradio Buendía, Aureliano Segundo (mistakenly so named for his twin brother), and José Arcadio 3rd) and the non-material or spiritual quests of the "Aureliano" line (Colonel Aureliano Buendía, José Arcadio Segundo, and Aureliano Buendía-Babilonia). Whereas the former line is preoccupied primarily with the *practice* of alchemy, the latter seems to be interested primarily in the spiritual and literary aspects of the ancient art, being drawn less to Melchíades's scientific gadgets and more to his enigmatic manuscript. Whereas the former line (of material transmutators) is perpetually condemned to failure, Halka argues that the latter holds out the promise of transformation through "magic realist" narration.[35] But while this division of alchemy into a materialist and a spiritual quest in *Cien años de soledad* is generally persuasive, it loses sight of the crucial and fundamental fact that, in the world of the novel, alchemy has a destructive effect on both materialist and spiritualist seekers, inhibiting the development of all of its men into emotionally mature human beings. As Brian Conniff has pointed out, all science in the novel ultimately exploits the inhabitants of Macondo;[36] and alchemy, specifically, is associated with the male characters' tendency toward madness and their incapacity for human love. Thus, José Arcadio Buendía's harebrained scientific pursuits include the use of his new magnifying glass for the purpose of solar warfare; his attempt to multiply alchemically the precious doubloons that his wife had inherited from her father end (to her dismay) in "un chicharrón carbonizado que no pudo ser desprendido del fondo del caldero" (5) (a large piece of burnt hog cracklings that was firmly stuck to the bottom of the pot; 8); and José Arcadio Buendía gradually withdraws into the seclusion of his alchemical laboratory, neglecting his domestic affairs and eventually becoming entirely insane to the point where he has to be tied to a tree.

And even the alchemical quests of the line of spiritual seekers, such as Colonel Aureliano Buendía, trap them in a cycle of repetition and stasis that ultimately spells their death. Thus, while Colonel Aureliano Buendías was born, fishlike, with his eyes open, the last of his line of spiritual seekers, José Arcadio Segundo, dies the same way (146). Indeed, as Shannin Schroeder has pointed out, Aureliano ultimately realizes "none of the benefits of alchemy" and his name is, in the context of alchemy, "ironic rather than prophetic."[37] Also, Kathleen McNerney and John Martin have argued that the "Buendías experience the solitude of alchemy without achieving its goals; rather than escaping from the tyranny of time, they become its victims, locked in its inexorable repetitive process, until the deciphering of the parchment brings the family chronicle to an end."[38] The alchemical madness of all of Macondo's men seems to be a disease that already afflicted their ancestors among the European discoverers and conquerors who came to America during the fifteenth and sixteenth centuries. It is the men's "herencia fabolosa" (151) of the conquest of America—the mythic quests for El Dorado, the Seven Cities of Cíbola, and the Fountain of Youth.[39] Thus, one of the things that José Arcadio Buendía is able to discover with his new magnet is

> una armadura del siglo xv con todas sus partes soldadas por un cascote de óxido, cuyo interior tenía la resonancia hueca de un enorme calabazo lleno de

piedras. Cuando José Arcadio Buendía y los cuatro hombres de su expedición lograron desarticular la armadura, encontraron dentro un esqueleto calcificado que llevaba colgado en el cuello un relicario de cobre con un rizo de mujer. (1)

(a suit of fifteenth-century armor which had all of its pieces soldered together with rust and inside of which there was the hollow resonance of an enormous stone filled gourd. When José Arcadio Buendía and the four men of his expedition managed to take the armor apart, they found inside a calcified skeleton with a copper locket containing a woman's hair around its neck; 2).

There is, then, a pervasive sense in *Cien años de soledad* that the men's alchemical quests are a form of delusion, a false consciousness that leads to their death and to Macondo's destruction—a point driven home dramatically in the last moments of the plot, when Melchíades's enigmatic manuscript is finally deciphered by Aureliano Babilonia, the last of the Buendías. At the moment in which he is initiated among the adept of the secrets of alchemy, he learns that he and all the Buendías have been but characters in the plot of Melchíades's prophecy—a plot which had made the Old World alchemist immortal but condemned the Buendías to 100 years of solitude and, ultimately, death. Moreover, in associating the madness of the Buendías with the skeleton of the Spanish conquistador—found with a locket containing the hair of the female lover he left behind in Europe—the novel interrogates the historical connections between alchemy, modern scientific pursuits, and the conquest of America. The violent legacy of the conquest still seems to haunt Macondo's community in form of the ghost of Prudencio Aguilar, whose throat was pierced by José Arcadio's spear after he had insulted his manhood. It is in light of the disastrous consequences of alchemy for Macondo that we must take a second look now at the novel's intertextual dialogue with Humboldt's writings about his famous journey to "The Equinoctial Regions of the New Continent." By associating Humboldtian "modern" science of the tropics with Melchíaden premodern alchemy, *Cien años de soledad* not only subverts the "rupture narrative" on which the legitimacy of modern science is predicated but also calls attention to the colonialist dimension of its formation during the sixteenth and seventeenth centuries.[40]

ENTANGLED MODERNITIES

Bruno Latour has provided a useful theoretical framework for thinking about García Márquez's critique of the Humboldtian hermeneutics of discovery. Modernity, Latour argues, can be seen as a sort of "Constitution" that depends on the interplay between two processes that he calls "purification" and "hybridization." While Purification separates nature from culture (mute things from speaking citizens, objects from subjects), Hybridization re-mixes them in cunning ways; that is, it redeploys "nature" in the realm of culture and "culture" in the realm of nature.[41] Moreover, Latour has alerted us to the *colonial nexus* from which this Modern Constitution emerged. He calls it the "External Great Divide"—the divide between the moderns ("Us"), who distinguish between nature and culture, and those premoderns ("Them") who do not: Medieval and non-Western people.

> We are the only ones who differentiate absolutely between Nature and Culture, between Science and Society, whereas in our eyes all the others—whether they are Chinese or Amerindian, Azande or Barouya—cannot really separate what is knowledge from what is Society, what is sign from what is thing, what comes from Nature as it is from what their cultures require. Whatever they do, however adapted, regulated and functional they may be, they will always remain blinded by this confusion; they are prisoners of the social and of language alike. Whatever we do, however criminal, however imperialistic we may be, we escape from the prison of the social or of language to gain access to things themselves through a providential exit gate, that of scientific knowledge.[42]

The colonial genealogy of Latour's Modern Constitution is manifest in the omnipresent references to America (Europe's "New World") in the iconography of the "New" (empirical and experimental) sciences of the seventeenth century. Thus, the seventeenth-century alchemist Noah Biggs, Fellow in the Royal Society of London, described his investigations into the structure of matter as an inquiry into the "America of nature."[43] Perhaps the visually most poignant image capturing the modern quest for Purification is the frontispiece of Bacon's *Instauratio Magna* (1620), which is patently lifted (as critics have noted) from Andrés García de Céspedes's earlier *Regimiento de navegación* (Madrid, 1606) (see figures 10.1 and 10.2):[44]

A sixteenth-century Spanish galleon passing through the Pillars of Hercules into the pure realm of nature in the New World, leaving behind all tradition, society, politics, and culture in the Old. But there is perhaps not a more memorable image exposing the Hybridization proliferated by the modern project of Purification than that of the sixteenth-century Spanish galleon found 300 years later in the South American jungle by the nineteenth-century Spanish American patriarch, José Arcadio Buendía, on his mad quest to find an opening to the Pacific Ocean.

> Siempre pendiente de la brújula siguió guiando a sus hombres hacia el norte invisible, hasta que lograron salir de la región encantada. Era una noche densa, sin estrellas, pero la oscuridad estaba impregnada por un aire nuevo y limpio.

Figure 10.1   Francis Bacon, frontispiece, *Instauratio Magna* (1620). *Source*: Courtesy of the Library of Congress.

Agotados por la prolongada travesía, colgaron las hamacas y durmieron a fondo por primera vez en dos semanas. Cuando despertaron, ya con el sol alto, se quedaron pasmados de fascinación. Frente a ellos, rodeado de helechos y palmeras, blanco y polvoriento en la silenciosa luz de la mañana, estaba un enorme galeón español. Ligeramente volteado a estribor, de su arboladura intacta colgaban las piltrafas escuálidas del velamen, entre jarcias adornadas de orquídeas. El casco, cubierto con una tersa coraza de rémora petrificada y musgo tierno, estaba firmemente enclavado en un suelo de piedras. Toda la estructura parecía ocupar un ámbito propio, un espacio de soledad y de olvido, vedado a los vicios del tiempo y a las costumbres de los pájaros. En el interior, que los expedicionarios exploraron con un fervor sigiloso, no había nada más que un apretado bosque de flores. El hallazgo del galeón, indicio de la proximidad del mar, quebrantó

Figure 10.2 Andrés García de Céspedes, Regimiento de navegación (Madrid, 1606).
Source: Courtesy of the John Carter Brown Library at Brown University.

el ímpetu de José Arcadio Buendía. Consideraba como una burla de su travieso destino haber buscado el mar sin en-contrarlo, al precio de sacrificios y penalidades sin cuento, y haberlo encontrado entonces sin buscarlo, atravesado en su camino como un obstáculo insalvable. (7)

(Always, following a compass, he kept on guiding his men toward the invisible north so that they would be able to get out of that enchanted region. It was a thick night, starless, but the darkness was becoming impregnated with a fresh and clear air. Exhausted by the long crossing they hung up their hammocks and slept deeply for the first time in two weeks. When they woke up, with the sun already high in the sky, they were speechless with fascination. Before them, surrounded by ferns and palm trees, white and powdery in the silent morning light, was an enormous Spanish galleon. Tilted slightly to the starboard, it had hanging from its intact masts the dirty rags of its sails in the midst of its rigging, which was adorned with orchids. The hull, covered with an armor of petrified barnacles and soft moss, was firmly fastened into a surface of stones. The whole structure seemed to occupy its own space, one of solitude and oblivion, protected from the vices of time and the habits of the birds. Inside, where the expeditionaries explored with careful intent, there was nothing but a thick forest of flowers. The discovery of the galleon, an indication of the proximity of the sea, broke José Arcadio Buendía's drive. He considered it a trick of whimsical fate to have searched for the sea without finding it, at the cost of countless sacrifices and suffering, and to have found it all of a sudden without looking for it, as it lay across his path like an insurmountable object; 12).

Whereas Bacon's ideas of scientific discovery and progress in the *Instauratio Magna* find their paradigm in the conquest of (American) nature by (European) culture (or "art"), in Macondo culture is swallowed up by nature, to the effect of inhibiting scientific progress. Having grown convinced that the site he chose for his New World settlement of Macondo is actually a peninsula, surrounded by water but without any orientation for where to turn next, Buendía falls into a deep despair: "Aquí nos hemos de pudrir en vida," he says to his wife, "sin recibir los beneficios de la ciencia" (7) ("We're going to rot our lives away here without receiving the benefits of science"; 13).

García Márquez's novel thus challenges us to contemplate the notion that the history of Latour's Great Modern Divides (culture/nature, moderns/premoderns, European subjects/non-European objects) began not with Robert Boyle's airpump during the so-called Scientific Revolution in seventeenth-century England (as Latour suggested) but rather with the Spanish conquest of America during the sixteenth century. Indeed, just as Bacon's famous allegory of the advancement of the "New Sciences" originates in the sixteenth-century Spanish conquest of America, so does García Márquez's trope of the entanglement of nature and culture in the American tropics. It appears there first in the English translation of Peter Martyr's *Decades*, originally written in Latin, by the English alchemist Richard Eden, who had published it as one of the earliest books about America to appear in the English language. It is also one of the earliest texts published in English to use the sixteenth-century neologism "to entangle" (from "tangle," a species of seaweed).[45] "The currents of the sea there [in America] clash so violently," Eden wrote, that the Spanish ships become "entangled with whirlepooles."[46] And the quicksands are so powerful there that they are called "vypers" by the Spaniards with good reason: "in them many shyppes are entangled, as the lycertes are implicate in the tayles of the vipers."[47] Whereas cunning Odysseus of old could choose between Scylla and Charybdis, becoming entangled in tropical America means being swallowed whole. But in the tropics, nature not only entangles European means of transportation and progress but also confuses the European order of things. Thus, fish—which are supposed to live in water—still fly in the air, and the sea is "euery where entangeled with Ilandes: by reason whereof, the keeles of the shippes often tymes rased the sandes for shalownes of the water."⁴⁸ In tropical America, it seems, nature was still in a primordial state of Chaos, when the four elements comprising nature were not yet fully separate. In Richard Eden's translation, then, to "entangle" means to mingle and confuse that which should be separate, according to the European order of things—the four elements, nature and culture, subjects and objects, time and space.

While the theme of the entanglement of nature and culture in the American tropics thus originates in the earliest European accounts about the New World during the sixteenth century, García Márquez's most immediate interlocutor in the inspiration of this passage was probably Humboldt. In his *Personal Narrative,* the Prussian naturalist had written that

> On the 1st of July we came across the wreck of a sunken ship. We could distinguish its mast covered in floating seaweed. In a zone where the sea is perpetually calm the boat could not have sunk. Perhaps its remains came from the northerly stormy area and were dragged there by the extraordinary whirling of the Atlantic Ocean in the Southern hemisphere.⁴⁹

After his arrival at Cumaná and during his first foray into the South American jungle, the Humboldtian philosophical traveler marvels at the "great seal" of tropical of nature but finds himself confused by its entangled profusion. Overawed, he does not know

> what shocks him more: whether the *calm silence of the solitude*, or the beauty of the diverse, contrasting objects, or that fullness and freshness of plant life in the Tropics. It could be said that the earth, overloaded with plants, does not have sufficient space to develop. Everywhere tree trunks are hidden behind a thick green carpet. If you carefully transplanted all the orchids, all the epiphytes that grow on one single American fig tree (Ficus gigantea) you would manage to cover an enormous amount of ground. The same lianas that trail along the ground climb up to the tree-tops, swinging from one tree to another 100 feet up in the air. As these parasitical plants form a real tangle, a botanist often confuses flowers, fruit and leaves belonging to different species.⁵⁰

A trope that pervades his naturalistic descriptions throughout, the entanglement of nature and culture conspires to effect the "solitude" of life in the tropics and their permanent state of cultural arrested development. Whereas in temperate Europe, historical change proceeded at a revolutionary pace, in tropical America history is static. Even very populous provinces appear almost deserted; because man, to find nourishment, cultivates but a small number of acres. These circumstances modify the physical appearance of the country and the character of its inhabitants, giving to both a peculiar physiognomy; the wild and uncultivated stamp which belongs to nature, ere its primitive type has been altered by art. Without neighbors, almost unconnected with the rest of mankind, each family of settlers forms a separate tribe. This insulated state arrests or retards the progress of civilization, which advances only in proportion as society becomes numerous, and its connections more intimate and multiplied. But, on the other hand, it is solitude that develops and strengthens in man the sentiment of liberty and independence; and gives birth to that noble pride of character which has at all times distinguished the Castilian race.[51]

One of the consequences of tropical man's solitude is his inability to preserve historical memory. Thus, in several passage that may well have inspired the outrageous episode of the insomnia plague in *Cien años de soledad*, Humbodt writes that in the tropics,

> everything in nature appears new and marvelous. In the open plains and amid the gloom of forests, almost all the remembrances of Europe are effaced; for it is vegetation that determines the character of a landscape, and acts upon the imagination by its mass, the contrast of its forms, and the glow of its colors. In proportion as impressions are powerful and new, they weaken antecedent impressions, and their force imparts to them the character of duration.[52]

The "absence of memory" seems to characterize not only the people of tropical America but of the New World at large, including even "these new people in the United States of America" as well as "the Spanish and Portuguese possessions." It is "not only distressing to the traveler, who becomes deprived of the pleasures of the imagination, but it also influences the bonds that tie a settler to the land he inhabits, the form of the rocks around his hut, the trees shading his cradle." Thus, in America,

> The settler vainly tries to name the mountains, rivers and valleys with names that recall his motherland; these names soon lose their charm, and mean nothing to later generations. Under the influence of an exotic nature new habits are born for new needs, national memories are slowly effaced, and those remembered, like ghost of our imaginations, are not attached to any time or place.[53]

While the "wild aspect" of nature has been destroyed in temperate climates by the cultivation of grain (graminées), man in the tropics has "less extended his empire" (*a moins éxtendu son empire*) and "may be said to appear, not as an absolute master, who changes at will the surface of the soil, but as a transient guest, who quietly enjoys the gifts of nature" (*bienfaits de la nature*).[54] Thus, whereas the Enlightenment philosophes Raynal, Buffon, and DePaw had subscribed to a New World exceptionalism that apprehended the biological and cultural differences of the entire Western hemisphere in terms of a "degeneration" of the biological and cultural forms of the Old World,[55] Humboldt re-shapes this economy of difference in two ways that are distinctive of his hermeneutics of (re-) discovery: First, he emphasizes latitude (as well as elevation) over longitude in explaining the climatological and environmental characteristics (the "character of the landscape") that explain the forms of human culture; in effect, he replaces a New World exceptionalism with a *tropical exceptionalism* the history of which reaches back to the late medieval cosmology of the famed alchemist Albertus Magnus and that still inspired Christopher Columbus.[56] Second, he apprehends cultural difference not in terms of a degeneration but rather in terms of progress (or rather, a lack thereof), hereby betraying the influence of the Romantic idea that man's original state of nature was the savage, not the pastoral state. Unlike Rousseau, however, he does not see this savage state as being noble in the least. Contemplating the custom among some Guyanan tribes to kill their children when they are born with deformities or as twins, he writes that "Such is the candor and simplicity of manners, such the boasted happiness of man in the *state of nature* [*état de nature*]! He kills his son, to escape the ridicule of having twins, or to avoid journeying more slowly; in fact to avoid a little inconvenience."[57]

While the cosmological crucible of the tropics thus offers superior opportunities for the discovery of natural secrets, it is incapable of producing culture for the same reason. With the development of culture being entangled by nature in the tropics, scientific progress is restricted to man living in the temperate zone, according to Humboldt's alchemical cosmology. Thus, in his *Cosmos* he later wrote that

> Notwithstanding the obstacles opposed in northern latitudes to the discovery of the laws of nature, owing to the excessive complication of phenomena, and the perpetual local variations and the distribution of organic forms, it is to the inhabitants of a small section of the temperate zone that the rest of mankind owe the earliest revelation of an intimate and rational acquaintance with the forces governing the physical world. Moreover, it is from the same zone (which is apparently more favorable to the progress of reason, the softening of manners, and the security of public liberty) that the germs of civilization have been carried to the regions of the tropics, as much by the migratory movement of races as by the establishment of colonies, differing widely in their institutions from those of the Phoenicians or Greeks.[58]

The Torrid Zone becomes in his writings the object of scientific discovery that reveals the secrets of nature to temperate man but not to tropical man himself, as such discovery requires the aid of human art and instrumentation the development of which are retarded by the tropical entanglement. In elaborating this Eurocentric cosmology of science, Humboldt stood in a long tradition of travel writers and natural historians who legitimated a modern hermeneutics of discovery in the idea that America was a "New World" that had been discovered by Europeans—a world "tan reciente, que muchas cosas carecían de nombre, y para mencionarlas había que señalarías con el dedo" (1) (so recent that many things lacked names, and in order to indicate them it was necessary to point; 1). But whereas Columbus or Bacon had legitimated this modern idea of discovery as a providential fulfillment of ancient apocalyptic prophecies of the impending millennium (scripturally, a time of rest and "the refreshment of the saints"),[59] Humboldt's scientific re-discovery of tropical America ends not in an eschatological apocalypse but rather in a revelation of another kind—the revelatory and transcendental aesthetic experience of the "calm" (Ruhe) of nature. Thus, in his *Cosmos,* he wrote that

> the knowledge of the laws of nature, whether we can trace them in the alternate ebb and flow of the ocean, in the measured path of comets, or in the mutual attractions of multiple stars, alike increase our sense of the calm [*Ruhe*] of nature, while the chimera so long cherished by the human mind in its early and intuitive contemplations, the belief in a "discord of the elements," seems gradually to vanish in proportion as science extends her empire.

It is this transcendent aesthetic experience of *Ruhe* (following *Reizung*) that legitimates the modern "scientific conqueror" (*wissenschaftliche[r] Eroberer*) in the secular age, in the absence of Christian apocalypse.

CONCLUSION

By re-reading Humboldt's scientific writings about the American tropics in light of their association with the enigmatic manuscript written by the ancient alchemist Melchíades in *Cien años de soledad* we are alerted to the important role that Humboldt played in the history of the idea that America was discovered by Europeans in the fifteenth century and in the history of modern scientific idea of discovery per se. If still in 1955, the famous French anthropologist Claude Lévi-Strauss could write, in his *Tristes Tropiques,* that nature in the tropics "displayed a higher degree or presence and permanence" than it does in the temperate zone, he betrayed his intellectual debt to Humboldt's alchemical cosmology elaborated some hundred years earlier—an alchemical cosmology that still underwrote the French anthropologist's modern scientific authority.[60] Humboldt's travel writings about the "second discovery" of America by temperate man, equipped with natural philosophy and scientific instrumentation, thus represent an important chapter in the alchemical (re-) invention of the Global South during the nineteenth century. While Humboldt's modern hermeneutics of scientific discovery may not be directly implicated in any specific imperialist geopolitical design, its logic depends of an idea of conquest that produces objects by erasing subjects. If the first (early modern) conquest had legitimated this Purification in the language of Christian alchemical apocalypticsim, Humboldt's crucial intervention in the history of the idea that America was discovered lay in the secularization of its millenarian telos in the language of the aesthetic sublime: the Romantic concept of *Ruhe*.

NOTES

1. García Márquez, *Cien años de soledad*, 31–32. The English translations are from García Márquez, *One Hundred Years of Solitude*, 73–74. All further references to these editions will appear parenthetically in the text.

2. Ochoa, *The Uses of Failure*, 83.

3. As far as I am aware, various scholars have noted the connection but not fully explored; besides Ochoa, ibid., see Clark and Lubrich, "Introduction," 31; also Williams, *Mario Vargas Llosa*, 138.

4. On the novel's meta-historical qualities, see Parkinson Zamora, *The Usable Past*, 81–82, 119–21; also González Echevarría, *Myth and Archive*, 1–42. On Humboldt's legacy in Mexico, see Ochoa, 80–110.

5. Bolívar qtd. In Ewalt, *Peripheral Wonders*, 191; also qtd. in Gilman, "Humboldt's American Mediterranean," 527; and Helferich, *Humboldt's Cosmos*, 303. I say "allegedly" because, though scholars frequently attribute this sentence to Bolívar, they usually do so by quoting from other secondary sources who do not cite their primary source. To date, I have not been able to verify the authenticity of this quote.

6. On the important role that apocalypticism plays in the modern fiction and culture of the Americas generally and in *Cien años de soledad* particularly, see Parkinson Zamora, *Writing the Apocalypse*; also, Parkinson Zamora, *The Apocalyptic Vision in America*.

7. See García Márquez, "The Solitude of Latin America."

8. See Conniff, "The Dark Side of Magical Realism." On the idea of America as a continuous colonialist tradition of Eurocentric "inventing," see Rabasa, *Inventing America*.

9. In my use of the terms "parody," "intertextualism," and "dialog," I am indebted to Bakhtin, *The Dialogic Imagination*.

10. Several Postcolonial critics have followed Mary Louise Pratt's seminal reading of Humboldt's "godlike, omniscient stance over both the planet and the

reader" as an "imperial eye" that is implicated in the nineteenth-century neocolonial exploitation of Latin America (Pratt, *Imperial Eyes*, 124). For an earlier exploration of the connection between what has been called "Humboldtian science" and imperialism, see Goetzmann, *Exploration and Empire*. In addition to being imperialist, Humboldt has also been charged with being 'derivative' by Cañizares-Esguerra in "How Derivative Was Humboldt?". More recently several scholars have come to Humboldt's defense, reminding us that he was not an agent of any European imperial power. In fact, following Kant, Humboldt had overtly condemned Europe's global imperialism and was one of the first European scientific travelers to give due credit to the cultural achievements of America's pre-Columbian civilizations; he vehemently condemned slavery, abhorred the development of a virulently racist ideology of Manifest Destiny in the United States, and anticipated contemporary eco-critical thinking. See Kutzinski and Ette, "Introduction." On the role that Humboldt's writings about New Spain may (inadvertently) have played in the justification of annexations, see Bernecker, "El mito de la riqueza Mexicana"; Pereyra, *Humboldt en América*, 193; and Quirarte, *Historiografía sobre el Segundo imperio de Maximiliano*, 11–21. On the politics of Humboldt's portrait of slavery, see Kutzinski and Ette, "Inventories and Inventions"; also Iannini, *Fatal Revolutions*, 281–289; for good overviews of the critical debates about Humboldt, see Kutzinski, Ette, and Dassow Walls, eds., *Alexander von Humboldt and the Americas*; Ette, *Alexander von Humboldt und die Globalisierung*; and Dassow Walls, *The Passage to Cosmos*. On Humboldt and contemporary eco-critical thinking, see Hey'l, *Das Ganze der Natur und die Differenzierung des Wissens*; and Wulf, *The Invention of Nature*.

11. O'Gorman, *La idea del descubrimiento de América* and *The Invention of America*. While O'Gorman's notion proceeded from an engagement with Heidegger's *Being and Time,* more recent critics, such as Walter Mignolo and José Rabasa have extended O'Gorman's notion from a poststructuralist perspective to argue that the invention of Latin America has been an ongoing process in which each writer writing about Latin America in European languages participates; see Mignolo, *The Idea of Latin America*; Rabasa, *Inventing America*; also Zavala, ed., *Discursos sobre la invención de América*.

12. On Humboldt's effacement of Latin American creole intellectuals in his narrative, see Cañizares-Esguerra, "How Derivative was Humboldt;" also Cañizares-Esguerra, "Spanish America, 737.

13. On the notion of "purification" in modern science, and particular on Boyle's air pump, see Latour, *We Have Never Been Modern*, 10–15; on "centers of calculation" and "immobile mobiles," see Latour, *Science in Action*, 215–257; on the notion of Humboldt as his own center of calculation, see Dettelbach, "Global Physics and the Aesthetic Empire," 264.

14. For a list and description of the instruments the two men unloaded at Cumaná, see Humboldt, *Voyage aux régions équinoxiales du nouveau continent*, 1: 106–114. All further references to the *Relation historique* pertain to this edition. English translations from Humboldt's French and German originals are mine unless indicated otherwise.

15. On Humboldt and La Condamine, see Safier, *Measuring the New World*, 55–56. On Humboldt's debt to Foster and other European men of science during the Enlightenment, see Browne, *The Secular Ark*.
16. Humboldt, *Examen critique de l'histoire de la géographie du Nouveau Continent*, 5–6.
17. Humboldt to David Friedländer, Madrid, April 11, 1799, in *Jugendbriefe Alexander von Humboldts*, 657.
18. Dettelbach, "Global Physics and the Aesthetic Empire."
19. Bacon, *The Works of Francis Bacon*, 4: 298; my emphasis.
20. See Dettelbach, 266. Dettelbach has helpfully placed Humboldt's conception of science in the context of cameralism, the "systematic science of administration that emerged and was codified in the curricula of eighteenth-century German universities and academies." A sort of *Staatswissenschaft*, a natural science placed in the service of the state, it had its roots in the seventeenth century, particularly in the reforms of natural philosophy proposed by Francis Bacon in England and in the work of alchemists such as Johann Becher patronized by courts in the Holy Roman Empire of the German nation, as well as in the Spanish imperial administration in the Americas. See Michael Dettelbach, "Describing the Nation." On the seventeenth-century precedents of this tradition (in particular Becher), see Smith, *The Business of Alchemy;* on the sixteenth-century precedents of this tradition, see my *The Alchemy of Conquest*.
21. Humboldt, *Versuche über die Gereitzte Muskel- und Nervenfaser*, 1.
22. Ibid., 3–4.
23. Humboldt to Joseph Banks, Freiberg, June 20, 1797, in *Jugendbriefe Alexander von Humboldts*, 584.
24. Humboldt, *Voyage aux régions équinoxiales du nouveau continent*, 1: 53–55.
25. Humboldt, *Cosmos*, 1: 34
26. On "theoretical curiosity," see Blumenberg, *The Legitimacy of the Modern Age*, 229–436; on da Vinci, see 364; on Humboldt, see 437–439. On Augustinian 'vain' and 'just' curiosity, see also Eamon, *Science and the secrets of nature*. For a critique of Blumenberg's argument for a distinctly 'modern' origin of curiosity, see Oberman, '*Contra vanam curiositatem*,' 17–18; and Peters, "The Desire to Know the Secrets of the World."
27. See Gaukroger, *The Emergence of a Scientific Culture;* on the importance of alchemy to the modern empiricist idea of discovery, see Newman, "From Alchemy to 'Chymistry,'" 497; Newman, *Atoms and Alchemy*; and Newman, *Gehennical Fire*.
28. Newman, *Promethean Ambitions*, 256–276; see also Janacek, *Alchemical Belief*.
29. Giorgio Agamben, *State of Exception*, 41, 25; Pinkus, *Alchemical Mercury*, 8–10, 26.
30. The historical literature on alchemy is vast and has recently been proliferating at an accelerated speed. For only a few works that have especially informed my argument here, see Newman, *Promethean Ambitions*; Newman, "From Alchemy to 'Chymistry';" Newman, *Atoms and Alchemy*; *Gehennical Fire*; Principe, *The Secrets of Alchemy*; Newman and Principe, *Alchemy Tried in the Fire*; Smith, *The Business of Alchemy;* Smith, *The Body of the Artisan*; Crisciani, *From the Laboratory to the*

Library; Eamon, *Science and the secrets of nature*; and De Vun, *Prophecy, Alchemy, and the End of Time*.

31. See Halka, *Melchíades, Alchemy, and Narrative Theory*, 3; also McNerney and Martin, "Alchemy in *Cien años de soledad*;" Schroeder, *Rediscovering Magical Realism in the Americas*, 39–57; and Robinett, *This Rough Magic*, 98–99.

32. See McNerney and Martin, "Alchemy in *Cien años de soledad*," 111.

33. See ibid., 107–108.

34. See Halka, 1–4, 16.

35. Ibid., 10–38.

36. See Conniff, "The Dark Side of Magical Realism", 179.

37. Schroeder, *Rediscovering Magical Realism in the Americas*, 49.

38. McNerney and Martin, "Alchemy in *Cien años de soledad*," 111.

39. See Gil, *Mitos y utopias del descubrimiento* for a survey of these myths.

40. On the rupture or "gap" narrative structuring the historiography and legitiamcy of modern science, see Robertson, "Medieval Materialism," 103.

41. Latour, *We Have Never Been Modern*, 34.

42. Ibid., 99–100.

43. Biggs, *The Vanity of the Craft of Physick*, 57; my emphasis. On Biggs, see Debus, *The Chemical Philosophy*, 499–512.

44. See Pimentel, "The Iberian Vision," 17–21; also, Eamon, "The Iconography of Scientific Discovery in the Renaissance."

45. According to the Oxford English Dictionary On-Line, the verb "to entangle" means "to intertwist (threads, branches, or the like) complicatedly or confusedly together; to intertwist the threads or parts of (a thing) in this way." On the trope of entanglement in recent historiography, see Bauer and Norton, "Introduction."

46. Eden, *The Decades of the Newe Worlde or west India*, 160r.

47. Ibid., 157r.

48. Ibid., 16r.

49. Humboldt, *Voyage aux régions équinoxiales du nouveau continent*, 2: 22. Wherever possible, I quote here from the (partial) English translation Alexander von Humboldt, *Personal Narrative of a Journey to the Equinoctial Regions of the New Content* (New York: Penguin Books, 1995), 41. Further references to this translation will appear parenthetically.

50. Humboldt, ibid., 2: 32 (50).

51. Humboldt, ibid., 3: 19–20 (80).

52. Humboldt, ibid., 4: 34 (131–132).

53. Humboldt, ibid., 3: 75 (76).

54. Humboldt, ibid., 3: 75 (76)..

55. See Gerbi, *The Dispute of the New World*, 405–417; and Brading, *The First America*, 514–534; and Cañizares-Esguerra, *How to Write the History of the New World*, 125–129.

56. See Wey-Gómez, *The Tropics of Empire*.

57. Humboldt, *Voyage aux régions équinoxiales du nouveau continent*, 7: 36.

58. Humboldt, *Cosmos*, 1: 36.

59. Humboldt, ibid., 1: 42. On the millennium as a time of rest, see Lerner, "The Refreshment of the Saints," 143–144; also Lerner, *The Power of Prophecy*; and Whalen, *Dominion of God*. On the connection between the Christian millenarian tradition and the history of the Western idea of progress, see Noble, *The Religion of Technology*, 21–42. It should be noted here about the quote from Humboldt that the German original does not use the word "empire" (*Reich*) in this context. In turn, the English translation does not use the phrase "wissenschaftliche[r] Eroberer" (scientific conqueror), which Humboldt had earlier used in the German original, but rather "scientific observer" (compare *Kosmos*. 1: 22; and *Cosmos*, 1: 41). But the Baconian connection between knowledge, power, and conquest, explicitly referenced by Humboldt (*Cosmos*, 1: 53), is clear. See also below, note 59.

60. Lévi-Strauss, *Tristes Tropiques*, 55.

WORKS CITED

Agamben, Giorgio, *State of Exception*. Translated by Kevin Attell. Chicago and London: The University of Chicago Press, 2005.

Bacon, Francis. *The Works of Francis Bacon*. Edited by James Spedding, Robert Leslie Ellis, and Douglas Denon Heath. 15 vols. New York: Hurd and Houghton, ca. 1900.

Bakhtin, Mikhail. *The Dialogic Imagination*. Edited by Michael Holquist. Translated by Caryl Emerson and Michael Holquist. Austin: University of Texas Press, 1981.

Bauer, Ralph. *The Alchemy of Conquest: Religion, Science, and the Secrets of the New World* Charlottesville: University of Virginia Press, 2019.

Bauer, Ralph, and Marcy Norton. Introduction: "Entangled Trajectories: Indigenous and European Histories." *Colonial Latin American Review* 26, no.1 (March 2017): 1–17.

Bernecker, Walther. "El mito de la riqueza mexicana. Alejandro de Humboldt: del analista al propagandista," in *Alejandro de Humboldt: Una nueva visión del mundo,* edited by Frank Holl, 95–101. Mexico City: UNAM, 2003.

Biggs, Noah. *The Vanity of the Craft of Physick*. London: Giles Calvert, 1651.

Blumenberg, Hans. *The Legitimacy of the Modern Age*. Translated by Robert M. Wallace. Cambridge, MA: MIT Press, 1999.

Brading, David. *The First America: The Spanish Monarchy, Creole Patriots, and the Liberal State, 1492–1867*. Cambridge: Cambridge University Press, 1991.

Browne, Janet. *The Secular Ark: Studies in the History of Biogeography*. New Haven: Yale University Press, 1983.

Cañizares-Esguerra, Jorge. *Nature, Empire, and Nation: Explorations of the History of Science in the Iberian World*. Stanford: Stanford University Press, 2006.

———. *How to Write the History of the New World: Historiographies, Epistemologies, and Identities in the Eighteenth-Century Atlantic World*. Stanford: Stanford University Press, 2001.

———. "Spanish America: From Baroque to Modern Colonial Science." In *The Cambridge History of Science*, edited by Lorraine Daston and Katherine Park, vol. 4, *Eighteenth-Century Science*, edited by Roy Porter, 718–38. Cambridge: Cambridge University Press, 2003.

Clark, Rex, and Oliver Lubrich, eds. *Transatlantic Echoes: Alexander von Humboldt in World Literature*. New York: Bergbahn Books, 2012.

Conniff, Brian. "The Dark Side of Magical Realism: Science, Oppression, and Apocalypse in *One Hundred Years of Solitude*." *Modern Fiction Studies* 36 no. 2 (1990): 167–79.

Crisciani, Chiara. *From the Laboratory to the Library: Alchemy according to Guglielmo Fabri* Cambridge, Mass: MIT Press, 1999.

Dassow Walls, Laura. *The Passage to Cosmos: Alexander von Humboldt and the Shaping of America*. Chicago: University of Chicago Press, 2009.

Daston, Lorraine, and Katherine Park, eds. *The Cambridge History of Science*. Vol. 3, *Early Modern Science*. Cambridge: Cambridge University Press, 2006.

De Vun, Leah. *Prophecy, Alchemy, and the End of Time: John of Rupescissa in the Late Middle Ages*. New York: Columbia University Press, 2009.

Debus, Allen G. *The Chemical Philosophy: Paracelsian Science and Medicine in the Sixteenth Century*. New York: Science History Publications, 1977.

Dettelbach, Michael. "Global Physics and the Aesthetic Empire: Humboldt's Physical Portrait of the Tropics," in *Visions of Empire: Voyages, Botany, and Representations of Nature,* edited by David Philip Miller and Peter Hanns Reill, 258–92. Cambridge: Cambridge University Press, 1996.

———. "Describing the Nation: Local and Universal in Humboldt's Administrative Practice and in Late Eighteenth-Century Cameralism," in *Alexander von Humboldt and the Americas,* edited by Vera Kutzinski, Ottmar Ette, and Laura Dassow Walls, 183–208. Berlin: Walter Frey, 2012.

Eamon, William. *Science and the Secrets of Nature: Books of Secrets in Medieval and Early Modern Culture*. Princeton, NJ: Princeton University Press, 1994.

———. "The Iconography of Scientific Discovery in the Renaissance," Internet blog http://williameamon.com/?p=465, accessed October 28, 2016.

Eden, Richard. *The Decades of the Newe Worlde or West India*. London: William Powell, 1555.

Ette, Ottmar. *Alexander von Humboldt und die Globalisierung*. Frankfurt, a. M.: Insel, 2009.

Ewalt, Margaret. *Peripheral Wonders: Nature, Knowledge, and Enlightenment in the Eighteenth Century*. Bucknell University Press, 2008.

García Márquez, Gabriel. *Cien años de soledad,* Edicion Conmemorativa. Madrid: Real Academia Española, 2007.

———. *One Hundred Years of Solitude*. Translated by Gregory Rabasa. New York: Harper & Row, 1970.

———. "The Solitude of Latin America." Nobel Lecture, 8 December, 1982. http://www.nobelprize.org/nobel_prizes/literature/laureates/1982/marquez-lecture.html, accessed in April of 2015.

Gaukroger, Stephen. *The Emergence of a Scientific Culture: Science and the Shaping of Modernity 1210–1685*. Oxford: Clarendon, 2006.

Gerbi, Antonello. *The Dispute of the New World: The History of a Polemic, 1750–1900*. Translated by Jeremy Moyle. Pittsburgh: University of Pittsburgh Press, 1973.

Gil, Juan. *Mitos y utopias del descubrimiento*. Madrid: Alianza, 1989.

Gilman, Susan. "Humboldt's American Mediterranean." *American Quarterly* 66, no. 3 (September 2014): 505–528.

Goetzmann, William H. *Exploration and Empire: The Explorer and the Scientist in the American West*. 1966; New York: Norton, 1979.

González Echevarría, Roberto. *Myth and Archive: A Theory of Latin American Narrative*. Cambridge: Cambridge University Press, 1990.

Halka, Chester. *Melchíades, Alchemy, and Narrative Theory: The Quest for Gold in Cien años de soledad*. Lathrup Village, Michigan: International Book Publishers, 1981.

Helferich, Gerard. *Humboldt's Cosmos: Alexander von Humboldt and the Latin American Journey that Changed the Way We See the World*. New York: Gotham Books, 2004.

Hey'l, Bettina. *Das Ganze der Natur und die Differenzierung des Wissens: Alexander von Humboldt als Schriftsteller*. New York/Berlin: Walter de Gruyter, 2007.

Holl, Frank, ed. *Alejandro de Humboldt: Una nueva visión del mundo*. Mexico City: UNAM, 2003.

Humboldt, Alexander von. *Voyage aux régions équinoxiales du nouveau continent, fait en 1799, 1800, 1801, 1802, 1803 et 1804*. Paris: A la Librairie Greque-Latine-Allemande, 1816. 13 vols.

———. *Examen critique de l'histoire de la géographie du Nouveau Continent*. Paris: Librarie de Gide, 1835.

———. *Jugendbriefe Alexander von Humboldts*. Edited by Ilse Jahn and Fritz G. Lange. Berlin: Akademie-Verlag, 1973.

———. *Versuche über de gereitzte Muskel- und Nervenfaser, nebst Vermutungen über den chemischen Process des Lebens in der Their- und Planzenwelt*. Berlin: Rottmann, 1797.

———. *Cosmos*. Translated by E. C. Otté. 2 vols. Baltimore: The Johns Hopkins University Press, 1997.

———. *Kosmos: Entwurf einer Physischen Weltbeschreibung*. 2 vols. Stuttgart und Tübingen, 1845.

———. *Personal Narrative of a Journey to the Equinoctial Regions of the New Content*. New York: Penguin Books, 1995.

Iannini, Christopher. *Fatal Revolutions: Natural History, West Indian Slavery, and the Routes of American Literature*. Chapel Hill and Colonial Williamsburg: The University of North Carolina Press for the Omohundro Institute of Early American History and Culture, 2012.

Janacek, Bruce. *Alchemical Belief: Occultism in the Religious Culture of Early Modern England*. University Park: Pennsylvania University Press, 2011.

Kutzinski, Vera, and Ottmar Ette. "Introduction." In *Views of the Cordilleras and Monuments of the Indigenous Peoples of the Americas: A Critical Edition*, edited by Vera M. Kutzinski and Ottmar Ette, 1–12. Chicago: University of Chicago Press, 2012.

Kutzinski, Vera, and Ottmar Ette. "Inventories and Inventions: Alexander von Humboldt's Cuban Landscapes." In *Political Essay on the Island of Cuba* by Alexander von Humboldt, edited and translated by Vera Kutzinski and Ottmar Ette, vii–xxiv. Chicago: University of Chicago Press, 2010.

Kutzinski, Vera, Otmar Ette, and Laura Dassow Walls, eds. *Alexander von Humboldt and the Americas*. Berlin: Walter Frey, 2012.

Latour, Bruno, *We Have Never Been Modern*. Translated by Catherine Porter. Cambridge, Massachusetts: Harvard University Press, 1993.

———. *Science in Action: How to Follow Scientists and Engineers through Society.* Milton Keynes: Open University Press, 1987.

Lerner, Robert. "The Refreshment of the Saints: The Time after Antichrist as a Station for Earthly Progress in Medieval Thought." *Traditio* 32 (1976): 97–144.

———. *The Power of Prophecy: The Cedar of Lebanon Vision from the Mongol Onslaught to the Dawn of the Enlightenment*. Berkeley: The University of California Press, 1983.

Lévi-Strauss, Claude. *Tristes Tropiques*. Trans. John Weightman and Doreen Weightman. 1955; London: Jonathan Cape, 1973.

McNerney, Kathleen, and John Martin. "Alchemy in *Cien años de soledad*." *West Virginia Philological Papers* 27 (1981): 106–12.

Mignolo, Walter. *The Idea of Latin America*. Malden, MA; Oxford : Blackwell, 2005.

Miller, David Philip, and Peter Hanns Reill, eds. *Visions of Empire: Voyages, Botany, and Representations of Nature*. Cambridge: Cambridge University Press, 1996.

Newman, William. "From Alchemy to 'Chymistry'." In *The Cambridge History of Science*, edited by Lorraine Daston and Katherine Park, vol. 3, *Early Modern Science*, 497–512. Cambridge: Cambridge University Press, 2006.

———. *Atoms and Alchemy: Chymistry and the Experimental Origins of the Scientific Revolution*. Chicago: University of Chicago Press, 2006.

———. *Gehennical Fire: The Lives of George Starkey. An American Alchemist in the Scientific Revolution* Chicago: University of Chicago Press, 1994.

———. *Promethean Ambitions: Alchemy and the Quest to Perfect Nature*. Chicago: The University of Chicago Press, 2004.

Newman, William, and Lawrence Principe. *Alchemy Tried in the Fire: Starkey, Boyle, and the Fate of Helmontian Chymistry*. Chicago: University of Chicago Press, 2002.

Noble, David. *The Religion of Technology. The Divinity of Man and the Spirit of Invention*. New York: Knopf, 1997.

Oberman, Heiko. *'Contra vanam curiositatem.' Ein Kapitel der Theologie zwischen Seelenwinkel und Weltall*. Zürich: Theologischer Verlag, 1974.

Ochoa, John. *The Uses of Failure in Mexican Literature and Identity*. Austin: University of Texas Press, 2004.

O'Gorman, Edmundo. *La idea del descubrimiento de América; Historia de esa interpretación y crítica de sus fundamentos*. Mexico City: Centro de Estudios Filosóficos, 1951).
———. *The Invention of America*. 1958; Westport: Greenwood Press, 1972.
Parkinson Zamora, Lois. *The Usable Past: The Imagination of History in Recent Fiction of the Americas*. Cambridge: Cambridge University Press, 1997.
———. *Writing the Apocalypse: Historical Vision in Contemporary U.S. and Latin American Fiction* Cambridge: Cambridge University Press, 1989.
———. *The Apocalyptic Vision in America: Interdisciplinary Essays on Myth and Culture*. Bowling Green: Bowling Green University Popular Press, 1982.
Pereyra, Carlos. *Humboldt en América*. Madrid: Editorial America, 1917.
Peters, Edward. "The Desire to Know the Secrets of the World." *Journal of the History of Ideas* 62, no. 4 (Oct., 2001): 593–610.
Pimentel, Juan. "The Iberian Vision: Science and Empire in the Framework of a Universal Monarchy, 1500–1800." *Osiris* 15, no. 1 (2000): 17–2.
Pinkus, Karen. *Alchemical Mercury: A Theory of Ambivalence*. Stanford: Stanford University Press, 2010.
Pratt, Mary Louise. *Imperial Eyes: Travel Writing and Transculturation*. London: Routledge, 1992.
Principe, Lawrence. *The Secrets of Alchemy*. Chicago: University of Chicago Press, 2013.
Quirarte, Martín. *Historiografía sobre el Segundo imperio de Maximiliano*. Mexico City: UNAM.
Rabasa, José. *Inventing America: Spanish Historiography and the Formation of Eurocentrism*. Norman: University of Oklahoma Press, 1993.
Robertson, Kellie. "Medieval Materialism: A Manifesto." *Exemplaria* 22, no. 2 (Summer 2010): 99–118.
Robinett, Jane. *This Rough Magic: Technology in Latin American Fiction*. New York: Peter Lang, 1994.
Safier, Neal. *Measuring the New World: Enlightenment Science and South America*. Chicago: University of Chicago Press, 2008.
Schroeder, Shannin. *Rediscovering Magical Realism in the Americas*. Westport, CT: Preager, 2004.
Smith, Pamela. *The Business of Alchemy. Science and Culture in the Holy Roman Empire*. Princeton: Princeton University Press, 1994.
———. *The Body of the Artisan: Art and Experience in the Scientific Revolution*. Chicago: University of Chicago Press, 2004.
Wey-Gómez, Nicolás. *The Tropics of Empire: Why Columbus Sailed South to the Indies*. Cambridge, MA: MIT Press, 2008.
Whalen, Brett Edward. *Dominion of God: Christendom and Apocalypse in the Middle Ages*. Cambridge, MA: Harvard University Press, 2009.
Williams, Raymond Leslie. *Mario Vargas Llosa: A Life or Writing*. Austin: University of Texas Press, 2014.

Wulf, Andrea. *The Invention of Nature: Alexander von Humboldt's New World.* New York: Knopf, 2015.
Zavala, Iris, ed., *Discursos sobre la invención de América.* Rodopi: Amsterdam and Atlanta, 1992.

Afterword
Djelal Kadir

This is not an Afterword. You know there is no such thing as "after word." I know you know what we have learned looking at a painting—that even the most inordinate eye strains, in vain, to reach the vanishing point that never keeps from receding. We learned this, too, reading a poem that sloughs off our readings and regenerates meanings that await our return to its lines and inter-lineal spaces. It's not surprising, then, that your list of book publications begins with the end, the apocalypse, and moves toward beginnings, the group portraitures, and familial collectives of your latest endeavor, where individual destinies and destinations are engendered. This predicament may well be at the root of our tireless impulse to read and to re-read, yet again. Words, we have learned, have no afterword except as more words they are after, hoping to catch up, only to discover that the pursued object runs ahead of the pursuing subject, varying the gap between the two but never managing to close it.

So, we know, you and I, that any closure is inexorably foreclosed. And the pretext of an Afterword is no more than a desideratum, forever a hopeful preface, no matter the postings in pagination, bookish, or otherwise. Shakespeare sealed that fate for us, those of us destined to a life of literature and its words, committing us in perpetuity to the parenthesis that opens with King Hamlet's ghostly peroration ("Remember me." 1.5.91), and closes with the imminent ghostliness of Prince Hamlet and the play's last words, after so many words: "The rest is silence"; 5.2. Yet, and yet again, like Hamlet, as solitary as a man's grief, we do not cease to hope for a friend, a Horatio, whom we might enjoin to tell what we might have descried in the squalor of the present and the nebula of things to come. We continue to echo, in this regard, the most brooding of Latin America's Avant-garde poets, the Peruvian César Vallejo, who would Hamletise even beyond his mortality, leaving us with the eternal question—"Y si despues de tantas palabras . . . ?" ("and, if after so many words. . . ?")— seeking to ensure that words remain in lapidary inscription by composing his own epitaph in his Parisian exile.

We have come to learn that the eye, ordinate or otherwise, is invariably an oyster with a grain of sand, if not a grain of salt, under its lids. So, we have discovered, anything that flows from that eye is inevitably baroque by its fated distortion and surprising asymmetry, as the Portuguese shuckers of oysters and language have defined "baroque" for us. Nothing/everything is new there, and, as you well know and teach, anything "neo-" is a complex illusion, a *trompe l'oeil* that aspires to conjure with time and time lines in search of novelty, only to discover that the pursuit of the new yields a pleonasm, that calling anything baroque new is to succumb to tautology. Hindsight, alas, is as furtive as an afterword, as yearned after a desideratum as is foresight, the latter no less a reaching for an alibi than the former. An alibi for any act of seeing is indispensable, an exculpatory expediency for what seeing inevitably skews in the plethora of vision and the plenitude of what you call "envisioning." The elaborate edifices of theology, theory, critical discourse, historiography, testimonial chronicle, epistles, confessions, and apostrophes, along with their visual ekphrases in art and architecture, have spawned libraries, cathedrals, universities, religious vocations, and academic professions. Invariably, they have labored, relentlessly, to forge the sought-after absolution and necessary justification that an alibi might provide.

And, so, as in all alibis, we find ourselves inexorably elsewhere, hoping somewhere else might yield a haven in the perpetual displacement that vanishing points and the rollicking roll of language impose. Like Teiresias—his metamorphoses and toggled transgendered avatars— perhaps the earliest protagonist of magical realism you have parsed so diligently, we have witnessed variegated species of snakes across our institutional paths, countenanced sightedness, blindness, and the vagaries of would-be second sight. But we have also discovered that, at the end of the day, the visions of the inordinate eye redound to the ordinary human fundamentals of friendship and solidarity that might see us through the pain of loss and the grievous perplexity of implacable solitude. In a dystopian time of viral plague and political pestilence, we find ourselves possessed in perpetuity by the departed we thought to have possessed in life. And those who remain with the remains of the day would celebrate what has accrued to our paths and paginated passages. One's happiest wish is that the exalting professions of the celebrants—the contributors to this volume— and the rightful recognition of the celebrated—you— coincide in the celebration.

When the world was all before us and happenstance our guide, we too sought to tack a course between the lessons that launched us and the novelties we thought to have invented. And here we are, once again, witnesses to that procession and its relay posts and paces toward the vanishing point. It might be best to read these postings by your academic progeny, as well as these words, as one would read the "This is just to say" plea taped to the fridge door by the pediatrician-poet from Patterson, New Jersey, William Carlos Williams, who sued for forgiveness for his compulsive consumption. And, though we have yet to cross through the third bank of the river to the other shore, it might be apposite to read these apostrophes of your scribbling brood as what the ancient Greeks called apotropaic professions honoring one's elders in order to ensure that they do as little damage as possible on exit and in their haunting visitations thereafter. Thereafter, of course, brings us back to Gertrude Stein's Hamlet and his ontological question, cribbed as "Is there a there there?" No, Hamlet's spectral perplexity about here and after was not about being or not being in Oakland, but neither was Gertrude Stein's inquest in Paris. Their respective interrogations were "What comes after for Denmark?" and "What comes after (for) Paris?" Whether the country of Hamletic ghosts, or the city of mud the literal Romans called Lutetia and the French would re-name after the ghost of the Trojan King Priam's son, theirs are spectral questions of ghostly geographies. Hamlet's is a proleptic query about Denmark's future, Stein's an analeptic speculation about an America with hardly a past and a ghost of a future in search of corporeality.

It's been two decades now since you and I set out to found the international organization that would explore the possibilities of Stein's question—of America as a hemispheric transnational phenomenon, the usefulness, uses, and abuses of its past, as you had already written, and its prospects for a salvageable future. As I write to you now, in this year of the plague, when the vengeful ghosts of the past have descended upon the squalid gore of the present, I recall Villa Serbelloni in Bellagio, the villa of Pliny the Younger. You recall, no doubt, his eloquent letters (he had been, after all, a student of Quintilian) that left us a haunting portrait of Rome's first-century social milieu, just as his uncle Pliny the Elder's histories had done for the natural (and supernatural) world(s) that pre-defined America before it was America. It was there, on the shores of Lake Como, that we gathered a quarrelsome quorum of international Americanists in the Spring of 2000 to launch the International American Studies Association (IASA) with the goal of pursuing the possibilities and historical quandaries telegraphed in Gertrude Stein's question. The agendas were as diverse as the two dozen participants from South and North America and from across the Atlantic and Pacific Oceans. And though you questioned the wisdom of that heterogeneous congeries, you understood the significance of holding close those less friendly to any endeavor, just as one must cleave to one's friends. And when I found myself the risible target, like Telemachus in Penelope's household at the mercy of the suitors, your succor did for me what Athena's aegis did for the earnest son of the far-flung Odysseus. And three years later, in Leiden, The Netherlands, we celebrated our first world congress, trying to take the measure of America as hemispheric phenomenon with the question "How Far Is America from Here?" The proceedings of that congress are published for posterity in the homonymous volume that you and I, along with Theo D'haen and Paul Giles, co-edited. It was a geographically and historically apt question, a question asked from that same spot in 1630 by the Pilgrims moored in Leiden, where they overstayed their Dutch hospitality by twenty years, and, finally, were about to resume their pilgrimage across the Atlantic in search of the "there" that might be there. It was also the time, when a few weeks earlier, in March of 2003, the dogs of war howled for blood and for shock and awe in a high-tech and lowbrow reprise of the 1258 Mongol sacking of Baghdad, the decimation of its patrimony and destruction of its libraries. The City of Heavenly Peace, as Baghdad was named at its founding, found itself asking the same question about the "there there" of its rampaging invaders from the other side of the planet, as would the peoples of Afghanistan, of Libya, of Palestine, of Syria in the ensuing years of the war-torn twenty-first century. And IASA's cavalcade and worldwide membership continue to span the globe asking analogous questions through its biennial world congresses. As a result, American Studies as a discipline has been dislodged from American-centered tautology as American discourse to become a multi-centered, multi-vocal, and worldwide scholarly and pedagogical colloquy among Americanists no longer beholden to or in thrall of their object of study and its myths.

The best of human achievements are occasional, and it is fit that you should be the occasion of this collective retracing of the paths your distinguished scholarly itinerary and pedagogical vocation have spanned and continue to traverse. The conversation among members of your academic circle gathered in this volume is multilateral, but, suggestively, it is also an intimate and resonant dialogue between you and each of the voices writing to you. That I should be designated to round out this pageantry is also fitting, having traversed the academic pathways of the last four decades with you in parallel and intersecting company, now in conversation, but just as often in silence, the mark of true friendship of those destined to walk together. As we came to know from our early readings in the Idylls of Theocritus and the Eclogues of Virgil, palaver has its pageantry and silence its decorum. And, so, it is meet that I resume our communion's silence now. Your work and mine, hopefully, will continue what has joined us since we have been in a conversation.

Dacha Otis,
Southwest Hills Portland, Oregon
2020

Index

Note: Page locators in italics refer to figures.

Abhinavagupta, 165n22
academic imperialism, 8, 10
Adams, James Truslow, 20n4
Adams, Rachel, 22n35
aesthetics, 7, 29, 84–85, 101–4, 110, 119n5
Afghanistan, 86, 208
Against the American Grain (Kutzinski), 8
AHA (American Historical Association), 3
AIDS, 107n20
Alarcón, Renato, 53n61
alchemy, xxiv, 180–85, 196n30
Aldridge, A. Owen, 8
Aleijadinho, 116
Allende, Isabel, 125
Almanac of the Dead (Silko), 18, 19
Alonso, Dámaso, 97
Al Qaeda, 82
altars: Day of the Dead, xx, 75–78, *76–77*, *79*, 83, 85; femicide and, 81; at Museo de Artes Populares, *80*
Alvarez Bravo, Armando, 58, *59*, *69*
Amauta (magazine), 40, 43
Ambassadors of Culture (Gruesz), 21n31

America Hispana (Frank), 40
American Baroque, 110, 119
American Historical Association (AHA), 3
American Indians, 107n16
American Literary History (journal), 22n35
American Renaissance (Matthiessen), 15
American Studies, 3–4, 10, 13–16, 35, 208
American Studies Association (ASA), 14
American utopias, 44, 51
American World Literature (Giles), 22n34
the Americas, Europe and, 41–44, 174–76. *See also* Carpentier, Alejo; *Cien años de soledad*; Humboldt, Alexander; New World Baroque; O'Gorman, Edmundo
The Americas, Otherwise (Zamora and Spitta), xii, 16
Anderson, Benedict, 93–94
Andrews, Chris, 31, 32
Ansermet, Ernest, 48
anti-imperialism, 12, 40

209

apocalypticism, 31, 176, 194n6
Apter, Emily, 29
Aquin, Hubert, 16
Arabs, alchemy and, xxiv, 180
La Araucana (Ercilla), 16
Archival Reflections (Juan-Navarro), 9
archive, 3, 18–20
Arenas, Reinaldo, 93, 104, 107n20
Argentina, 39, 44–45, 48, 50–51
Aridjis, Eve, 87
Aridjis, Homero, 87
Armstrong, Louis, 98
Arnald of Villanova, 180–81
El arpa y la sombra (Carpentier), 105
art, xxi–xxii, 102, 110–11, 113, 115–16, 120n12
art of the glance, xxiii, 143–47
ASA (American Studies Association), 14
atman, brahman and, 148, 167n53
Attridge, Derek, 12
Atwood, Margaret, 16
Auerbach, Erich, 6
Autonomía cultural americana (Ballón), 8

Bachelard, Gaston, 60, 61, 64, 67
Bacon, Francis, 193, 196n20; Humboldt and, 178, 180, 198n59; *Instauratio Magna*, 178, 186, *187*, 189
Bailey, Gauvin, 113
Ballón, José, 8
Barbusse, Henri, 41–43
Barcha, Mercedes, 126, 128
Bard, Patrick, 85
baroque, xii; aesthetic, 101–3, 110; *Carpentier's Baroque Fiction*, 105; Hispanic Baroque Research project, 121n44
the Baroque: as alternative expression of modernity, 110; American Baroque, 110, 119; with art and science, 111, 115–16; Brazilian, 116; in church interiors, 113; as cinematic, 113;
complexity theory and, xxii, 111, 113–16, 119, 121n44; Counter-Reformation and, xxi, 78–79, 99, 102–5, 107n16, 110; Deleuze on, 106n14; as destabilizing order, 110; Echevarría on American Indians and, 107n16; ellipses and, 110–11, 115–17; European, 103, 118–19; folk, xx, 75–78; form as disorderly, 109–19; Fuentes on, 101; gold and, 93; "How the Baroque Learned to Speak Spanish," 119n5; "Meditations on the Baroque," 119n5; memento mori, 86; Neo-baroque, xx–xxii, 102, 104–5, 110, 117–18, 119n5; New World Baroque, 27, 75, 107n16, 110, 116, 119; *On the (New) Baroque*, 119n5; politics and debate, xxi, 104, 110; revolution and, 103, 110; Roman Catholic Church and, 78–79; science and, xxi; as subversive, 103; systems thinking and, xxi, 111–13; theory of, 103, 116–18; wealth displays and, 93, 101; "What is Baroque?," 120n12
"The Baroque and the Neobaroque" (Sarduy), 117–18
"Baroque curiosity" (Lezama Lima), 107n16, 119
Baroque New Worlds (Zamora and Kaup), xii, 119, 119n5
Barroco (Sarduy), 116, 117
Barroco de Indias, 103
Barroco y modernidad (Chiampi), 119n5
Barth, John, 8
Batista, Fulgencio, 60, 99
Bauer, Ralph, 5, 20n9
Becher, Johann, 196n20
Being and Time (Heidegger), 195n11
bel composto, art and, 113
The Believers (Schlesinger), 84
Beltrán Leyva, Arturo, 85
Berger, Mark, 53n60

Berkeley, George, 32
Bernini, Gian Lorenzo, 79, 113, 116, 120n12
Berthollet, Claude, 178
Bhabha, Homi, 137–38
the Bible, 17, 64, 102
Biemann, Ursula, 88n7
Big Bang theory, 103, 117
Biggs, Noah, 186
Bilingual Aesthetics (Sommer), 29
Blackburn, Alexander, 95
Blanco (Paz), 143, 156–57, 162, 167n53, 168n63
Blog del Narco, 82
Blumenberg, Hans, 180
bodies, 68, 128, 160; drug-related violence and, 78–80, 82, 84, 87, 88n7; sacredness of, 157
Bolaño, Roberto, 31–35
Bolívar, Simón, 173, 194n5
Bolton, Herbert Eugene, 3–5, 7, 13, 17–18, 20n3
Bolton thesis, 3–5, 16, 21n13
Bonaparte, Napoleon, 176
Bones in the Desert (*Huesos en el desierto*) (González Rodríguez), 81, 88n8
Bonpland, Aimé, 176–77
Borges, Jorge Luis, 16, 31, 48, 138n2
Borromini, Francesco, 116
Bourgainville, Louis Antoine de, 177
Bowers, Maggie Ann, 125
Boyle, Robert, 176, 189
brahman, 148, 151–52, 156, 159, 167n53
Braider, Christopher, 116
Brazil, 6, 22nn39–40, 33, 50
Brazilian Baroque, 116
"Bread and Wine" ("Brot und Wein") (Hölderlin), 57, 69
"Breaking the Circle of Perfection" (Stengers), xxii
"Breaking the Circle of Sufficient Reason" (Stengers), 111, 115
Brickhouse, Anna, 20n9, 30

"Brot und Wein" ("Bread and Wine") (Hölderlin), 57, 69
Buell, Lawrence, 14
butterfly symbolism, 126–27

Cabell, James Branch, 30
Calderón, Felipe, 86–87
Callois, Roger, 44
The Cambridge History of the American Novel (Cassuto, Eby and Reiss), 14, 15
cameralism, 196n20
Canada, 6, 15, 16, 18, 22n40
Candide (Voltaire), 29, 95, 97
Cañizares-Esguerra, Jorge, 110, 194n10
cannibalism, 84–86
Cantú, Roberto, 167n53
Capra, Fritjof, 111–13. *See also* systems thinking
Caravaggio, 116
Carpentier, Alejo, xx–xxi, 93–106, 106n11
Carpentier's Baroque Fiction (Wakefield), 105
Carrá, Carlo, 67
"Carta a León Felipe" ("Letter to León Felipe") (Paz), 146, 165n14
Carter, Angela, 125
Carvalho, Joaquim de Montezuma de, 6, 21n11
Cassuto, Leonard, 14, 15
Castro, Fidel, 99, 129
catastrophe, mistranslation of, 33–35
Celestina's Brood (González Echevarría), 119n5
cena lezamiana (feast), 101
Central Intelligence Agency (CIA), 31, 33
"Cerca del cabo Comorín" ("Near Cape Comorin") (Paz), 146, 156
Cervantes, Miguel de, 17, 39, 94–96
Césaire, Aimé, 59
Changó, el gran putas (Zapata Olivella), 17
chemistry, 178, 179

Chevigny, Bell Gale, 8
Chiampi, Irlemar, 119n5
Chirico, Giorgio de, 67
Christ, fish symbol, 183
Christianity, 39, 107, 180, 181
church interiors, the Baroque in, 113
CIA (Central Intelligence Agency), 31, 33
Cien años de soledad (*One Hundred Years of Solitude*) (García Márquez), 16, 194n1; alchemy and, 181–85; apocalypse in, 176; Catholic culture in, 128–29; criticism of, xxiv; critique of Humboldt, 173–98; encyclopedic novels and, 17; with entanglement of nature and culture in American tropics, 189–93; irony in, 131–33, 138; Kafka and, 129–31, 134–37; magical realism, 125–38, 174–75; Melchíades in, 173–75, 181–85, 193; with political allegorization of West and un-West, 132–33; popular Catholicism in, 127–29; popular religion and, 127; travel writings of American tropics and, xviii–xxiv, 194; utopia of life and, 177. *See also* magical realism
Cienfuegos, Camilo, 99
cinematic, the Baroque as, 113
circle, 115–17
Cirlot, Juan Eduardo, 61, 64
Claros del bosque ("Clearings in the Forest") (Zambrano), 61
Clarté (journal), 42
class, feminism and, 53n55
classicism, 112–13
Claudet, Paul, 44
"Clearings in the Forest" (*Claros del bosque*) (Zambrano), 61
Codeau, Jacques, 44
codices, Mesoamerican, 19
Cohn, Deborah, 9, 33
coincidentia oppositorum (countering opposition), 102

The Collected Poems of Octavio Paz, 1957–87 (Weinberger), 164n1
Columbia University, 22n35
Columbus, Christopher, 18, 39, 173, 192, 193
Comolli, Jean-Louis, 82–83
Comparative American Studies (journal), 13, 22n41
Comparative Cultural Studies, 164
Comparative Literature, 7–8, 15
Comparative Literature (journal), 22n41
comparative studies, xi, 8, 22n41, 22n50
complexity theory, xxii, 111, 113–16, 119, 121n44
conceptual revolution, science and, 114
Concierto barroco (Carpentier): excess of lack or price of revolution, 98–106; jazz and, 97–98; picaresque and, xx–xxi, 92–96, 101–2
"Confluences" (Lezama Lima), 66, 68
Conniff, Brian, 184
Cook, James, 177
Copernicus, 103, 109, 115–16
Cortázar, Julio, 8
Cortés, Hernán, 98–99
cosmology, xxi–xxii, 109–11, 114–17, 192–94
Cosmos (Humboldt), 179, 192–93
Costa-Gramunt, Teresa, 167n53
Cotes, Tranquilina Iguarán, 126–27
countering opposition (*coincidentia oppositorum*), 102
Counter-Reformation, xxi, 78–79, 99, 102–5, 107n16, 110. *See also* the Baroque; Neo-baroque; Roman Catholic Church
crime-beat press (*nota roja*), xx, 85
Critical Inquiry (journal), 12
Cross, Elsa, 167n61
Cuba, 60, 88n2, 98–99, 104–5, 107n20, 129
Cuban Revolution, 94, 99–100, 104, 105
"Cuento de dos jardines" ("A Tale of Two Gardens") (Paz), 156, 168n63

Cultural Studies, 10, 164
culture, xv, 8, 10, 21n31, 40, 144, 158; Catholic, 128–29; comparison and Paz, 162–64; of modernity with trauma, 174; nature and, xxiv, 175–76, 186, 189–90, 193
Cultures of United States Imperialism (Kaplan and Pease), 10

Daesch/ISIS videos, 82–83
Damrosch, David, xi
"Dándole de comer a los cerdos" (De la Fuente), 86
Dante, xv, 17, 61, 63, 64
Dara Shiko (prince), 152
A Dark Meadow Invites Me ("Una oscura pradera me convida") (essay) (Lezama Lima), xv, 60, 64–69
da Vinci, Leonardo, 180
Dawn in Russia (Frank), 41
Day of the Dead altars, xx, 75–78, 76–77, 79, 83, 85
death: folk Baroque and, xx, 75–78; violent, xx, 79–87, 88n7, 89n33. *See also* La Santa Muerte
Decades (Martyr), 189
The Decline of the West (Spengler), 58
De la Fuente, Pilar, 86
Del amor y otros demonios (García Márquez), 127
Deleuze, Gilles, 106n14, 119n5
DeLillo, Don, 17
Descartes, René, 111
Dettelbach, Michael, 196n20
D'haen, Theo, 208
Dharmakirti, 159, 168n63
Dhingra, Anil, 168n63
The Dialectics of Our America (Saldívar), 9
Diario libre (newspaper), 104
Diccionario de la real academia española, xviii
Dictionary of Symbols (Cirlot), 61
Dimock, Wai Chee, 14

Disciplinary Conquest (Salvatore), 53n60
dissipative structures theory, 111
"Distant Neighbor" ("Prójimo lejano") (Paz), 147
Distant Star (*Estrella Distante*) (Bolaño), 31–35
Doce cuentos peregrinos (García Márquez), 127
Donegan, Kathleen, 33
Don Quixote (Cervantes), 94–96
El Dorado, 18, 184
d'Ors, Eugenio, 48
Do the Americas Have a Common History? (Hanke), 21n13
Do the Americas Have a Common Literature? (Pérez Firmat), 6
The Double Flame (*La llama doble*) (Paz), 159–62, 164
drug-related violence, Mexico, xx, 79–87, 88n7
Duncan, Robert, xiv–xv, 58–64, 66, 68–69
Durix, Jean-Pierre, 137

Early American Literature (Aldridge), 8
East Slope (*Ladera Este*) (Paz), 143, 146–47
Eby, Clare Virginia, 14, 15
Echevarría, Bolívar, 107n16, 119n5
Eden, Richard, 189–90
Egginton, William, 119n5
Egypt, ancient, 180
Einstein, Albert, 117
Eiss, Paul K., 85–87
Eliot, T. S., 166n37
ellipses, 110–11, 115–17
"Encyclopedic Narrative" (Mendelson), 17
encyclopedic novels, 5, 12, 16–20
Enemigo rumor ("Inimical Murmur") (Lezama Lima), 60
entanglement, 28, 75, 175, 185–93, 197n45

Epic, decay of, 106n1
The Epic of America (Adams, J.T.), 20n4
La epopeya de la máxima América ("The Epic of Greater America") (Bolton), 3–5, 17, 20n4
Ercilla, Alonso de, 16
erotic, question of, 159–62
La escena contemporánea (Mariátegui), 42–43
Espuela de Plata (magazine), 60
Essai sur la géographie des plantes (Humboldt), 176–77
Estrella Distante (*Distant Star*) (Bolaño), 31–35
Europe, the Americas and. *See* the Americas, Europe and
European Baroque, 103, 118–19. *See also* the Baroque
"La exclamación" ("Exclamation") (Paz), 146–47
Experiments on Stimulated Muscle and Nerve Fibers (*Versuche über die Gereitzte Muskel-und Nervenfaser*) (Humboldt), 178–79
La expresión americana (Lezama Lima), 67

Faber, Sebastiaan, 53n59
La Familia, with violence, 84
Faulkner, William, 31–33
feast (*cena lezamiana*), 101
"Felicidad en Herat" ("Happiness in Herat") (Paz), 153–54
Felski, Rita, 11–12
femicides, xx, 79–81, 84, 86, 89n33
feminism, 46, 53n55
FIAR (*Forum for Inter-American Research*) (journal), 22n41
filming, of torture, 82–83
The First Gentleman of America (Cabell), 30
fish symbol, Christ, 183
Fitz, Earl E., 5, 8, 9, 22n39
Florida International University, 22n35

The Fold (Deleuze), 119n5
folk Baroque: death and, xx, 75–78; *horror vacui* and, 76, 78. *See also* La Santa Muerte
Forum for Inter-American Research (FIAR) (journal), 22n41
Foster, Georg, 177
Foucault, Michel, 76
Four Quartets (Eliot), 166n37
Fox, Claire F., xiii, 13, 15, 16
Frank, Waldo, 52n4, 53nn60–61; Latin America and, xv–xvi, 37–39, 41, 49–51; on literary friendship, 37; Mariátegui and, xv–xvi, 38–44, 53n61; Ocampo and, xv–xvi, 38–39, 44–51
Freud, Sigmund, 11, 116
friendships, transamerican: Europe and Americas, 41–44; Frank and Mariátegui, xv–xvi, 38–44, 53n61; Frank and Ocampo, xv–xvi, 38–39, 44–51; pan Americanism, xv–xvi, 37–39
Frontline (documentary series), 86
Fuentes, Carlos, 7, 8, 16–20, 28, 101
Fulano Suárez (fictional character), 30, 31

Gadre, Vasant G., 168n88
Gallimard, Gaston, 44
Gandhi, Leela, 37
Ganguly, Shayma, 165n10, 166n36, 169n96
García, Joel, 75
García Barcha, Rodrigo, 128
García Bernal, Gael, 87
García de Céspedes, Andrés, 186, 188
García Lorca, Federico, 127
García Márquez, Gabriel "Gabo," 8; *Del amor y otros demonios*, 127; *Doce cuentos peregrinos*, 127; Kafka influencing, 129–31, 134, 135–37; magical realism and, xxii–xxiii, 125, 138n8; Nobel Prize address, 174; with old wives' tales, 126–27; "La

Santa," 127–28. *See also Cien años de soledad*
García Mena, Gilberto, 81
gay science, poetic, 59–60
Gaztelu, Angel, 68–69
Gesamtkunstwerk, xxii, 84, 113
Giles, Paul, 22n34, 208
glimpsing, xxiii, 149, 163, 165n3. *See also* art of the glance
Glusberg, Samuel, 37, 39, 46–47
Gnostics, 63
gold, 93, 97, 180, 183, 184
Góngora, Luis de, 96–97, 116
González Echevarría, Roberto, 18, 119n5
González Rodríguez, Sergio, 81, 88nn8–9
"Good Neighbor" policy, 3
Granma (yacht), 99, *99*, 104
Gravity's Rainbow (Pynchon), 17
El Greco, 116
Greeks, ancient, 192, 206, 207
Greenberg, Janet, 53n55
Greenberg, Martin, 130
Gropius, Walter, 48
Gruesz, Kirsten Silva, 21n31
Guatemala, 33, 89n33
Guevara, Ernesto "Che," 88n2, 99
Guiraldes, Ricardo, 48

Hacia el comienzo (Paz), 143
Halka, Chester, 183–84
Hamlet (Shakespeare), 205
Handel, George Friedrich, 97
Handley, George, 9
Hanke, Lewis, 21n13
"Happiness in Herat" ("Felicidad en Herat") (Paz), 153–54
Hauser, Arnold, 113
Hawkins, Gay, 80
Hawthorne, Nathaniel, 28, 32
The H.D. Book (Duncan), 59
Heidegger, Martin, xv, 57–59, 61, 63, 67–69, 195n11
heliocentrism, 109, 115

"Hemispheric American Novels" (Lazo), 14–16
Hemispheric American Studies, 4, 14–15
Hemispheric American Studies (Levander and Levine), 14–15
"The Hemispheric Novel in the Post-Revolutionary Era" (Murphy), 14
Hemispheric Studies, xi, xiv, 9, 20; Bolton thesis and, 3–5, 16, 21n13; with Literature of the Americas, xiii, 10–16
Hernández, Eunice, 168n63
Hernández, José, 16
Hidalgo, Jacqueline, 83
"La higuera religiosa" ("The religious fig") (Paz), 156
"Himno entre ruinas" ("Hymn among Ruins") (Paz), 154
Hinduism, 158, 161, 167n55
Hispanic Baroque Research project, 121n44
Historia comparada de las literaturas americanas (Sánchez), 5
historical memory, solitude and, 191
History and Memory in the Two Souths (Cohn), 9
Hölderlin, Friedrich, xv, 57, 69
"The Homosexual in Society" (Duncan), 60
homosexuals, 59–60, 107n20
horror vacui (horror of the vacuum), 76, 78. *See also* the Baroque
"How Derivative Was Humboldt?" (Cañizares-Esguerra), 194n10
"How the Baroque Learned to Speak Spanish" (Young), 119n5
Huesos enel desierto (Bones in the Desert) (González Rodríguez), 81, 88n8
Humboldt, Alexander, 194n10, 197n49; Bacon and, 178, 180, 198n59; critique of, 173–98; crucible of tropics and, 176–81; entangled modernities and, 185–93; Melchíades

and, 173–75; *Ruhe* and, 176, 193–94; with travel writings of American tropics, xviii–xxiv, 175–77, 194. *See also Cien años de soledad*
Humboldtian science, 178, 180, 194n10, 196n20
Hurtado, Albert L., 20n3
"Hymn among Ruins" ("Himno entre ruinas") (Paz), 154

IASA (International American Studies Association), 22n41, 207, 208
IAS/EAS (International Association of Inter-American Studies), 22n41
Ibero-American Novel Project, 33
ICLA (International Comparative Literature Association), 7
Ilarregui, Gladys, 169n96
Imagined Communities (Anderson), 93
imperialism, 8, 10, 12, 14, 18, 40, 194n10
Inca (*Ollantay*), 16
incomplete glimpses (vislumbre), 102, 145, 163, 165n10
India, 143–64, 168n88, 169n96. *See also* ineffable, epistemology of; *Vislumbres de la India*
Indian epigrams (*kavyas*), 144–45
ineffable, epistemology of: art of glance and, xxiii, 143–47; cultural comparison and, 162–64; Dharmakirti and, 159; *The Monkey Grammarian* and, xxiii, 143, 147–52, 154, 166n37, 169n96; with question of erotic, 159–62; sacred and sensory, 152–59; vislumbre and, 145, 165n10; *Vislumbres de la India* and, xxiii, 143, 145
infinity, 109–10
Infortunios de Alonso Ramírez (Siguenza y Góngora), 93
"Inimical Murmur" (*Enemigo rumor*) (Lezama Lima), 60
In Light of India. See Vislumbres de la India

The Inordinate Eye (Zamora), xii, xiii, xix, 110, 119n5, 164, 205–6
Instauratio Magna (Bacon), 178, 186, *187*, 189
intellectual history, 7, 13, 22n34, 53n61, 177
"Inter-American Literary Relations" (ICLA conference), 7
inter-American literary studies, 6
Inter-American literature. *See* Literature of the Americas
International American Studies Association (IASA), 22n41, 207, 208
International Association of Inter-American Studies (IAS/EAS), 22n41
International Comparative Literature Association (ICLA), 7
"Introducción a la Esferaimagen" (Introduction to the Sphereimage) (Lezama Lima), 59
irony, magical realism and, xxiii, 125, 131–33, 138
ISIS/Daesch videos, 82–83
isobar, 178
isotherm, 178, 180

Jackson Turner, Frederick, 3–4
James, William, 37
los Jardínes de Humaya, 87
Jay, Martin, 119n5
jazz, 97–98
Jews, racism and, 47
John of Rupescissa, 180–81
John the Baptist, xx, 86, 88
Juan-Navarro, Santiago, 9

Kadir, Djelal, 14
Kafka, Franz, xxiii, 125, 129–31, 134–37
Kant, Immanuel, 194n10
Kaplan, Amy, 10
Kaup, Monika, xii, 106n14, 119, 119n5
kavyas (Indian epigrams), 144–45
Kenyon Review (magazine), 60

Kepler, Johannes, xxi–xxii, 109–11, 115–17. *See also* the Baroque
Keyserling, Hermann, 44, 50
Khare, R.H., 168n88
Knechtel, John, 80
"The Knowledge of Verses" ("Rigveda"), 158, 167n55
Koestler, Arthur, 115–16
Kristeva, Julia, 85–86
Kutzinski, Vera M., 8, 194n10
Kwa, Chunglin, 121n44

Lacan, Jacques, 44
La Condamine, Charles Marie, 177
Ladera Este (East Slope) (Paz), 143, 146–47
Laguardia, Gari, 8
Lambert, Gregg, 119n5
Laplace, Pierre Simon, 178
La Rochelle, Drieu, 48
Latin America, xxii, xxiv, 9, 175, 195; with culture of modernity, 174; Frank and, xv–xvi, 37–39, 41, 49–51; literature, xi–xii, 7, 18, 33. *See also* Paz, Octavio
Latin American Studies, history, 53n60
Latour, Bruno, xvi–xvii, 12, 175, 185–86, 189
Lavoisier, Antoine, 178
Lawrence, T.E., 48
Lazarillo de Tormes (1554), 94–96
Lazo, Rodrigo, 14–16
League of American Writers, 41
Le Corbusier, 45
"Lectura de John Cage" ("Reading John Cage") (Paz), 155–56
Leibniz, Gottfried Wilhelm, 116
"Letter to León Felipe" ("Carta a León Felipe") (Paz), 146, 165n14
Levander, Caroline F., 14–15, 22n35
Levine, Robert S., 14–15, 22n35
Lévi-Strauss, Claude, 193
Lezama Lima, José, 58–59, 61–62, 104, 110; "Baroque curiosity," 107n6, 119; *cena lezamiana* and, 101; Cuban history and, 60; imaginary eras, concept of, 8; "Una oscura pradera me convida," xv, 60, 64–69
Lispector, Clarice, 16
literary friendship, 37
Literature and the Delinquent (Parker), 95
Literature of the Americas (1982–2020): Bolton thesis, 3–5, 16, 21n13; hemispheric studies, xiii, 10–16; one hemisphere, many nations, xiii, 6–10; *summa Americana*, xiv, 5, 16–20
La llama doble (*The Double Flame*) (Paz), 159–62, 164
Lomnitz, Claudio, 75
López Matoso, Antonio, 93
Lowe, Lisa, 34
Löwy, Michael, 52n12
Luigi, Pier Luigi, 113
Lukacz, Gyorgy, 106n1
Lunes de revolución (newspaper), 104
Luther, Martin, 102

magical realism (marvelous real, *real maravilloso*): *Cien años de soledad* and, 125–38, 174–75; in *Concierto barroco*, 105; five essences of, xxiii, 125, 133–37; García Márquez and, xxii–xxiii, 125, 138n8; irony and, xxiii, 125, 131–33, 138; literary techniques, 125, 138n2; old wives' tales, xxiii, 125–27; with phenomenological morphing after Kafka, xxiii, 125, 129–31; political allegorization of divide between West and un-West, xxiii, 125, 132–33, 137–38; popular Catholicism, xxiii, 125, 127–29; as postcolonial literature, xxii, 137–38; writers, 139n28
Magic(al)Realism (Bowers), 125
Magnus, Albert, 192
Mahayana Buddhism, 167n61
Mahler, Gustav, 68
Maiorino, Giancarlo, 110

Majstorovic, Gorica, 48
Mallea, Eduardo, 46
Maluenda, Amalia, 34
Malverde, Jesus, 82
manuscript, of Melchíades, 174–75, 183–85, 193
Maravall, Antonio, 102, 103
The Marble Faun (Faulkner), 32–33
Mariátegui, José Carlos, xv–xvi, 38–44, 52n12, 53n61
Martí, José, xiv, 46, 58
Martin, Gerald, 126
Martin, John, 184
Martín Fierro (Hernández), 16
Martyr, Peter, 189
marvelous real. *See* magical realism
Marx, Karl, 11
Matthiessen, F.O., 15
"El mausoleo de Humayún" ("The Mausoleum of Humayun") (Paz), 154–55
Mbembe, Achille, 83
McClennen, Sophia, xiii, 14
McNerney, Kathleen, 184
meadow, xv, 60–69
"Meditations on the Baroque" (Echevarría), 119n5
Melchíades (fictional character), 173–75, 181–85, 193. *See also Cien años de soledad*
Melgar, Lucía, 88n9
Melis, Antonio, 43
Melville, Herman, 15, 17
memento mori, 86
Memorias (Mier), 93
memory, xxiv, 9, 67–68, 93, 191
Ménard, Pierre, 31
Mendelson, Edward, 17
"Mensaje a los escritores mexicanos" (Message to Mexican Writers) (Frank), 39
The Metamorphosis (Kafka), 129–31, 134, 136
metaphor, meadow as, 60–61

Mexico, 88n2, *100*, 100–101; drug-related violence in, xx, 79–87, 88n7; Ni Una Más protests in, 88. *See also* La Santa Muerte
Middle Ages, xxiv, 180, 181
Midnight's Children (Rushdie), 137
Mier, Fray Servando Teresa de, 93
Mignolo, Walter, 195n11
Mistral, Gabriela, 37
mistranslation, xviii–xix, 29–30, 33–35
La modernidad de lo barroco (Echevarría), 119n5
modernity, 110, 119n5, 174, 185–93
Molloy, Sylvia, 49
monarchical absolutism, 102
Monegal, Emir Rodríguez, 17
El mono gramático (*The Monkey Grammarian*) (Paz), xxiii, 143, 147–52, 154, 166n37, 169n96
Monsiváis, Carlos, 85
Morrison, Toni, 125
Motezuma (Vilvaldi), 98, 106n11
muerte artera (violent death), 78, 82–83, 85
Muerte de Narciso (Lezama Lima), 59, 60
La muerte de Artemio Cruz (Fuentes), 17
Muhammad (prophet), 126
murder, 31, 34, 80–81, 83
Murphy, Gretchen, 14
Museo de Artes Populares, 80
Museo Dolores Olmedo, Calaveras altar at, 76, *76–77*
Muslims, 39
mutilation, sexual, 89n33
mystical experience, orgasm and, 160
mythopoetics, xv, 59

Nadie parecía (magazine), 60
NAFTA (North American Free Trade Agreement), 86–87
narcomedia, 85
natural science, 110–11, 196n20

nature: culture and, xxiv, 175–76, 186, 189–90, 193; secrets of, 178–79
Ndalianis, Angela, 119n5
"Near Cape Comorin" ("Cerca del cabo Comorín") (Paz), 146, 156
necroaesthetics, 84–85. *See also* La Santa Muerte
necrofridge, 87
Nehru, Jawaharlal, 163
Neo-baroque, xx–xxii, 102, 104–5, 110, 117–18, 119n5. *See also* the Baroque
Neobaroque Aesthetics and Contemporary Entertainment (Ndalianis), 119n5
Neobaroque in the Americas (Kaup), 119n5
neocolonialism, in Latin America, xxiv, 175, 195
neoliberalism, 78, 80, 84, 88, 89n36
New Americanists, 10, 13–15
New American Poetry, 58
Newman, William, 180
new realism, xvi–xvii, xxi, xxvn5, 111–12
Newton, Isaac, 111, 116
New World Baroque, 27, 75, 107n16, 110, 116, 119. *See also* the Baroque
Nicolson, Marjorie, 109
Niemeyer, Oscar, 116
Nietzsche, Friedrich, 11
Ni Una Más protests, 88
non-dualism, 168n62
North American Free Trade Agreement (NAFTA), 86–87
North-South artistic flows, 7
nota roja (crime-beat press), xx, 85
nothingness (*Súnyata*), 167n61, 168n63
La nouvelle revue francaise (magazine), 44
novela total (total novel), 17
Novum Organum (Bacon), 178
Nueva historia de la literatura americana (Sánchez), 5
Núñez, Estuardo, 20n10

Ocampo, Victoria, xv–xvi, 38–39, 44–51, 53n55
occult, Christianity and, 181
"Often I Am Permitted to Return to a Meadow" (Duncan), xv, 60–64
O'Gorman, Edmundo, xvi, xvii, 16, 175, 195n11
Ogorzaly, Michael, 53n61
Okri, Ben, 138
old wives' tales, magical realism, xxiii, 125–27
O'Leary, Peter, 60
Ollantay (Inca), 16
Olson, Charles, 64
One Hundred Years of Solitude. *See Cien años de soledad*
On the (New) Baroque (Lambert), 119n5
the Open, 61, 68
The Opening of the Field (Duncan), 60
Order Out of Chaos (Prigogine and Stengers), 114–15
organic chemistry, 179
orgasm, mystical experience and, 160
Orígenes (magazine), 60
Ortega y Gasset, José, 44, 47, 50
Ory, José Antonio de, 154, 167n61
"Una oscura pradera me convida" (A Dark Meadow Invites Me) (essay) (Lezama Lima), xv, 60, 64–69
Ospedale della Pietà, 97
Our America (Frank), 40, 44
Ovalle, Paula, 85
Oxford English Dictionary On-Line, 10, 197n45

Pacheco Romero, Medardo, 134
Padilla, Heberto, 105
Palestine, 208
pan Americanism, xv–xvi, 37–39
Panofsky, Erwin, 120n12
Panorama (journal), 21n11
Panorama das literaturas das Américas (Carvalho), 6, 21n11

Paradiso (Dante), 63
Parker, Alexander, 95
parody, 175, 194n9
Parra, Eduardo Antonio, 85
Pascal, Roy, 129–30
Paz, Octavio, 28, 164n1, 165n2, 165nn9–10, 168n88; Abhinavagupta and, 165n22; with absolute truth, 166n36; art of glance and, xxiii, 143–47; *Blanco*, 143, 156–57, 162, 167n53, 168n63; "Carta a León Felipe," 146, 165n14; "Cerca del cabo Comorín," 146, 156; "Cuento de dos jardines," 156, 168n3; with cultural comparison, 162–64; eroticism and, 159–62; "La exclamación," 146–47; "Felicidad en Herat," 153–54; with glimpsing, xxiii, 149, 165n3; *Hacia el comienzo*, 143; "La higuera religiosa," 156; "Himno entre ruinas," 154; India and, 143–64; India influencing, xxiii, 143, 152, 167n61, 169n96; *Ladera Este*, 143, 146–47; "Lectura de John Cage," 155–56; *La llama doble*, 159–62, 164; "El mausoleo de Humayún," 154–55; *El mono gramático*, xxiii, 143, 147–52, 154, 166n37, 169n96; "Prójimo lejano," 147; rendering of *kavyas* by, 144–45; "Retórica," 145; "Tumba del poeta," 156; *Vislumbres de la India*, xxiii, 143–45, 152–54, 158–59, 161–62, 167n61. *See also* ineffable, epistemology of
Pease, Donald E., 10
Pedwell, Carolyn, 47
PEN Club of Mexico newsletter, 39, 40
Percy, Walker, 8
Pérez Firmat, Gustavo, 6, 13, 19, 21n13, 22n35
Performing the Border videoessay (Biemann), 88n7
Personal Narrative of a Journey to the Equinoctial Regions of the New Content (Humboldt), 179, 190, 197n49
Peru, 33, 40, 41
Peruvian Socialist Party, xv, 40
phenomenological morphing, xxiii, 125, 129–31
Philosopher's Stone, 131, 182–83
physical geography, 178
picaresque, xx–xxi, 92–96, 101–2
Pigafetta, Antonio, 174
Piglia, Ricardo, 49
Pike, Frederic, 53n61
Pinochet, Augusto, 31
place, selfhood and, 7
Platonic coupling, yogic and, 160–61
pleonasm, 206
Pliny the Elder, 207
Pliny the Younger, 207
poetic illusion, 106
Poetics of Space (Bachelard), 60
"Poetry and Knowledge" (Césaire), 59
political allegorization, xxiii, 125, 132–33, 137–38
politics, xv, xxi, 37, 40, 104, 110
polycentrism, xiv, 38
Popol Vuh (Quiché-Maya), 16
Porter, Russell, 138n8
Portugal, 4
postmodernism, xvi–xvii, xxvn5
Postslavery Literature in the Americas (Handley), 9
Poulin, Jacques, 18–19
Pound, Ezra, 58
Pratt, Mary Louise, 194n10
Prigogine, Ilya, xxii, 111, 113–19
Prime Mover, 116
print journalism, 93
Proceed with Caution (Sommer), 9, 29
"Prójimo lejano" ("Distant Neighbor") (Paz), 147
Protestantism, 102
Ptolemy, 115
Pujol, Oscar, 165n10
purgatory, 134, 135

purification, 182, 185–86, 194, 195n13
Puritans, 3, 20n9
Pynchon, Thomas, 8, 16–17

Quiché-Maya (*Popol Vuh*), 16
Quijano, Aníbal, 51
Qu'ran, 126

Rabasa, José, 195n11
Rabelais, François, 17
racism, 40, 47, 194n10
Radway, Janice, 14
Rahab (Frank), 40
Ransom, John Crowe, 60
"Rappaccini's Daughter" (Hawthorne), 28, 32
"Reading John Cage" ("Lectura de John Cage") (Paz), 155–56
real maravilloso. See magical realism
Rediscovering the New World (Fitz), 9
Regimiento de navegación (García de Céspedes), 186, 188
Reguillo, Rossana, 83–84
Reinventing the Americas (Laguardia), 8
Reiss, Benjamin, 14, 15
relativity theory, 117
religion, 78, 102, 127, 180, 181, 183. *See also* Roman Catholic Church
"The religious fig" ("La higuera religiosa") (Paz), 156
retombée, xxi–xxii, 110, 117
"Retórica" (Paz), 145
Review of International American Studies (RIAS) (journal), 22n41
Revista Canadiense de Estudios Hispánicos (journal), 28
Revista Occidente (magazine), 47
Reyes, Alfonso, 37, 39, 48
Reyes, Rubiela, 126–27, 138n6
RIAS (*Review of International American Studies*) (journal), 22n41
Ricoeur, Paul, 11
Rig Veda, 158–59
"Rigveda" ("The Knowledge of Verses"), 158, 167n55

Rilke, Rainer Maria, 58, 61, 67–68
Rise of the Novel (Watt), 94–95
Rochon, Lisa, 80
Roger, Heather, 80
Rolland, Romain, 41–43
Roman Catholic Church, 3, 68–69, 75; the Baroque and, 78–79; Counter-Reformation and, xxi, 78–79, 99, 102–5, 107n16, 110; magical realism and popular Catholicism, xxiii, 125, 127–29; purgatory and, 134, 135; La Santa Muerte and, xx, 86
Romans, ancient, 207
Romero Romero, Enriqueta, 83
Roosevelt, Franklin D., 3
Roosevelt, Theodore, xvi
Rougement, Denis de, 160
Roush, Laura, 81
Rubens, Peter Paul, 116
Ruhe (solitude), 176, 193–94
Rushdie, Salman, 125, 137, 138

sacred, 152–59, 161–62
"Sad chairs" (Hawkins), 80
Sadowski-Smith, Claudia, xiii, 13, 15, 16
Saldívar, José David, 9
Salvatore, Ricardo, xiii, 53n60
Sánchez, Luis Alberto, 5–7, 15–17, 20n10, 38, 48
"La Santa" (García Márquez), 127–28
La Santa Muerte: Day of the Dead altars, xx, 75–78, 76–77, 79, 83, 85; drug-related violence and, xx, 79–87, 88n7; femicides, xx, 79–81, 84, 86; as folk Baroque, xx, 75–78; John the Baptist and, xx, 86, 88; *muerte artera* and protection from, 78, 82–83, 85; necrofridge and, 87; *nota roja* and, xx, 85; Roman Catholic Church and, xx, 86; torture, xx, 78, 80–84, 89n33; Trees of Life, xx, 76–77, 85; la Virgen de Guadalupe and, xx, 82, 86
La Santa Muerte (Aridjis, H.), 87

La Santa Muerte/Saint Death (documentary film), 87
Santa Rosa de Lima, 128, 139n13
Sarduy, Severo, xxi–xxii, 103–5, 110–11, 116–18
Sarlo, Beatriz, 44, 45
Scarlatti, Domenico, 97
Schlesinger, John, 84
Schroeder, Shannin, 184
science, xxi–xxii, 110–11, 116, 195n13, 196n20; chemistry, 178, 179; complexity theory and, 114–15; gay, 59–60; religion and, 180, 181
"Scopic Regimes of Modernity" (Jay), 119n5
Searle, John, xvi, 16–17
Sedgwick, Eve, 11, 12
selfhood, place and, 7
sensory, sacred and, 152–59
The Seven Arts (journal), 40
sexual energy, sacredness of, 161–62
sexual violence, 89n33
Shades of the Planet (Dimock and Buell), 14
Shakespeare, William, 205
Siguenza y Góngora, Carlos de, 93
Silko, Leslie Marmon, 18, 19
silver, 96–97, 99–102, *100*
Sing-Akademie zu Berlin, 106n11
The Singularity of Literature (Attridge), 12
slavery, 16, 18, 51, 194n10
Soledades (Góngora), 96
solitude, 176, 184, 191, 193–94. *See also Cien años de soledad*
"The Solitude of Latin America" (García Márquez), 174
Sommer, Doris, 9, 29–30
Soteno, Alfonso, 88n2
Soviet Union, 163
Spain, 4, 18, 39, 41, 98
"Spanish American Literature Compared with That of the United States" (Umphrey), 21n15

The Spanish Background of American Literature (Williams, S.T.), 15, 16
Spanish translations, xiii
Spengler, Oswald, 58
spiritual hunger, 102–3
spiritual traditions, India, 152, 167n61
Spitta, Silvia, xii, xiv, 16
Srinath, C.N., 167n53
Stein, Gertrude, 58, 207
Stein, William, 53n61
Stengers, Isabelle, xxii, 111, 113–19
Stravinsky, Igor, 44
Suárez, Juán Luis, 121n44
subversive, the Baroque as, 103
sufficient reason, principle of, 116
summa Americana, xiv, 5, 16–20
Súnyata (nothingness), 167n61, 168n63
Supervielle, Jules, 48
Sur (magazine), 46–49
Sylva Sylvarum (Bacon), 178
syncretism, 75
synecdoche, 138. *See also* magical realism
systems thinking, xxi, 111–13

"A Tale of Two Gardens" ("Cuento de dos jardines") (Paz), 156, 168n63
technology, 93
Teiresias, 206
terra incognita, 6, 16–20
Terra nostra (Fuentes), 16–20
Tertullian, 68
The Theater of Truth (Egginton), 119n5
theory of the Baroque, 103, 116–18
Theory of the Novel (Lukacz), 106n1
"This is just to say" (Williams, W.C.), 207
"Thoughts in Havana" (Lezama Lima), 58
"Tomb of the Poet" ("Tumba del poeta") (Paz), 156
torture, xx, 31–35, 78, 80–84, 89n33
total novel (novela total), 17
Touching Feeling (Sedgwick), 11

"Toward a Hemispheric American Literature" (seminar), 22n35
traditions, aesthetics and, 7
transamerican literary studies, xii
translation, xiii, xviii–xix, 28–30, 32–35
transmission, translation and, 28–29, 34
Trash (Knechtel), 80
trauma, culture of modernity and, 174
travel, 106n5; accounts, 96, 98, 178–80; *Concierto barroco* and, 96–98; writings of American tropics, xviii–xxiv, 175–77, 194
Trees of Life, xx, 76–77, 85
Tristes Tropiques (Lévi-Strauss), 193
Trotsky, Leon, 42
truth, absolute, 166n36
"The Truth and Life of Myth" (Duncan), 59
"Tumba del poeta" ("Tomb of the Poet") (Paz), 156

Umphrey, George W., 7, 21n15
Unamuno, Miguel de, 41
Under Northern Eyes (Berger), 53n60
United Nations, 99
United States (U.S.), 8–10, 21n15, 52n4, 89n36
The United States and Latin America (Pike), 53n61
Universidad de San Marcos, 20n10
University of Virginia, 33
University of Western Ontario, 121n44
The Unsettlement of America (Brickhouse), 30
The Usable Past (Zamora), xii, xiii, 9, 27
Uses of Literature (Felski), 11–12
utopia, 44, 51, 174

Valenzuela Arce, José Manuel, 86
Valery, Paul, 46
Vallejo, César, 205–6
vanishing point, 205, 206
Vedic Creation Hymn, 158–59
Velázquez, Diego, 116

Venezuela, 33, 176
Verbum (magazine), 60
Versuche über die Gereitzte Muskel- und Nervenfaser (Experiments on Stimulated Muscle and Nerve Fibers) (Humboldt), 178–79
Viaje de Perico Ligero al País de Los Moros (López Matoso), 93
La vida alucinante (Arenas), 93
Vilvaldi, Antonio, 98, 106n11
violence: drug-related, xx, 79–87, 88n7; necrofridge, 87; sexual, 89n33. *See also* torture
violent death (*muerte artera*), 78, 82–83, 85
la Virgen de Guadalupe, xx, 82, 86
Virgin of the Rocks (da Vinci), 180
Virgin Spain (Frank), 39
vislumbre (incomplete glimpses), 102, 145, 163, 165n10
Vislumbres de la India (*In Light of India*) (Paz), 159, 167n61; art of glance and, 144–45; epistemology of ineffable and, xxiii, 143, 145; with question of erotic, 161–62; with sacred and sensory, 152–54, 158
"Vislumbres de la India" (Gadre), 168n88
Vitier, Cintio, 104
Vivaldi, Antonio, 97–98, 104–6
Volkswagen Blues (Poulin), 18–19
Voltaire, 29, 95, 97
Le voyage aux régions equinoxiales du Nouveau Continent, fait en 1799–1804, par Alexandre de Humboldt et Aimé Bonpland (Humboldt and Bonpland), 177

Wakefield, Steve, 105
Waldo Frank (Ogorzaly), 53n61
Wallace, David Foster, 17
Wallerstein, Immanuel, 51
Watt, Ian, 94–95, 106n1
wealth, displays of, 93, 101
Weinberger, Eliot, 164n1

West, political allegorization of un-West and, xxiii, 125, 132–33, 137–38
"What Are Poets For?" (Heidegger), 58
"What is Baroque?" (Panofsky), 120n12
Whitman, Walt, 15, 58, 63
"Why Has Critique Run Out of Steam?" (Latour), 12
Wieder, Carlos, 31–34
Williams, Stanley T., 15–16
Williams, William Carlos, 8, 58, 207
Wölfflin, Heinrich, xxii, 112–13
women, xx, 79–81, 84, 86, 88n7, 89n33
Woolf, Virginia, 44–45, 48
writers, magical realism, 139n28
Writing the Apocalypse (Zamora), xiii, 5–9, 12, 16, 21n22, 31, 194n6

Xirau, Ramón, 67, 68

yogic coupling, Platonic and, 160–61
Young, Allen, 119n5

Zambrano, María, xv, 61–62, 64, 67
Zamora, Lois Parkinson, xi, 35, 75, 103, 138n2; *The Americas, Otherwise*, xii, 16; on baroque, 110; *Baroque New Worlds*, xii, 119, 119n5; *The Inordinate Eye*, xii, xiii, xix, 110, 119n5, 164, 205–6; *The Usable Past*, xii, xiii, 9, 27; *Writing the Apocalypse*, xiii, 5–9, 12, 16, 21n22, 31, 194n6
Zapata Olivella, Manuel, 17
Zavattini, Cesare, 128

About the Contributors

Priscilla **Archibald** is professor of Spanish at Roosevelt University. Her scholarly interests include Andean Studies and American Hemispheric Studies. She is the author of *Imagining Modernity in the Andes* (Rowman & Littlefield, 2011) and has published articles in numerous journals, including *Social Text*, *Revista Iberoamericana*, and *Revista canadiense de estudios hispánicos*. She is currently writing a book about intellectual and cultural exchange between Latin Americans and Anglo-Americans in the 1920s, 1930, and 1940s. Over the years she has taught a wide range of subject matter, including interdisciplinary courses on modern and colonial Latin American literature, on literary and cultural theory and about the issue of immigration. She has been a Fellow at the Society for the Humanities at Cornell University, was the recipient of a Fulbright Scholarship to Santiago, Chile and is currently a Scholar-in-Residence at the Newberry Library. Archibald received a Masters in Comparative Literature from the University of Chicago and a Ph.D. in Latin American Literature from Stanford University.

Antonio **Barrenechea** is a professor of Literature of the Americas at the University of Mary Washington. He is the author of *America Unbound: Encyclopedic Literature and Hemispheric Studies* (University of New Mexico Press, 2016) and is co-editor of "Hemispheric Indigenous Studies," a 2013 special issue of *Comparative American Studies*. He is currently working on *One Hemisphere, Many Nations: The Americas in Literary History*, a book-length manuscript that recovers the centrality of languages and literatures in the global humanities. It traces Literature of the Americas from the Good Neighbor era, through the Cold War rise of a comparative discipline, and into the "Hemispheric Turn" of the 2000s.

Ralph **Bauer** is a professor of English and Comparative Literature at the University of Maryland, College Park. His research interests include the literatures and cultures of the colonial Americas, early modern studies, hemispheric studies, and the history of science. His publications include *The Cultural Geography of Colonial American Literatures: Empire, Travel, Modernity* (Cambridge University Press 2003, 2008); *An Inca Account of the Conquest of Peru* (University of Colorado Press, 2005); (co-edited with José Antonio Mazzotti) *Creole Subjects in the Colonial Americas: Empires, Texts, Identities* (University of North Carolina Press, 2009); (co-edited with Marcy Norton), "Entangled Trajectories," a special issue of *Colonial Latin American Review* (2017); (co-edited with Jaime Marroquín Arredondo) *Translating Nature: A Transcultural History of Early Modern Science* (University of Pennsylvania Press, 2019); and *The Alchemy of Conquest: Science, Religion, and the Secrets of the New World* (University of Virginia Press, 2019).

Anna **Brickhouse** is Linden Kent Memorial Professor of English and American Studies at the University of Virginia. She has published two books—*Transamerican Literary Relations and the Nineteenth-Century Public Sphere* (Cambridge University Press, 2004) and *The Unsettlement of America* (Oxford University Press, 2014)—and is currently working on a book about catastrophe and American literary history.

Wendy B. **Faris** is professor emeritus of English at the University of Texas at Arlington. She is the author of *Carlos Fuentes* (Ungar Publ., 1983), *Labyrinths of Language: Symbolic Landscape and Narrative Design in Modern Fiction* (Johns Hopkins University Press, 1988), and *Ordinary Enchantments: Magical Realism and the Remystification of Narrative* (Vanderbilt University Press, 2004); she co-edited (with Lois Parkinson Zamora) *Magical Realism: Theory, History, Community* (Duke University Press, 1995). She has recently published articles on Ben Okri's *Dangerous Love*, Haruki Murakami's *1Q84*, and is currently working on the relations between modernist painting and literature.

Stephen M. **Hart** is professor of Latin American Film, Literature, and Culture at University College London. His recent monographs and edited volumes on Latin American literature and film include: *A Companion to Magical Realism* (co-edited with Wen-Chin Ouyang; Tamesis 2005), *Gabriel García Márquez* (Reaktion Books, 2010), *César Vallejo: A Literary Biography* (Boydell and Brewer 2013), *Latin American Cinema* (Reaktion Books, 2015), and *Santa Rosa de Lima: La evolución de una santa* (2017).

Djelal **Kadir** is the Edwin Erle Sparks Professor Emeritus of Comparative Literature at Pennsylvania State University. He is the Founding President of the International American Studies Association and former Editor of the international quarterly *World Literature Today*. His authored books include: *Juan Carlos Onetti* (Twayne, 1977), *Columbus and the Ends of the Earth: Europe's Prophetic Rhetoric as Conquering Ideology* (University of California Press, 1992); *The Other Writing: Postcolonial Essays in Latin America's Writing Culture* (Purdue University Press, 1993); *Questing Fictions: Latin America's Family Romance* (University of Minnesota Press, 1987) and *Memos from the Besieged City: Lifelines for Cultural Sustainability* (Stanford University Press, 2011). He is the co-editor of the *Routledge Companion to World Literature* (2012; 2nd ed. 2022), the co-editor of *Literary Cultures of Latin America: A Comparative History* (Oxford University Press, 2004), and of the *Longman Anthology of World Literature* (2004). He has authored over 100 articles and has developed and taught a number of graduate seminars ranging from classical literary theory of Greek and Latin antiquity to colonial and contemporary American literatures to comparative modernisms and postmodernism. He is a founding Board member of Synapsis: The European School of Comparative Studies, a Senior Fellow and Executive Board member of The Stockholm Collegium of World Literary History, and a member of the founding Board and teaching faculty of the Institute for World Literature.

Monika **Kaup** is professor of English at the University of Washington. Her scholarship focuses on twentieth-century American and Latinx literature, hemispheric American literature, the Baroque/neobaroque/New World Baroque, and critical theory. Her books include *Neobaroque in the Americas: Alternative Modernities in Literature, Visual Art, and Film* (University of Virginia Press, 2012) and *Baroque New Worlds: Representation, Transculturation, Counterconquest* (co-edited with Lois Parkinson Zamora; Duke University Press, 2010). Her most recent study, *New Ecological Realisms: Post-Apocalyptic Fiction and Contemporary Theory* (Edinburgh University Press, 2021), deals with revisioning realism in the eras of post-critique and of climate change and showcases a new context-based concept of the real.

John **Ochoa** is associate professor of Spanish at Pennsylvania State University. His scholarship focuses on Mexican cultural and intellectual history, literature of the Americas (esp. travel literature), and Latina/o studies. He is the author of *The Uses of Failure in Mexican Literature and Identity* (University of Texas Press, 2005) and of *Fellow Travelers: How Road Stories Shaped the Idea of the Americas* (University of Virginia Press, 2021).

Silvia **Spitta** is the Robert E. Maxwell 1923 professor of Arts and Sciences and professor of Spanish and Comparative Literature at Dartmouth College. Her areas of interest include *indigenismo*, Latin American and Latinx material and visual culture, and border culture. She is the author of *Against Ruins: El Cusco de Martín Chambi/Del archivo a las calles. El Cusco de Martín Chambi* (2020), *Between Two Waters: Narratives of Transculturation in Latin America* (2006), the award winning *Misplaced Objects: Collections and Recollections in Europe and America* (2009), and with Boris Muñoz, *Más allá de la ciudad letrada: Crónicas y espacios urbanos* (2003), and with Adriana López-Labourdette and Valeria Wagner *Des/Memorias: Prácticas y discursos mnemónicos en las Américas* (2016). She is currently working to preserve Andean photography archives and she curated a city-wide exhibition of the photographs of indigenous photographer Martin Chambi in Cusco in 2014 and the exhibit "Baldomero Alejos" in 2019 in Ayacucho, Peru.

Christopher **Winks** is associate professor and Chair of Comparative Literature at Queens College/CUNY. He is the author of *Symbolic Cities in Caribbean Literature* (Palgrave Macmillan, 2009), and he has published articles, reviews, and translations (from French and Spanish) in many journals and edited collections. He is the editor and co-translator with Adriana González Mateos of *Los danzantes del tiempo*, a bilingual English-Spanish anthology of Kamau Brathwaite's poems that received the 2011 Casa de las Américas prize. Current translation projects include *Labyrinth*, a bilingual English-Spanish anthology of the selected writings of Cuban poet Lorenzo García Vega (Junction Press, forthcoming) and the poetry of Haitian surrealist Magloire Saint-Aude.

www.ingramcontent.com/pod-product-compliance
Lightning Source LLC
Chambersburg PA
CBHW020115010526
44115CB00008B/835